The Monastery

The MONASTERY

A Study in
Freedom, Love, and Community

GEORGE A. HILLERY, JR.

Foreword by Andrew Greeley

Westport, Connecticut
London

Library of Congress Cataloging-in-Publication Data

Hillery, George A.
    The monastery : a study in freedom, love, and community / George
A. Hillery, Jr. ; foreword by Andrew Greeley.
        p.   cm.
    Includes bibliographical references and index.
    ISBN 0–275–94173–6 (alk. paper)
    1. Monastic and religious life.   I. Title.
BX2385.H55   1992
255—dc20   91–46757

British Library Cataloguing in Publication Data is available.

Library of Congress Catalog Card Number: 91–46757
ISBN: 0–275–94173–6

First published in 1992

Praeger Publishers, 88 Post Road West, Westport, CT 06881
An imprint of Greenwood Publishing Group, Inc.

Printed in the United States of America

The paper used in this book complies with the
Permanent Paper Standard issued by the National
Information Standards Organization (Z39.48–1984).

10 9 8 7 6 5 4 3 2 1

This book is dedicated to
the monks,
who are my brothers.

Contents

Illustrations

FIGURES

CHARTS

TABLES

Foreword

Ten years ago there were two different attitudes about the future of Cistercian monasteries in the Catholic Church. A prominent priest psychologist told me in a tone of voice that tolerated no dissent, "They're finished, and they should be finished. We have no room for masochism in the New Church."

A layman, president of a Benedictine college and a distinguished historian, presented the opposite opinion: "It is absurd to think that a social institution which has responded to human needs for the past millennium and a half will disappear overnight."

The priest, by the way, later left the active ministry and married.

I think that by now the issue is settled. The community Professor Hillery has so gently studied will survive. And flourish. Eventually. The historian was right and the psychologist was wrong, a not infrequent event in contemporary Roman Catholicism, which, alas, is much more likely to listen to the psychologist than to the historian.

Professor Hillery has had the great good fortune to capture his monastery on the rebound from the traumas of the era after the Vatican Council, a time when everything from the past was called into question, often with little depth and no wisdom. Clearly the monastic life (like much else in Catholicism) needed to be reevaluated. It was time and past time to sort out that which was essential from that which was medieval. Unfortunately the baby was often thrown out with the bath water (and as I have remarked elsewhere, the Baby's Mother too).

Many of those who were the most diligent reformers inside the monastic orders seemed to have been the first to leave after the reforms were accomplished—as if they needed for their own emotional stability the rigid rules they had overturned.

The emphasis in the New Church was on relevance—which often meant the latest fads and fashions—and on "modernizing"—which often meant becoming indistinguishable from any other social activists. Sadly, many religious orders, especially teaching nuns, committed collective suicide because of the haste and the shallowness of their "reforms." Even the Jesuits, the most powerful order in the Church, have gone through a severe crisis in which many of their members have seemed to repudiate almost everything for which St. Ignatius stood.

To complicate this transitional trauma, the Trappists had to cope with the giant, brilliant, enigmatic, and finally tragic figure of Thomas Merton— in some ways the most important American Catholic of the middle decades of the century. His ambivalences and agonies about his Trappist vocation reflected, perhaps in a distorting mirror, the crisis of the whole community.

Professor Hillery's monastery, it seems to me, has weathered the worst of the storm. The crisis is not over; the baby and the bath water still must be separated. But there now seems to be a solid consensus on which the future is to be built. Indeed, to this outsider the Benedictine tradition has survived the roller coaster of the last quarter century with more gracefulness than have many of the other Catholic traditions—perhaps because with its age there has come both flexibility and resilience.

If I had to guess, I would predict that the Cistercian future will place much greater emphasis on the dignity and the fulfillment of the individual person, on psychological maturity as both a requirement and a result of the monastic vocation, and on a rhythm of involvement with and retreat from the world. I also suspect that there will be a great variety of ways of affiliating with the tradition, both within the monastery community and on its margins.

Professor Hillery has presented us with, among other things, an excellent benchmark from which to watch the emergence of a new Trappist tradition that is also very old.

I told Professor Hillery when he asked me to write this introduction that I have never doubted for a second my lack of a monastic vocation. In fact, I often have a hard time understanding it. He responded that the monks have something to tell us. Surely they do. But what?

I suspect they tell us about the fragility and the importance of life, and the importance of love and communities of love. As G. K. Chesterton once remarked, life is too important ever to be anything but life.

I've often wanted to make a retreat in a monastery. Professor Hillery's book has compelled me to make a reservation for such a retreat.

I won't stay, but I may go back again and again.

People who can echo that last sentence may be an important part of the Cistercian future.

                                                    Andrew Greeley

Preface

Why write a book about monasteries? Statistically speaking, monks make up only a minuscule portion of our population. But what is apparently insignificant may turn out to be of critical importance. And what we see at first sight might as likely be less significant. So with monasteries. I began studying these groups precisely because they appear to be an exception among communities. They had no family, in the usual sense of the word. How could such a community exist? This is still an important question. But as I searched for an answer, a much more significant topic emerged.

I believe that monasteries have something very important to say to the world, not just to theologians or sociologists. It took me many years to face the conclusion that the monasteries studied here were actually committed to the realization of love, not physical, possessive, exclusive erotic love but a spiritual, detached, inclusive, and very real agapé love. I argue that without this love, these monasteries would not exist. More important for those of us who do not live in monasteries, this dedication to agapé throws in stark silhouette the fact that communal organizations are created to attain broad goals, and the most important of these is love. To the degree that love is absent in a community, the community is seriously deficient. In this sense, I contend that all communal organizations should be based on love, if they are to approach their potential. This love extends from the eros of married couples, to the affection in the family generally, to the friendship of neighbors and others. The monasteries suggest further that agapé can strengthen all of these loves. Unfortunately, either because of their positivism or their materialism, love is not a popular topic among sociologists. It is a lack that can only contribute to the poverty of the discipline. I hope that this book can help to make up for that deficiency.

"Where there is no vision, the people perish," says the proverb. During the so-called Dark Ages, monks were reputed to have kept civilization alive.

This function is still extant today. In a world where material values are given highest preference, the monks remind us that there are other, spiritual values. Thus, in our present "Dark Ages" of material ascendency, monasteries still preserve a spark of civilization.

But the role of love in the normal communal organization, as well as in the nation, is another story. The task of the present study is to examine love as it actually operates in an ongoing system, the Trappist-Cistercian monastery. Few people have seen monasteries. Fewer have been able to study them at close range. I consider it a privilege to have been permitted to live with the men who inhabit them for more than a year during the last two decades and to have shared with them as much of their life as a married Protestant can. I believe that they have a place in the world, and not a small part of that place is what they can teach us about community.

Research for this book took nearly 20 years. It is thus hardly possible to name all who have assisted in its completion. I hope that those who are not mentioned here realize that my gratitude is nonetheless real.

Dom John Eudes Bamberger, Order of Cistercians of the Strict Observance (O.C.S.O.), introduced me to Trappist-Cistercian life at a time when separation from the world was more rigorous than today. He was the first of numerous monks who patiently initiated me into monasticism. Others who were particularly helpful were Dom David Bock, Dom David Wechter, Dom Edward McCorkell, Dom Brendan Freeman, Dom Emmanuel Spillane, Dom Thomas Davis, Dom Christian Carr, Father Kenneth Tietjen, Father Raphael Simon, Father Andrew Gries, Father Paul Valley, Father William Wilson, Brother Fabian Osowski, Brother Stephen Verbest, Brother Kevin Knox, and Brother Robert Simon (all O.C.S.O.). In addition, every monk I have met has taught me about Cistercian monasticism, and I thank them all.

A Ford Foundation Faculty Research Fellowship (1969–70) enabled me to investigate the relationship between monasteries and communes, and helped me see the importance of understanding the monastery if one is to understand community. Discussion with various colleagues since then has sharpened my thinking. They include James L. Price, Ira L. Reiss, Gene Summers, Charles Perrow, Robert Nisbet, William E. Snizek, Rosabeth Moss Kanter, Ruth S. Cavan, Hart Nelsen, George C. Homans, Beverly Fuller, Ellsworth R. Fuhrman, Charles L. Taylor, David H. Demo, Mark L. Wardell, Steven K. Paulson, Daniel Bradburd, Virginia Kerns, James H. Dorsett, and Madeline Hillery Scavo, are among those who pushed me most. Bradley Hertel, Charles J. Dudley, William H. Swatos, Jr., Norman Lea, Benjamin Zablocki, and several anonymous readers have read the entire manuscript in various drafts. It is better for their criticisms.

In addition to making comments on the manuscript, Charles J. Dudley spent many hours debating with me the concepts of freedom and love, and though we seldom agree, each of our ideas keeps impacting on the others so that I am not always certain where his ideas start and mine end. But the responsibility for what has been written here, as regarding all those who have helped, must be mine.

Clifton Bryant, Alan Bayer, and Cornelia Flora, the department chairs who were with me through most of this study, helped in numerous ways, especially in providing resources and encouragement.

Others have provided more special help. Many secretaries typed bits and pieces of the manuscript, but Cindy Crawford, Phyllis Light, Allison Craft, and Machell Schmolitz did most of it. Among the graduate students, I should note Colleen Wihelm, Paula C. Morrow, Pat Edwards, Marie Gabriel, Nancy Mannikko, and Andrea Burrows. Sr. Marie Augusta Neal kindly granted permission to use some of the statistics gathered for The Research Committee of the Conference of Major Religious Superiors of Women's Institutes of the United States of America.

Finally, to my wife, Iris, as always, goes a special thanks. She did without much so that I could work on this book, because she understands the special place it has in my life.

Beginning

Chimes sound across the quadrangle formed by the monastery buildings. I quickly get up and dress, pick up my Psalter, and hurry to the church. Another day of research in the monastery has begun. It is now 3:25A.M. Most of the monks are kneeling or standing in their stalls, on either side of the sanctuary. Several guests are with me in the far end, the part reserved for visitors. A knock sounds from the abbot's stall. Those monks who are kneeling stand up, and all form into two lines facing the altar. They make the sign of the cross. The cantor* sings,

> O come, bless the Lord,
> all you who serve the Lord,
> who stand in the house of the Lord,
> in the courts of the house of our God.

The rest of the monks respond,

> O Lord, open my lips,
> And my mouth shall declare your praise.

And so the Night Office begins. Several psalms are sung, in plainsong, antiphonnally, one line of monks singing one verse, the other side responding with another verse. After each psalm, the monks bow and sing, "Glory be to the Father and to the Son and to the Holy Spirit. As it was in the beginning, is now, and ever shall be, world without end, Amen." Then, the lights are extinguished save for one spotlight from the ceiling of the church, which shines on a lectern. The rest of the church is in darkness. A monk reads

*Specialized terms are defined in the Glossary.

from the Old Testament. After several minutes of silence, the lights go on, and the monks continue singing the psalms.

Four A.M.: The Night Office is over. I leave with the guests and unlock the door leading to the cloister, marked Private, walk down the cloister hall and into the refectory. A few monks are already eating. Breakfast is taken whenever one wishes, until 6:00 A.M. My own consists of a large slice of the monastery bread and margarine, some honey, cheese, and coffee.

After breakfast, I return to my room in the guest house. The silence surrounds me, so deep I can almost hear it. This silence is a part of a peace that is nowhere as intense and pervasive as in a Trappist monastery. I kneel to pray as the monks have taught me (with a few variations of my own). First, I quiet my mind, offering myself to God. Then I focus attention on a single word, repeating it with each breath, again, and again, and again. Eventually, the word is forgotten, and I am conscious only of the presence of God.

I pray for 20 minutes. Gradually I come back to my thoughts, repeating the Lord's Prayer very slowly. Then I read the Bible. It is now 5:30. I change into my shorts and go jogging. When I return, I shower, dress, and go to Mass (usually I skip the Office of Lauds). This is a weekday, and the guest end of the chapel is only half full. Father Charles is the principal celebrant, and since this is the feast day of a saint, he preaches the sermon about him, noting the perseverance of the saint, and how he would not deny his God, even under torture, which consisted of frying him alive. Father Charles has a wry sense of humor and could not resist commenting that the saint told his tormentors to turn him over, since he was done on one side. Then came the pun: he observed that this saint must have loved football, since he was the first patron saint of the gridiron.

The kiss of peace before Communion is always an emotional charge for me. Each member of the congregation of visitors and guests shakes hands with his or her immediate neighbors, and it is virtually always a firm and generous handshake with a big smile. The monks embrace. Most do so joyfully. Some are stiff, almost as if they were holding their neighbor apart rather than embracing. And though the monks do not give the "kiss" to the guests, there still seems to be the same emotional charge.

I always enjoy watching Father Charles take Communion. He appears totally absorbed. As a Protestant, I do not commune in this church, since the bishop is opposed, and so I have the opportunity to watch more closely. The expressions on the faces of the waiting communicants vary from matter of fact to intense. Some come with folded hands, some with rosaries. Some are regulars, appearing virtually every day. They do not go into the monastic part of the church. A priest and a brother bring them the bread and the wine. And there is the same variation of expression on the faces of those serving.

After Mass, I go to my room to prepare for the day. I am to help Father

Kevin in the bakery. It is a good job. The smell of yeast greets me. I like kneading the dough most. The warmth is almost as if it is alive—which in a sense it is, at least the yeast.

While we work, we often talk. Father Kevin does this mainly because he knows I need to understand what is happening in the monastery and about the life. Once he mentioned that he felt God really created grapes and wheat so we could have wine and bread so we could have the communion. He spoke also of the time he went to Indonesia with one of the other monks.

After work, I go to my room, where various monks come by for interviews. I have long ago given up using a tape recorder—too many of the monks are affected by its presence. And rarely do I take notes. The act of writing can be as inhibiting as a tape recorder. I have learned to listen to various parts of the conversation as if I were going through a house: now we are on the front steps, now on the porch, now in the living room, and so forth. Then, when I recreate the interview after the monk has left, I merely go through the house, recalling what was said, starting with the last room. It works well as long as the notes are reconstructed soon after the interview.

I usually skip the Office of Terce and work until Sext. This is one of the "little hours"; the psalms are shorter, and are repeated more frequently (every Monday, Wednesday, and Friday or Tuesday, Thursday, and Saturday, rather than every other week). One of my favorites comes from Psalm 122 (Psalm 123 in the Protestant Bible—I quote here from Gelineau's [1963] version, which has been prepared especially for liturgical singing):

> To you have I lifted up my eyes,
> you who dwell in the heavens:
> my eyes, like the eyes of slaves
> on the hand of their lords.
>
> Like the eyes of a servant
> on the hand of her mistress,
> so our eyes are on the Lord our God
> till he show us his mercy.

At the close of Sext, there is always the prayer: "May God's help remain with us always and with our brothers who are away." I find it beautiful in itself, and it reminds me that in spite of their commitment to remaining in the monastery and being separate from the world, there have always been occasions for monks to be out of the abbey.

Dinner follows Sext. Again I unlock the door marked Private, thinking as I do of the rare opportunity I have of sharing the cloister with these men. I try to be discreet. I act as an anthropologist and fade into the background. There is much to observe in the refectory, even though almost no talking is permitted.

Today the menu is lettuce and tomato salad, (meatless) pizza, string beans, beets, and cake for dessert. We file past the tables, each of us helping ourselves to the pizza and vegetables. The dessert will be served by monks who are appointed to that task for the week. The monks feel that there is a virtue in waiting on their brothers, and though they could get everything cafeteria style, this duty of serving is retained.

After grace, the monks begin eating, in silence. They communicate by sign language. The only ones who speak are the abbot, saying grace before and after meals, and the appointed reader for the week. The reader begins with a passage from the *Rule* of St. Benedict. He then continues from the reading of yesterday, the autobiography of Dorothy Day, founder of the Catholic Worker. The abbot rings a small handbell by his plate, as a signal for the reader to stop. Immediately, all of the monks rise, and the abbot says grace. Those who have not yet finished eating then continue. The others leave.

After dinner, the monks are allowed a siesta. Not all of them take it, but I do, gladly. Though I am able to function fairly well after a few days of adjusting to the early beginning of the monastic day, I am never at the abbey long enough to be completely comfortable with it (the monks say it takes six months). When I awake, I go to the Office of None, then work for a while on my field notes. There is not too much to do, since most of the morning was occupied in the bakery. When I am done, I decide to visit my friend the hermit. I walk past the orchard, past the quarry, through the woods, and after 45 minutes finally reach his house—one room, perched on top of a small cliff. He is happy to see me, as he always seems to be. We talk of his studies of the early desert fathers and their own hermit life. After a while, we have tea, sharing some of his dried toast. As I crunch it noisily, he smiles and says, "So it does make a loud sound when you are eating it. Living here alone, I sometimes wonder how loud it is."

His hermitage is small but well designed, measuring approximately ten by ten feet. He cooks on a coleman stove. His table also serves as a bed. He has a small closet built into one corner in which he can pray. He does not go out to visit except for his biweekly trips to the monastery for supplies. "But," he says, "if someone comes to visit me, I take that to be the will of the Lord." And, as I can attest, he receives visitors graciously.

I am "home" again at the monastery in time for Vespers. I eat supper first. Again there are only a few monks in the refectory, since supper is served from 4:00 until 5:30 P.M. (just before Vespers) and one eats when he pleases (or if one is fasting, he does not eat at all and thus does not call attention to his fasting).

Vespers is for some reason that I cannot explain my favorite office. It signals the end of work (though some monks have finished much sooner). The evening shadows on the walls of the church give it a hint of gold. Though not Gothic in the true sense, it shares some of the characteristics of Gothic churches in changing appearance with the change in light through the course of the day, except that the changes here are more subtle.

After Vespers, I go for a walk in the front of the abbey. A few other guests are walking also. I strike up a conversation with one, a now sober alcoholic who has made his first retreat here and is very impressed, especially with the peace. "If someone had tried to tell me about it," he said, "I could not have believed him." He is convinced that this will not be his last visit.

The final office for the day is Compline, sung by the monks from memory. The reason for memorizing this office is not apparent during summer, when light lasts well past 8:00 or 9:00 P.M., but in winter the justification is evident, for this office is sung in darkness. The monks begin with a traditional hymn, followed by Psalms 4 and 90 (91 in the Protestant versions), concluding with the hymn to Mary "Salve Regina." They then file by the abbot, who blesses them with holy water. It is a few minutes before 8:00 P.M., time to retire. The Great Silence has begun. There will be no conversations until after Mass the next day.

Such is a sample of one day in which I did research in Trappist monasteries over a period of almost 20 years. (For a more complete account of the research methods, see Appendix A.) What impressed me particularly was the love and the freedom these men expressed in their daily lives. This book is an attempt to describe and explain that love and freedom.

Introduction

> If it were true—as conceited shrewdness proud of not being deceived, thinks—that one should believe nothing which he cannot see by means of his physical eyes, then first and foremost one ought to give up believing in love.
>
> —Kierkegaard. *The Works of Love* 1962: 13.

The Christian monastery, in its beginnings more than 1500 years ago, was not conceived as an experiment. Rather, it began as an effort by groups of men and of women to live a more holy life. But in prohibiting any kind of genital sexual expression, the monastery became in effect an experiment, and a quite radical one, for it dispensed with a pivotal component of the normal community, the family. In order to build a community under such a restriction, the monastery had to emphasize (whether intentionally or unintentionally) features of community life we tend to take for granted: love and freedom.

Thus, the major themes of this book are freedom, love, and community. Since each of these terms is encumbered with a multitude of definitions, any definition will necessarily conflict with others. Granted this arbitrary quality, these terms are briefly defined here. In this book, communal organizations refer to such things as villages, cities, and of course monasteries, not to businesses, prisons, or political parties. Freedom means having choices. Love means doing the best one can for the beloved.

Parts of this chapter were adapted from George A. Hillery, Jr., "Gemeinschaft Verstehen," *Social Forces* 63, December 1984, 307–34.

SOCIOLOGISTS AND THE STUDY OF LOVE

A basic principle that guides the discussion is that communal organizations are most fully developed when they emphasize love, and that love can only be obtained in freedom. The principle cannot be verified here. The task is more limited. What do monasteries have to teach us about the role of love in communities? Love may be seen as varying between two extremes. At one end, it is focused on two persons who seek a mutual response. It is highly possessive and exclusive, and is essentially undisciplined. This is eros. At the other extreme, love is detached from personal gain, excludes no one, is universal, and is highly disciplined. This type is agapé. All forms of love vary between these extremes. (For a more complete discussion of love, see Chapter 3.) The monastery seeks to cultivate agapé to such an extent that it can replace all forms of love, particularly eros.

Sociologists do not like the concept of love. From 1971 to 1985, only one article on love appeared in nine of the major sociological journals (Lantz 1987—book reviews are not included in this count). Similarly, altruism had only three articles and affection, only ten. Friendship was represented somewhat better with 27 articles, but contrast this with crime (66 articles) and power (84). And yet, millions of marriages have been based on love, and Parsons goes as far as to say that kinship always orders eros (Parsons 1966:12). Mother love (affection) is synonymous with motherhood. Certainly, love is as old as recorded history. Confucius gave a great deal of attention to it, as did both the ancient Greeks and the Hebrews. It is something for which people have given their lives, including committing suicide.

Obviously, love is important to human beings, and it is essentially a social act, but most sociologists do not care to investigate it. Perhaps the aversion is due to the subjectivity of the concept. Cuzzort and King (1989:357) put the matter succinctly: "It appears that the more rigorously scientific we become in the social sciences, the more we remove ourselves from what we want to understand. The more we tolerate subjective human qualities, the less scientific we are."

But sociologists have been studying subjective phenomena for decades. Something else is probably also responsible for the neglect. I believe that the answer is found to some extent in the experiential nature of the phenomenon. Love must be experienced to be known at all. If it is not experienced, people have a tendency to deny its very existence.

Whatever the reason for the neglect, I want to show that love, especially agapé, exists in the monastery—imperfect, of course, but an ideal for which people will strive.

Perhaps a lesson can be learned from another concept studied by the masters. Marx, Durkheim, and Weber were not religious men. Marx tried to explain religion away by referring to it as an opiate. We learned nothing from this approach. Durkheim recognized that religion was important to people, and gave us *The Elementary Forms of Religious Life* (1915). Weber also took religion seriously. Though he admitted to being religiously "tone deaf," he produced a series of brilliant works on religion, of which *The Protestant Ethic and the Spirit of Capitalism* (1930) is only one of the best known.

The lesson, as I see it, pertains to love as well as religion. We may not agree with others about the importance we attach to a given phenomenon. We may believe that it is useless. But we may learn something if we try to discover why others think it meaningful.

It does no good to deny that love exists or to try to explain it away. Millions of people have experienced something. A more profitable approach is to try to discover how to work with it. We can do so only by knowing the conditions under which love is said to exist. This book intends to contribute to such an endeavor.

SYSTEMS OF TRUTH

Probably the most critical problem in comprehending monasteries is that one is not able to observe them adequately with the conventional understanding of the meaning of truth. That is, if one attempts to understand monasteries purely through what can be seen, heard, felt, touched, and tasted, one will not understand monasteries. This is true because the monastery is based on such largely immeasurable concepts as love and prayer. To consider only prayer, not only is it outside of the realm of sensory experience, but a certain type developed by these monks, contemplative prayer, cannot even be conceptualized (see Chapter 10). Yet prayer is central to monastic life.

There are systems of truth other than positivistic science that are also valid. To understand the meaning of truth, one must first understand the assumptions that are made (the metaphysics) and the method that is used to know something (the epistemology). Two main metaphysical assumptions are made about truth: that it is physical or that it is spiritual. (A third assumption is that both assumptions are valid.) There are numerous epistemologies. One may know something exists by an objective approach: something is true if I can show you how I observe it, and if you do what I tell you and come to the same conclusion, then it is true. However, there are numerous true (or real) experiences that have nothing to do with objectivity. The sounds of a Beethoven symphony, the taste of oysters or martinis must be experienced to be known, but they are nonetheless a kind of truth. This method of knowing may be called experiential.

There are other epistemologies (one knows by intuition, one knows because one trusts someone in authority, etc.), but these will do for our purposes. To simplify the discussion, we use only two extreme assumptions of reality and two methods of knowing: the spiritual and physical assumptions

Figure I.1
Selected Types of Truth

Epistemology
(method of knowing)
is only:

Metaphysical
assumption
that reality
is only:

	Experiential	Objective
Spiritual	Mystical	Theological
Physical	Sensory	Scientific

on the one hand and the experiential and objective methods on the other. The resultant typology (see Figure I.1) is an ideal or pure type. Any of the four truths is certainly more complicated than depicted here: science contains value judgments, theology is not always objective, and so on. There are also more than four kinds of truth; in fact, there are as many truths as there are metaphysical assumptions and epistemologies. The main objective of the typology is to show that there is more than one kind of truth. Recognizing the limitations, the four types may be described as follows: (1) scientific truth must ultimately be objective and based on physical evidence; (2) sensory truth is also based on physical things, but it can be known only through experience; (3) theological truth assumes the reality of the spiritual world, but relies on objective evidence (such as scripture references) for its conclusions; and (4) mystical truth concerns spiritual experiences, such as Paul's conversion on the road to Damascus (Acts 9:1–11).

This study uses all four kinds of truth and thus expands our conception of what sociology is about. One of my objectives in studying the monastery is to reintegrate sociology with its allied disciplines. I want to understand the monastery on its own terms but at the same time to link that understanding with the rich methodology of sociology. I will occasionally dabble into the psychology of the monks to grasp such things as the meaning of polity in the monastery. Without a knowledge of history, the importance of the *Rule* of Benedict, the strictness of the Trappist interpretation, and the significance of the Second Vatican Council would be lost. And throughout the book, I use a holistic, anthropological approach. In short, this volume attempts to reintegration of all sorts of knowledge—all sorts of truth—in order to understand a particular community.

I pay as much if not more attention to experiential knowledge than statistics. My objective in studying the Trappist monastery is to understand it. If something relevant can be objectively measured, such as the population of monks or their financial condition, I measure it. If measures can be approximated, I approximate them, such as the monks' report on their interpersonal conflicts, or their attitudes on freedom. But if the subject can be neither measured nor approximated, if it is essential to understanding monasticism, and if I can experience it, then I experience it and report that experience as best I can.

This effort cost more than a few days of handing out questionnaires and a few weeks of manipulating data in a computer. It cost more than a year of my life, a year that I could have invested in other things. The collection of data did not come easily (to say nothing about the analysis). This does not mean that I did not enjoy it. It became a labor of my own love as the monks accepted me into their cloister. Nevertheless, it had a price.

One of the questions that has become increasingly bothersome in my understanding of sociology is why we have not gone significantly beyond Weber, Durkheim, and Marx in our understanding of the human social condition. Why can sociology be so boring? Perhaps, just perhaps, we have assumed the existence of an impossible goal—that all the significance elements of the social experience can be measured. Charles J. Dudley and I are investigating sociology as a study of freedom as well as order (see Chapter 2 for our initial venture in this direction). Once one realizes that freedom is essential in understanding the social experience, then other now-neglected areas insist that they also be examined. Such things as prayer and love are such areas.

A NOTE ON OBJECTIVITY AND SUBJECTIVITY IN SOCIOLOGY

The use of truths other than scientific raises the problem of objectivity and bias. I mean by objectivity the ability to reason without allowing one's own values to interfere with one's judgement. It is in the interest of objectivity that the scientific method (scientific truth) is employed. One should note, however, that the scientific method is no guarantee of a lack of bias, especially in the social sciences.

In the first place, the very desire to be objective is a value that leads to bias. In choosing the scientific approach exclusively, one thereby rules out of consideration anything that cannot be studied through this form of truth, such as (in the present instance) love and prayer. Second, personal and cultural biases still operate even within subject matters that are amenable to science. For example, why have there been such negative reactions against the Nazi medical experiments?

There is also an implicit assumption that only in scientific truth can one be free of bias, or that one cannot be free from bias when one is operating within a value system. As should be evident from the previous discussion, we all have values. The question is whether a given value will produce biases, not whether one will have values. I would argue that objectivity and a lack of bias is not something to be attained automatically by the use of some system. Objectivity is an art. This statement can be most readily illustrated by considering performance in games. We may start with the observation that all game players are value oriented—they want to win. This can be a very emotional experience. But in many if not most games, such as football, tennis, chess, bridge, and poker, one must be able to put oneself in the role of the opponent. Some are better at role taking than others. Those who are best able to assume roles are the best artists and will be most likely to win, *in spite of their emotional value toward winning.*

In view of such problems with objectivity, two possible remedies may be used. One was proposed by Melvin Williams some years ago when he argued "for an environment of free competition between opposite biases" (1943:139–40). The other remedy is a logical accompaniment: One should make evident one's values and thus one's potential biases. Of course, this can never be done completely. It would take extensive psychological counselling to make us conscious of even most of our biases, but nevertheless, one is better able to work with one's values when aware of them. My most relevant values are my Christian Protestantism and my love for the monks. Knowing this, the reader is better prepared to judge whether my values lead to biases. (See Appendix A.)

Sociology has been in a deconstructionist mode for some time. However, arguing in the same manner as Cuzzort and King (1989), the more we try to understand society from a deconstructionist perspective, the more we lose in the understanding of process. For example, one cannot understand the monastery without understanding love, and the key to understanding love is not to be found in analysis. It follows that this study is more than a study of a monastery. It is a study in the untidy subjective, the elusive process.

In the chapter on deviance (13), we shall encounter Br. Jacob, a monk who was a constant thorn in the side of many in the abbey. But he served a useful purpose. He helped define the community boundaries. In order to understand the boundaries of a community, we must know more than the location of the city limits or the counties that comprise the Standard Metropolitan Statistical Area. To try to know the monastery merely by counting—whether abbots or outhouses—is an insult, not only to the monks, but to sociology itself. What we will discover is that the boundaries of this community are defined by emotions and not by physical markers, even though the markers exist.

Accordingly, those who are convinced that sociology can only proceed as a science should stop reading here, if they have not already done so. Nothing more that I could say is likely to persuade them that what follows has any value.

THE SIGNIFICANCE OF THE MONASTERY FOR COMMUNITY

Christian monasteries have deliberately excluded erotic love. In doing so, they introduce simplifications that are instructive in several ways. My initial interest in these groups arose from the conviction that monasteries were one of the extreme experiments in communal living. They had completely and successfully eliminated the biosocial family. Experiments have always had strategic value in a field where experimentation is difficult and often impossible.

The commune probably showed the importance of the monastery most clearly. The connection is found in the intense commitment and the practice of placing the welfare of individuals above material considerations (Hillery and Morrow 1976). Monasteries are also the most long-lived communes in history, because they have continued for centuries and have shown repeated ability to renew themselves according to their basic ideals. In contrast, the life span of most communes extends not even a generation, and almost none last more than a hundred years. Thus, the monastic "experiment" has been a relatively permanent one, especially as compared with other attempts to modify community life.

The radical nature of this experiment is seen in comparison with other communal endeavors. Whereas free love has been attempted in the Kibbutz (Spiro 1956, 1958), and whereas the Oneida community attempted group marriage (Carden 1969), the monastery eliminated not only sexual love and marriage but even sexual relations. Only the Shakers approximated the success of monasteries in removing the family, but lacking a mother church from which to draw recruits, the Shakers are now almost extinct.

Another reason for a study of monastic life concerns the future of monasteries themselves. In part because of the recommendations from the Second Vatican Council, changes have occurred that could drastically alter their existence—and even possibly lead to their disappearance, at least in the industrial West. If so, it is imperative that a sociological study be made of them while there is time. But if the monks are about to embark on another period of renewal, as I believe may be the case, then a useful baseline has been prepared for future investigation.

RELATED RESEARCH

Studies of monasteries are rare. Probably the most complete is *The Plan of St. Gall,* by Walter Horn and Ernest Born (Horn and Born 1979; see also Price 1982). Although their chief interest is in the *plan* of this ninth-century monastery, they also comment enough on the activities of the monks that one may achieve a fairly reasonable picture of what life in this monastery must have been. However, there are several important differences from what I am trying to do.

1. Whereas both studies are historical in that they represent a certain period of time (820–830 A.D. for St. Gall, 1969–87 for my study), *The Plan of St. Gall* is historically reconstructed, and my work is reported from living monks.
2. The discussion concerns a plan, especially in its ideal sense. One never knows how much of the plan is conjectural and how much actually existed. More pointedly, what went on at St. Gall? We can say that much was probable, but we cannot answer that question with certainty. Though my work may suffer the same criticism, the criticism can only be in part, for I begin with description of what I experienced, and my goal is to portray the life as it is. The objective of Horn and Born is to study a plan. The life of the monks is incidental. My own concern is exactly opposite. I am primarily concerned with the life, and the monastery's plan is incidental.
3. St. Gall is a Benedictine monastery; the one I study is Trappist, which involves several reforms from the Benedictine movement. To mention only four, there is less emphasis on liturgy, more emphasis on prayer and penance, greater seclusion from the outside, and today, no separation between choir monks and lay brothers.

Several works that claim to be analyses of communities are actually concerned with orders (for example, Choukas 1935; O'Toole 1964; Ramold 1964). The order (see Hill 1973) is a collection of either communal or formal organizations, two quite distinct types of human groups (see Chapter 3). At any rate, the order is not a single communal organization. Even those reports that discuss a single monastery focus on only one aspect. Hill (1967) and Sampson (1968) wrote of the novitiate or training function. Azarya (1984) treated the interesting case of a refugee community (vill) within a monastery. However, we have no detailed account of the monastery operating in its own right as a communal organization.

One may obtain a view of one Trappist abbey through the works of and about Thomas Merton. The best descriptions given by him are *The Sign of Jonas* (1953) and *Conjectures of a Guilty Bystander* (1966). *The Seven Storey Mountain* (1948) is mostly about his life outside the monastery. Good biographies abound (Furlong 1985; Hart 1974). Mott (1984) is especially good for details of Merton's personal and social life, and Kramer (1984) for an appreciation of his interior (or prayer) life. But as valuable as such readings are, they are limited in that they give the perspective of one monk.

The only sociological study that emphasizes the role of agapé love in Christian and other forms of monasticism is Sorokin's *The Ways and Power of Love* (1954, Chapters 20 and 21). Based on an extensive range of sources, this work shows how widespread the monastic practices of agapé were. His thesis thus is much the same as that developed in this book. The difference is that the present study focuses on what happened in one monastery during the decades following the Second Vatican Council (1963–65). Sorokin discusses various monastic movements in Islam (Sufi), Buddhism, and especially Christianity from St. Basil the Great to Sts. Theresa of Avila and Francis de Sales—a span of twelve centuries. Nevertheless, Sorokin's work provides a good introduction to this one. Indeed, the pertinent chapters have been reprinted by Benedictine monks (Sorokin 1973) and are used by both Benedictines and Trappists in their novitiates.

THE ABBEY

The monastery being studied belongs to the Order of Cistercians of the Strict Observance (O.C.S.O.), popularly known as Trappists, an order in the Roman Catholic Church. It was initially chosen because it displayed what seemed to be then (Hillery 1971) a curious mixture of freedom and discipline (only much later did the importance of love emerge). No monastery can represent all others, just as no single case can represent an entire population. But at least the monastery under consideration falls near the middle of the various statistical distributions that I have examined. (Though the focus is on a single monastery, comparisons with others in the United States are made at various points in the discussion.)

The monastery is given the fictitious name of Our Lady of the Palisades (the name is taken from some cliffs in the region). Technically, it is an abbey, a type of monastery that enjoys a certain independence and autonomy under the control of its own abbot (superior). This means not only that it is mainly exempt from the authority of the local bishop but also that it is largely independent from other monasteries. The abbey is within an hour's drive of a small city, but is otherwise isolated. The monastery was founded in approximately 1850 from a mother house in Europe. When this study began in 1969, there was an official population of 94 monks, but only approximately 70 were physically present. By 1991, no more than 42 still lived in the community.

The monastery traces its founding to the 17th century in France, particularly as the movement was consolidated by de Rancé, abbot of La Grande Trappe (whence the name "Trappists"). The history of this order has been repeatedly punctuated by various reforms (of which the present efforts at renewal in the abbey may well be another beginning). The Trappists themselves are a reform of the Cistercians, and thus they call themselves Cistercians of the Strict Observance. The Cistercians in turn were a reform (in

1098) of the Benedictines, who were founded in the sixth century A.D. (See Chapter 1.)

The monastic way of life practiced by these monks implies separation from the world and from active ministry and a permanent residence in a "family" of monks living in a rural area, governed by an elected superior (or abbot). The monks live by the labor of their hands, in poverty (or in a condition approaching that), with common ownership of all property.

The purpose of the monastery is inextricably involved in efforts toward renewal following the recommendations of the Second Vatican Council (Vatican II) of 1962–65. Earlier, a quite famous monk could write that the monks have "as their purpose the Liturgical praise and contemplation of God, not only for the sanctification of their own souls, but as representatives of the whole Church before the throne of God" (Merton 1962: 384).

Today, the purpose cannot be stated so categorically. The monk is not as certain, for example, of how representative he is "of the whole Church." He knows (or should) that he has been called to the monastery by God, and he knows that prayer is an indispensable part of this call. Beyond that, purposes differ with different monks, from those who feel called to a life of intensive prayer, to those who feel called to follow in the *Rule* of St. Benedict, to those who believe that their way of life is a witness of God's will for the world, to those who consider the monastery as a place to which the outside world may come for spiritual recuperation and re-creation. And by no means has this list exhausted the possibilities.

Of course, the purposes of the monks do not vary randomly. There is a structure to the monastery into which these purposes fall. First, there is the *Rule* of St. Benedict to which Cistercian monasteries are committed to follow as closely as is practical. There is the emphasis on prayer, both liturgical and contemplative. There are the vows and the promises of chastity, obedience, poverty, stability, and conversion of life. There are also numerous minor details that make up the "way of life" of *this* particular monastery. This means that a monk might be called to one monastery and not to another within the same order. This book will be explaining much of that "way of life."

For the order in general, there are three central activities: liturgy, labor, and *lectio divina* (the three Ls, as they are termed by some monks). Liturgy includes the Mass and the offices (minor rites that are a duty of the monks, consisting of psalms, prayers, hymns, etc. lasting from 15 to 30 minutes— see Chapter 10) that are said daily. Labor refers to the occupation to which the monk is assigned by the abbot: baker, tractor driver, guest master, and so on. *Lectio divina* means literally divine reading or study. More broadly it concerns efforts toward "self-improvement and self-searching, contemplation and meditation. In the later stages of growth the person is essentially alone." (Chapter papers 1971:42).

Realizing, then, that the purpose of the monastery is as varied as is the variation among monks, it may be said that Trappists come together to search for God, to pray to God, and to help each other in these efforts.

THE TIME OF STUDY

Research among the Trappists started in the fall of 1966. It began at the abbey in the fall of 1969 and continued actively through 1984, though observations are still being made as of this writing. In addition, a very important source of information was *A Report of the Survey of Contemplatives* (Research Committee of CMSW 1969). Sister Marie Agusta Neal, S.N.D., was the head of the research committee that designed and sponsored the survey. Administration to 1,114 nuns was done in the summer and fall of 1968. It is a counterpart for contemplatives of the sisters' survey of 1967 in which 135,106 active sisters participated. The contemplative survey, however, concerns mainly contemplative sisters. Trappists were the only male organization participating (235 responded at the same time, 66 from Palisades Abbey). The results of the survey are found in two references: a tabulation of the marginal totals for the 649 questions (Research Committee of CMSW 1969) and a report by Sister Neal (Neal 1970). The marginal tabulations are used here, and though one may glean a vast amount of information from them in this form, the extent of statistical manipulation of the data is limited. (For more detail on data I collected, see Appendix A.)

Thus, the time frame used in this book extends for more than 15 years. Understandably, not all of the monastery was studied at once. Accordingly, what happens in one chapter will not always correspond in time with what happens in another chapter. Since most of the material is based on participant observation, such differences are unavoidable, and the reader should be aware of them.

I have attempted to correct for such gaps in information by bringing the reader up to date where necessary. However, there is always a judgmental decision about what is necessary, which changes are significant and which are not. The point is that this study is not a history of what happened from 1969 to 1987. It is an account of what was present during varying periods in that segment of time. The focus during this time segment shifts from topic to topic.

Not all parts of the monastery change at the same rate. The basic architectural design is a modern variant of Gothic, including the renovated church. This design has existed for decades. The economic system, however, changes radically from year to year, as profits replace losses, as one system of enterprise follows another. Thus, in certain areas, such as some of the basic monastic beliefs, one point in time is as good as any. For others, such as the size of the population, the economy, or the succession of abbots, greater care must be made in noting the changes.

One should, in addition, maintain an appropriate time perspective. Although 18 years is approximately one-fourth of a man's life, it is 13 percent of the monastery's life and one percent of the life of the order. Thus, how "long" a time period is involved depends on one's point of view.

PLAN OF THE BOOK

Part I places the monastery in its historical and sociological contexts. Chapter 1 traces the history of the order and the abbey. Chapters 2 and 3 examine the major themes, freedom, love, and community, particularly as they are manifested in the monastery. In Part II, the entire community is considered in detail. The major purpose of this analysis is to show the context in which freedom, love, and community operate. The basic question that guided the writing was, What is necessary to understand the monastic community? Some features of the life appear more important than others, such as the major themes. But one cannot fully understand the monastery without knowing also the place of the guest house in monastic life, the attachments to their family of orientation, the way in which they earn their living, the functioning of their government, and so forth.

The chapters in Part II are arranged according to the kind of data available. Statistical data existed for much of the material in Chapters 4 through 9. Though participant observation is used throughout the study, it becomes more of the mainstay in the chapter on prayer (Chapter 10) and those that follow. Thus, the first five chapters in this section provide an observational grounding or empirical basis, whereas more subjective elements, based on my own experience, characterize the remainder. Neither type of data is superior, but the two types are suitable to different topics, and they require different treatment.

The question is, then, How does the monastic community operate? How does it function? The goal of the monks is to be continually striving for agapé. How do they do this? And how do they survive in the process? To answer these questions, many things must be considered. They are all part of the ethnographic analysis.

And now, a warning to the reader. It is easy to fall in love with the Trappists, and thus it is easy to romanticize them. But we must be careful not to force them into our own preconceived molds. These are not museum pieces from the Middle Ages. They are fully modern, 20th-century men, trying to find God by means of a model which, though ancient, is still viable in this technocratic age. The reader should allow them to tell their story in their own manner and not be shocked, as one visitor was, that they are in many ways very much like some other neighbors we may happen to know.

Part I

The Historical and Sociological Context

Chapter 1

The Historical Context

Palisades Abbey exists in a broader historical context that is almost two thousand years old. Thus, it has developed numerous customs and practices and multitudinous relationships. This chapter traces the origin of these practices and connections, especially the influence of the Roman Catholic Church, the Benedictine and Cistercian Orders, and for Palisades, the ties developed throughout the world. To assist the reader in following the discussion, a chronological summary has been prepared (see Table 1.1).

ORIGINS: FROM THE THIRD CENTURY TO BENEDICT

The beginnings of Christian monasticism can not be precisely dated. Christians living a common life are first mentioned in the Book of Acts (Chapters 2 and 4), but whether this pattern included celibacy is unknown. More closely approximating monasticism in the sense of *monachus* (one who lives alone), is St. Paul of Thebes (228–341 A.D.), who was not a monk in that he lived in a community, but rather is said to have been the first Christian hermit. It became the custom for hermits to gather around those noted for their sanctity. One of these, Anthony (251–356 A.D.), son of a well-to-do Egyptian peasant, heard the words of Jesus read by a priest: "If you would be perfect, go sell what you possess and give to the poor, and you will have treasure in heaven; and come, follow me" (Matt. 19:21). This was in 271. Anthony obeyed and turned to a solitary life in the desert. For those attracted to him (essentially hermits), he had enclosures (or *lauras*) built, separate cells scattered over a limited area. This tentative monasticism

---

Little effort in this chapter has been made to be original. Secondary materials are the only sources before 1950. The aim is to provide the reader with historical background.

Table 1.1
Chronology of Events in Benedictine and Cistercian Monasticism

Dates	Events
228-341	St. Paul of Thebes, first Christian hermit.
251-356	St. Anthony, tentative monasticism.
286-346	St. Pachomius writes first monastic rule.
529-534	Dates attributed to the writing of the Rule of Benedict.
1097	Benedictine reform at Molesme Abbey under Robert.
1098	Citeaux founded: first Cistercian monastery.
1106	Cistercians placed directly under protection of the Pope.
1113	Bernard arrives at Citeaux with 30 companions.
1116	Charter of Charity composed by Stephen: organizing Cistercian monasteries into a loose federation.
1153	Death of Bernard.
1315-1317	Famine in Europe.
1347	Black Death.
1337-1453	Hundred Years War.
1378-1417	Great Schism in the Roman Catholic Church.
1666	Papal Bull separated the Strict (Trappist) from the Common Observance among the Cistercians.
1790	French Assembly declared all property of the Church belonged to the French Nation.
1791	Lestrange takes 21 Trappist monks to Switzerland.
1824?	Petit Clairvaux monastery founded in Nova Scotia-- beginning of Trappist life in America.
1849	Gethsemani and New Melleray Abbeys founded in America.
1962-1965	Second Vatican Council ("Vatican II").

was developed further by St. Pachomius (286–346 A.D.), also in Egypt. A convert from paganism, after some years as a hermit he felt called to provide a monastic life for others. He wrote the first monastic rule (Anon. 1944: 3–4; Knowles 1969: 13–14), which assumed chastity and poverty. To these he added obedience, not simply as a mark of respect, as a hermit would give to an elder, but as a condition of monastic life. The first of his monasteries was at Tabenne, upper Egypt, in 315, and he eventually collected thousands of hermits into monastic communities (Knowles 1969:14).

During this period an abundant literature was produced on the spiritual life. I will only mention here examples from "Some Sayings of the Desert Fathers" and from the works of Cassian.

It was said of Abbot Agatho that for three years he carried a stone in his mouth until he learned to be silent.

A monk ran into a party of handmaids of the Lord on a certain journey. Seeing them he left the road and gave them a wide berth. But the Abbess said to him: If you were a perfect monk, you would not even have looked close enough to see that we were women.

Abbot Pastor said: the virtue of a monk is made manifest by temptations. (Merton 1960: 30–32.)

The *Institutes* and *Conferences* of John Cassian were written between 415 and 429. Cassian lived for 15 years among the hermits and from this experience presented their teachings to the monks in monasteries in France (Knowles 1969:15). His works heavily influenced the development of monasticism in the West. "Quotations abound in the rule of St. Benedict and the *Conferences* were read every night before compline in early medieval monasteries" (Knowles 1969:15).

According to Knowles (1969:25) monasticism "spread gradually and sporadically as a plant spreads from seeds that are blown abroad." Athanasius, Anthony's friend and biographer, was probably the most effective agent in the diffusion, for "his *Life of Antony* was a Christian classic in his lifetime" (1969:25).

In the next century (about 480 A.D.), Benedict (from the Latin, meaning blessed one) was born in Nursia, Italy, of a noble Roman family. When he completed his studies, he left Rome and later took residence in a cave, where he became a hermit. Eventually, disciples came in such numbers that he built monasteries for them, the most famous of which was Monte Cassino. The date he wrote his celebrated *Rule for Monasteries* is unknown, though 529 to 534 is suggested by Steidle (1952:33). The *Rule* was not entirely original, but it survived and spread throughout Europe, north to England and west to Germany by the eighth century, and ultimately all over the globe.

Thus, the beginnings of the monastic movement were not the action of one or even a few men. It was a reaction of many to the corruption they saw in life around them, with the conviction that the only hope for salvation was to flee from the world and escape to the desert, where temptations at least seemed more obvious, if not simpler. Benedict came at the end of this period, at its crystallizing point, and codified what was then known into his *Rule*. Its longevity is partly due to the efforts of many.

FROM BENEDICT TO THE FOUNDING OF THE CISTERCIANS

Knowles (1969:35–36) gives a picture of the daily life in an Italian monastery in the sixth century. It was a small structure of stone with a tile or shingled roof. Around were offices, outhouses, and, further away, farm sheds. The rooms were on one floor. None were large, since dormitory, refectory, and oratory were intended for approximately 15 monks. The oratory had a simple altar. Kitchen, novices' quarters, and guest house were either separate or additions to the main block. There was a workroom and a reading room but no cloister.

The appearance was of a large family at work. Psalms were chanted and lessons sung in monotone. There was no daily Mass, though Communion was usually given every day by the abbot. The Night Office began at 2 A.M., Lauds at daybreak, Prime at 6 A.M., and Terce, Sext, and None followed at three-hour intervals. Vespers was at the last hour of daylight, Compline after supper, usually in darkness and sung by memory. In summer and from Easter to mid-September and Sundays the main meal was at noon and supper. A single meal was allowed on fast days, with a drink and some bread in the evening. Between the offices, one did reading, domestic work, or manual work.

The monks at first were neither priests nor scholars, and the ritual was simple. During the next two centuries (by the rise of Charlemagne in 770), the typical Western monastery had changed radically. It became an extensive complex built around open courts, with a large church, dormitories, and other rooms for the monks, novices, and the ill and elderly. It also housed offices for administering large estates. It "was becoming a storehouse of relics and objects of art, visited by crowds of pilgrims, while in the cloister were stored illuminated service books, manuscripts and liturgical treasures" (Knowles 1969:39). Most people, at least by middle age, were in some order (according to Knowles). Manual work was felt to be unfitting, and the monastery with its writings and artistic craft work was the center of European cultured life. Liturgy grew in quantity and solemnity. "The 'monastic centuries' had begun" (Knowles 1969:39).

During the early Middle Ages, observance of the *Rule* was not uniform. There was a tendency to lessen the severity of asceticism, as for example, allowing more clothing and mitigating the fasts (Anon. 1944:14). At the monastery of Molesme, under the Abbot Robert, first steps were taken in 1097 to return to the essentials that Benedict advocated. In 1098, permission to inaugurate a reform was granted by the apostolic legate of France, with the condition that (among other things) the founders leave the Abbey of Molesme and start a new monastery. This monastery was eventually called Citeaux (the monks were known as Cistercians).

The desire for a more strict interpretation of the *Rule* was not prompted by laxness or scandal at Molesme. Nevertheless, the decision of Robert and those who decided to leave prompted severe antagonisms from the other monks, and it was several months before they left. The monks of Molesme, meanwhile, appealed to the Pope, requesting the return of their abbot. The Pope agreed, and Robert resumed his former position. Under Alberic, the new abbot of Citeaux, manual labor was increased and external ministries (such as pastoring local churches) was abandoned, so that the contemplative life could become the main focus (Anon. 1944:30). Lay brothers were introduced; they had no vote in Chapter (the community of monks), but were otherwise treated as monks. The lay brothers were to enable the monastery to be self-sustaining and the choir monks to fulfill their liturgical duties. The white habit came into being at this time, because of the wording of the *Rule*: "The monks should not complain about the color or the coarseness of [the garments], but be content with what can be found in the district where they live and can be purchased cheaply" (Doyle 1948:Ch. 55:76). In consequence, the Cistercians did not dye their habits black, as was the Benedictine custom. The scapular (combined apron and hood), which is now black, was initially either brown or black and was not technically a part of the habit but was a protective garment used during work (Anon. 1944:34).

The first church built of stone (a material for which Cistercians still seem to have a fondness) was consecrated November 16, 1106. It also was dedicated to the Blessed Virgin Mary, the beginning of an unbroken Cistercian tradition (Lekai 1977:16). Of at least equal significance was the bull of papal protection secured by Alberic from Pope Paschal II. Known as the "Roman privilege," the bull ordained that the monks of the new monastery "be secure and free from any annoyance ... under the special protection of the Apostolic See" (Lekai 1977:17). Not only did this bull implicitly approve the discipline of these monks, but it assured them the freedom and security indispensable to future growth.

Under Stephen, who followed Alberic as abbot, a stricter observance was made of enclosure and simplicity in ornamentation. Postulants, however, were lacking, and the community was getting older and was decimated by plague. In 1113 (according to recent evidence—Lekai 1977:19), Bernard (then 22 years of age) and thirty of his relatives and friends entered the monastery. Other postulants came quickly. The third new foundation, or daughter house, the famous Clairvaux, was established within two years of

Bernard's coming, and he was put in charge. Other daughter houses were rapidly founded.

No community is self-sufficient, and Stephen recognized this fundamental sociological fact. In 1116, he called the superiors of the four daughter houses to Citeaux (La Ferte, Pontigny, Clairvaux, and Morimond) to regulate their dependence on the mother house. He prepared a draft of what was to be known as the Charter of Charity, which was unanimously accepted, though it was to undergo revision for the next 50 years (Lekai 1977:27). The purpose of the charter was to supplement the *Rule* in bringing the abbeys into close relation without disturbing their autonomy. The abbot of Citeaux had the duty to visit every monastery but could not interfere with its internal operations. This position is today known as the "Father Immediate." Taxes among the houses were abolished, though any abbot could appeal for material help. General convocations (Chapters) were instituted with regular visits (Visitations) among the abbeys, especially by the Father Immediate of any mother house. The abbot was to visit the daughter houses, examine their administration, and restore order and "fervor where these had relaxed" (Anon. 1944:55). The charter encouraged hospitality, regulated precedence among abbots, established procedures for abbatial elections, and specified punitive measures against unworthy or negligent abbots (Lekai 1977:28).

CISTERCIAN EXPANSION THROUGH THE TWELFTH CENTURY

It is characteristic of religious movements that they have periods of growth and decline, and in some, the decline is followed by a new growth. This happened among the Benedictines, though not in all houses. The spiritual renewal that occurred in Citeaux led to a distinct separation from the Benedictine Order. The growth of the Cistercians was comparable to that of Citeaux after Bernard's arrival. During Stephen's tenure (1109–33), 73 abbeys were founded. At Bernard's death in 1153, there were 343 houses, and when the order was dissolved in France in 1790, there were between 700 and 727. The average size of the individual monasteries is not known, but Citeaux, certainly one of the larger houses, had 700 monks. The Abbey of Vaucelles, founded in 1132 as the 13th daughter house of Clairvaux, in 1232 had 303 choir monks and 103 lay brothers (Anon. 1944:75).

Though Bernard was not the founder of the order, nor even its general head, his authority was on a par with the abbot of Citeaux. "He even eclipsed the venerable Founders, SS. Alberic and Stephen, by his singular personality and varied endowments both of nature and grace. But for all that, the order did not assume his name, although this has been done by several of its branches" (Anon. 1944:113). His influence went far beyond his abbey and even his order. For example, according to the *Columbia-Viking Desk Encyclopedia* (Bridgewater 1960: 103), holiness of life, immense capacity of mind, force of character, and burning eloquence made him the most powerful figure of his day.... He led the successful fight to seat Pope Innocent II and was the adviser of Pope Eugene III.... His preaching [ordered by Eugenius III—Anon. 1944:89] launched the Second Crusade. Bernard was notable also for...his protection of the weak (e.g., the Jews of the Rhineland) from the powerful.

THE DECLINE OF THE CISTERCIANS

Just as the Benedictines had a lively expansion during the early Middle Ages, so the Cistercians began their own growth; and as with the Benedictines, they too had their decline. The Cistercian Order was clearly a product of the 12th century. It reached its peak in number of new foundations in 1150. In that year alone it started more than 100 new houses (Lekai 1977:46). But where hundreds of monasteries were founded in the 12th century, only 50 new foundations appeared between 1250 and 1300, during the first half of the 14th century there were only ten, and the next 50 years saw only five (Lekai 1977:91). After an auspicious start, the following centuries constituted an extended period of decline (until dissolution in 1790).

Several causes for the decrease may be noted. First is the very success of the order itself. Even St. Bernard asked one of his abbots "not to trouble him with querulous complaints about the administration of his house, as he [Bernard] had plenty of troubles of his own, not to be burdened with those of other abbots" (Anon. 1944:165). There were too many houses, spread too far apart, founded too rapidly, to permit successful integration. Another factor was the decline in the spirit of poverty. "That devotion to labor which had been the strength of Citeaux resulted in a temporal prosperity, and in the end proved noxious; the monasteries became wealthy, and Cistercian simplicity inevitably disappeared" (Anon. 1944:171). Not least important was the dissension among some of the major abbots, involving especially the abbot of Citeaux: "Bickering and wrangling went on intermittently at the General Chapters for centuries," ending only with the end of the order in the French Revolution (Anon. 1944:172).

There were also external factors. From 1315 to 1317, a famine occupied all of Europe; 30 years later the bubonic plague appeared, the Black Death, decimating in three years as much as a third of the population, and even more in the monasteries. The Hundred Years' War (1337–1453) had its own famine and depopulation. The Great Schism of the West (1378–1417), creating as it did rival papal powers, weakened the authority of the ecclesiastical hierarchy. The Renaissance challenged the supremacy of faith as the arbiter of truth. The Protestant Reformation destroyed all monasteries of England, Scotland, Ireland, Holland, Norway, and Sweden and almost all in Germany and Switzerland (Anon. 1944:172).

Probably the most insidious factor was the custom of appointing commendatory abbots, whereby secular authorities and even the Pope had the
right to designate superiors. Often these were not monks—some were even
children. Their usual concern was only collecting the benefices from an
abbey. With no interest in the spiritual let alone the material welfare of the
monks, the custom of having abbeys *in commendam* led to the ruin of
monasteries, not only financially but in number of vocations as well. Cistercian abbeys came under its influence in the 14th century and eventually
the practice spread to include Italy, France, Spain, Hungary, Germany,
Ireland, and Scotland. The relative lack of commendatory abbots in England
may be attributed in part to the suspicion of the English "that the pope
acted habitually as a French Agent" (Lekai 1977:105).

TRAPPIST ORIGINS AND SPREAD FROM EUROPE TO
WORLDWIDE SCOPE

One may speculate that just as any organization may contain the seeds
of its own demise, so also it contains the seeds of its renewal. Abuses in
the 15th century "were as much in evidence as were the necessity and
intention to correct them" (Lekai 1977:109). Various reforms were attempted, one of the successful being the Strict Observance. The date for its
beginning is usually given as 1598, when Octave Arnolfini, a 19-year-old
Italian noble, was appointed commendatory abbot of La Charmoye Abbey.
In 1606, with two other monks, he signed a document that called for reform,
especially in following the *Rule* without dispensation, which meant abstain-
ing from meat. Their resolve met with much resistance, and skirmishes
between the "Abstinents" and the "Ancients," as they came to be called,
continued for years, involving not only popes but the king of France.

Relations between the two observances became more strained with the
appearance of Armond Jean de Bouthillier de Rancé, abbot of the monastery
at La Trappe. The papal bull of 1666 separated the Strict from the Common
Observance as a "distinct legal entity within the Order" (Lekai 1977:148).
However, de Rancé was not satisfied. He instituted an even more strict
interpretation of the *Rule* than practiced under the Strict Observance. He
"gradually sharpened the rigor of the fasts and suppressed the little relax-
ations that hitherto had been tolerated by the Congregation of the Strict
Observance" (Anon. 1944:243). Only salt was permitted as seasoning and
only two dishes of cooked food were served at dinner. Fish, eggs, and butter
were eliminated. "He reintroduced the hard couch as was befitting a Cistercian religious, restricted active correspondence with the outside world,
and suppressed the recreation period after dinner and the weekly walk out
of the enclosure" (Anon. 1044:244).

Not only did de Rancé go beyond Abstinent standards of severity, but
after 1667 he ceased to attend sessions of either the General Chapter or the

Strict Observance. Known for his learning, piety, and eloquence, he also possessed, Lekai (1977:147) notes, "temper, ostentatious asceticism and inflexibility." Though his actions did not bode well for the harmony of the order, his extreme commitment and dedication provided an intransigent nucleus from which the order could again grow after a near disastrous pruning.

In 1790, the French Assembly declared that all property of the Church in France belonged to the nation. In effect, this ruling meant the end of French monastic life. Lekai (1977:172–73) observes, "The forces that finally triumphed against the monks were in no way provoked by the misdeeds of individuals or communities; they arose out of principle and directed their fury not against abuses, but against monasticism as an ideal, as a way of life." Many monks died in French prison camps or in the penal colony of French Guiana. Others fled to the various countries of Europe, only to be followed by the invading French Armies of Napoleon. The monastery at La Trappe, however, undertook to preserve the Cistercian way of life. Augustin de Lestrange (1754–1827), the last novice master at La Trappe, took 21 monks of his community to Switzerland, settling in the abandoned charterhouse of Valsainte on June 1, 1791. Here, under his leadership, the monks "outdid one another in introducing even greater mortifications" (Lekai 1977:181). With no heating, sleeping on the floor with only a blanket and a straw pillow, and their diet restricted to bread, water, and boiled vegetables, such severity did not deter vocations. When the Trappists returned to France in 1815, they experienced even further growth. By 1855, there were 23 abbeys, with four houses in Belgium, two in the United States, and one each in Ireland, England, and Algeria. By 1894 the abbeys more than doubled, extending to Germany, Italy, Austria-Hungary, Holland, Spain, Canada, Australia, Syria, Jordan, South Africa, and China, totalling 56 monasteries with 3,000 monks and 600 priests (Lekai 1977:184).

Meanwhile, the Cistercians were still trying to achieve their separate identities. In 1834 a decree from Rome combined all French abbeys into one congregation. However, the Trappists were generally disenfranchised among the Cistercians, not being allowed to vote in the General Chapters. In 1892, the "Order of Reformed Cistercians of Our Lady of La Trappe" was formed, and in 1902 reference to La Trappe was dropped, the Trappists becoming the Order of Reformed Cistercians or of the Strict Observance, "true heirs to all Cistercian rights and privileges" (Lekai 1977:189). The abbeys studied in this book are all part of this order.

TRAPPISTS IN AMERICA

The date of the establishment of the first Trappist monastery in America is not clear. Unsuccessful efforts were started toward the end of the 18th century. In 1815, Father Vincent de Paul Merle was accidentally left behind

by one of these monastic expeditions at the Canadian port of Halifax. After
living as a missionary among the Indians for almost a decade, he founded
the small monastery of Petit Clairvaux in Nova Scotia with the help of some
monks from Bellefountains Abbey in France. The destructive effects of two
fires prompted a move to Lonsdale, Rhode Island, where the monks built
Our Lady of the Valley, which itself burned. They then moved to Spencer,
Massachusetts, founding St. Joseph's Abbey in 1849. Since the monks lacked
a permanent place during their earlier years, historians generally do not
designate them as the first monastery in America, but the monks at St.
Joseph's Abbey are descended from the monks of Nova Scotia who began
monastic life in America in 1815, more than three decades before Gethsemani, which is regarded as the first or "proto" abbey in this country. New
Melleray was founded in 1849, a few months later than Gethsemani. All
other nine Trappist-Cistercian houses for men in the United States descended
from these three abbeys.

PALISADES ABBEY

The monastery known in this work as Palisades Abbey was founded before
1850 from one of the daughter houses of a French monastery. The monks
settled in America on a thousand acres of farm land that contained two
small frame buildings, one of which they used as their dwelling and church.
Along with the appointed superior, there were two priests and four brothers
(Hoffman 1952:63). A few months later, sixteen additional monks were
sent from the mother house in Europe, but an epidemic of cholera reduced
their numbers to ten. Another contingent soon followed: four priests and
13 lay brothers. After one of the monks defected during the journey, the
total strength of Palisades was brought to 33 monks.

Crop failures in two successive years forced the sale of 120 acres. A
number of novices left, some because of what they felt to be a "spirit of
laxity" (Hoffman 1952:85). Part of this attitude probably came from long
hours of work; the monks at times went to bed at 9:00 P.M. and arose again
by 3:30 or 4:00 A.M. "In short, severe manual labor was substituted for
duties of a . . . more sacred character, and . . . there was little room for peace
or order or regularity" (Hoffman 1952:86). But considering the crop failures, such efforts should be seen as acts of survival. The prior, in fact, tried
to raise money through donations, something Trappists are not supposed
to do. During these first years, the monks also acted as parish priests and
taught at a school for boys.

Under more capable financial administration, economic conditions of the
monastery improved, but no American applicants stayed long. Also, early
efforts to obtain the status of abbey, with its consequent independence, were
not successful. By 1858, there were 60 monks. One of the brothers in the

abbey had died (the first death in the monastery) and one was ordained to the priesthood (again the first).

The Civil War increased the price of agricultural products. More land was purchased, new buildings were erected, and so much was done that an abbot making the regular visitation complained that the degree of activity in the monastery was not consonant with the atmosphere of a Trappist house (Hoffman 1952:134). In 1862 Palisades became an abbey and elected its first abbot (who at the time was the community's prior). This abbot had been preceded by seven different priors and superiors in more than twelve years. The abbey was quite isolated from the nearest town, in keeping with the custom in Trappist communities of settling in secluded places. The guest house could accommodate eight. The graveyard was occupied by six brothers and two seculars. One newspaper reporter was particularly impressed by "the silence that enveloped [the monks] like an atmosphere. Signs of busy life and activity were abundant, and monks were moving...everywhere. But there was no noise—no shouts nor laughter. All was as still as death, broken only by the occasional sharp ring of the hammer on the smithy anvil, and by the lowing of the cattle on the hills" (Hoffman 1952:149).

By 1875, part of the stone structure that now forms the main building had been built. However, though prosperity was evident, those making the regular visitations were not pleased. One in particular remarked that the intensive business efforts were spiritually unhealthy for the order, frequent travel by the brothers was dangerous to contemplative life, and too much money was being spent on machinery (Hoffman 1952:158). Eventually (in 1887), the abbot and his prior began to examine more closely the business activities of the procurator. The monastery was found to be heavily in debt. High interest rates and constant losses in selling livestock made the situation worse. The procurator tried to remedy things by investment in the stock market, but this too failed, and the total indebtedness reached almost one quarter of a million dollars. Bonds were issued to solve the problem, but it was years before the affair was settled. At the time of this financial crisis, there were 67 monks in the community, but two years later in 1889, the number had fallen to 53. (See Figure 1.1)

Palisades Abbey had its second abbot in 1894, who, like the first, was born in Europe. The election of the third abbot in 1897 was postponed several years because of the heavy debt and a lack of vocations. This dearth of applicants continued for almost 30 years. In 1892, there were 43 members; in 1901, only 34; eight years later, 27; by 1918, the low point had been reached at 17 (five of whom were priests). Yet even with this decline, under the third abbot the debt on the monastery was cleared, modern farming methods and machinery were introduced, and new land was added. In 1917, when this abbot died, he became the first abbot of Palisades to be

Figure 1.1
Population Change

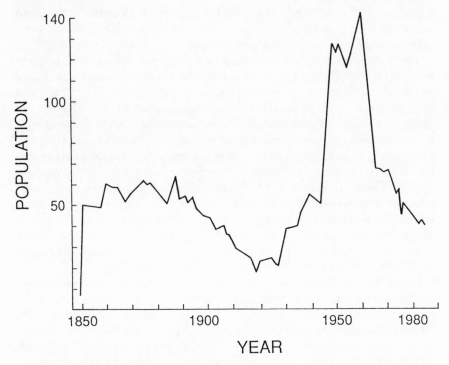

YEAR

buried in America. The fourth abbot was elected in 1935. During his administration, the present guest house was started, electricity came to the monastery, and the first automobile arrived.

The population of the abbey had been slowly increasing, and when this abbot died in 1944, there were 51 monks. The fifth abbot died after only two years in office, but already the flood of monks that was to come had started. By 1950, there were 135 monks; by 1952, the numbers were even higher (Hoffman 1952:205), many of these being veterans of World War II.

The next significant development was the Second Vatican Council (October 1962 to December 1965). Many things may be attributed to the council, among them a greater openness to other religions. The monastery's population had increased steadily and markedly since 1920. From 20 monks, it peaked at 144 monks in 1960. Consistent declines have been registered since. By 1980, the numbers were once again below 50. Only one novice made his solemn profession between 1970 and 1983.

One cannot give the Second Vatican Council responsibility for the decline. The entire American culture was undergoing a revolution in those days. Youth was searching for new things to which they could be dedicated. The old, especially the "establishment" and anything connected with it, was suspect. Monasteries were seen as part of the establishment. Nor were monasteries well understood, even by Catholics. Because of Vatican II, the attitude was less tenable that the monks were "the Marines of the Church," as one monk phrased it. Finally, the monks were trying to clarify for themselves the purposes to which they were dedicated, and thus were less certain of their goals. Whatever the cause, population decline is one of the most severe crises faced by Palisades Abbey, as it is for almost all of the Trappist-Cistercian monasteries in the United States.

The abbey established its first daughter house during the tenure of the sixth abbot, whom we shall call Dom Edward. Eleven monks (three of them priests) were assigned to start the foundation, and others soon followed. Unfortunately, the soil at the new monastery was quite poor, but even this has been turned to advantage, for the community has been able to earn its living by making concrete blocks. Shortly after, two experimental houses were begun, composed of only four monks each. Neither house proved successful. In each case, the monks were "searching for community." The monastic search is, of course, for God.

The ninth abbot, Dom Daniel, supervised the remodeling of the church. The former church occupied the second floor of one of the wings. The monks removed all interior structures, including the flooring of the second story, providing a much more spacious interior. An architect designed a structure of elegant simplicity—plain wood and stone. This design, in the neo-Gothic setting of the rest of the building, gives a sense of expanse not unlike the medieval Gothic, without the more polished and darker appearance. Few developments have occurred that enhanced more the atmosphere of worship. The church was completed in 1976.

At the same time, Dom Daniel was bringing the monks to a deeper spirituality. He led them in searching for inner direction rather than external compliance. For example, he urged the monks to pay less attention to guests and more to their own prayer life. His leadership is a response to the repeated recommendations of previous visitors to have monks observe the rules of silence and enclosure more carefully. Dom Daniel also reduced the number of guests and stopped the practice of tour buses stopping at the abbey "to view the sights." Noisy farm machinery was abandoned, in particular, an expensive alfalfa dehydration plant ("the dehy"). The result of this and other measures has been an increase in the peaceful atmosphere generally prevailing in Trappist-Cistercian monasteries.

I began my studies of Palisades Abbey in 1969 during Dom Daniel's term of office.

CONCLUSION

Since World War II, there have been dramatic changes in the Order of the Cistercians of the Strict Observance. The first category of changes had to do with solitude: the modification of the rule of silence, the installation of private rooms, more emphasis on contemplative prayer, and permission for the existence of hermits within the order. The second set of changes concerned contact with the outside world: saying the office in the vernacular, allowing more letters and visits, and interaction with Protestants. A third set of changes centered on the structure of monastic life itself, such as eliminating the Chapter of Faults (see the Glossary), dropping distinctions between choir monks and lay brothers, limiting the abbot's time in office, placing more emphasis on screening candidates, and putting less emphasis on detailed rules. These are not all of the changes, but they are those that have drastically affected the monastic way of life and probably contributed to a decline in new applicants, if only until the monks learned to adjust.

These changes are interrelated. Contact with the outside influences solitude and both of these are influenced by changes in the structure of the life, and vice versa. Changes in solitude had probably the greatest impact. Because speaking is now permitted, monks are able to know one another better. Before the change in the rule of silence, as one monk said, "you could hide your animosity under a cloak of pious silence," when you were really almost ready to murder someone. With the change, more privacy was required, hence the need for private rooms, or monastic cells. The increase in emphasis on contemplative prayer had been continuing at least since 1947 (Mott 1984:233), and permission for Thomas Merton to become a hermit at Gethsemani came almost 20 years later (1965), but the two are not unrelated. As one monk put it, the presence of hermits "reminds us of our need for solitude," and solitude is especially conducive to contemplative prayer.

The monastery was being opened to the outside. The extreme emphasis on isolation decreased markedly. This study, for example, could not have been conducted before World War II because I am a Protestant. Dropping the use of Latin in the office upset many monks. But, as one of the brothers said, "You can get into the rhythm of a song, even if you don't know the words. But without the vernacular, the meaning isn't there."

The order was seeking a deeper interpretation of monasticism. Before World War II, salvation was almost equated with following rules. After, one had to search for God more intently. The Chapter of Faults is a case in point. This was a meeting in which the monks accused themselves or others of violations of the *Rule* (see Glossary). One brother commented on the ending of the Chapter: "Some were concerned: 'What are you going to replace it with?' But now there is more openness, a greater willingness to unite, more love. It helped us shape up, maybe, but it devolved from this. Today in America, it didn't work. It became petty and bickering...and trivial. Perhaps it was an attempt to communicate within a situation of strict silence and solitude. But the rules were constricting. They made asceticism negative rather than positive."

The general pattern of change 20 years after the survey is of consolidation following innovations that were almost revolutionary. Some customs are being reinstituted after having been temporarily abandoned (such as more frequent use of bells at the canonical hours). But important changes continue. The monks have turned a significant corner in the centuries-old existence of their order. How far these changes will reach probably cannot be determined within our lifetime.

These changes represent one of the most far-reaching "revolutions" in monastic history, especially since many of the events were also happening in the larger Church. It is difficult to maintain one's perspective in a revolution, except to know that one is in a revolution. But at the very least, monasteries can no longer be considered museum pieces. They are very much a part of the twentieth century.

Even from as brief a survey as this, one can be impressed with the tenacity of the monastic movement. It is an inseparable part of Christianity, needing only the nucleus of such a system as the *Rule* to give it substance. The movement has been able to withstand both prosperity and persecution. Undoubtedly, the large numbers who have left in the last decades and the relative lack of new vocations does not offer much hope. But two decades are a small fraction of almost two thousand years.

Such, then, is the background of Palisades Abbey and the monastic movement to which it belongs. Whether the period in which this research was done is representative cannot be said, but one can argue that no time is representative. We may be witnessing a beginning or an end. In either case, the place of the monastic movement in history is established. What follows is a detailed account of one segment of that history, probably more detailed than any that has been done to date.

Chapter 2

Freedom and Discipline

with Charles J. Dudley

Freedom is basic to the *Rule* of St. Benedict. The novice is clearly informed of "all the hard and rugged ways by which the journey to God is made" (Doyle 1948: Chapter 58:79). The *Rule* is to be read to him several times.

Then, having deliberated with himself, if he promises to keep it in its entirety and to observe everything that is commanded him, let him be received into the community. But let him understand that, according to the law of the Rule, from that day forward he may not leave the monastery nor withdraw his neck from under the yoke of the Rule which he was free to refuse or to accept during that prolonged deliberation. (Doyle 1948: Chapter 58:80)

Even with so strong a statement, however, the door to the monastery is never completely sealed. In closing this same chapter, the *Rule* states, "if he should ever listen to the persuasions of the devil and decide to leave the monastery (which God forbid), he may be divested of the monastic clothes and cast out." The point is, he can decide to leave. He has a choice.

My first observations in the monastery presented an apparent paradox. Though the monks lived a highly regimented life, they acted otherwise as if they were free men. When the study was in its early stages, I made the following remarks:

Can it be said that the monasteries maximize the freedom of their members? Certainly, alternatives are curtailed: For example, the monks are celibate; they fast and

Parts of this chapter have been adapted from Charles J. Dudley and George A. Hillery, Jr., 1979. The results given in earlier studies do not match exactly those reported here, for several reasons: (1) factor scores were used for some measures; (2) different weights were employed; and (3) many more groups have been added.

maintain extensive periods of silence. But to talk to these men . . . is to be impressed with the lack of manifest antagonism. The point is that the monk is where he is . . . for . . . the most significant choice of his life. Deprivations are an important part of this call, but they are . . . chosen by him, and they can be renounced whenever he so wishes. The monastery is the place where he is free to follow his call to the maximum of his ability (Hillery 1971: 58–59).

DATA COLLECTION AND TYPES OF FREEDOM

Questions concerning freedom were raised from the beginning of the study. First, there was the meaning of freedom. Further, how is freedom related to social structure? As the study proceeded, the relation of cohesion and alienation became important. In short, what is the impact of freedom on both the monastery and the monks?

The most basic question seemed to be, What is freedom? Subjective freedom appeared to involve at least two features (Hillery 1971). First, freedom depends on having choices: the more choice, the greater the freedom. But second, any choice requires discipline, since once a choice is made, others have been ruled out. Therefore, there are at least two kinds of subjective freedom: (1) ego freedom, wherein one is free to make choices; and (2) disciplined freedom, wherein one must exercise restraint in giving up some things in order to have others.

At this point in the research, I was investigating two communes: one was highly structured, operated by the Lutheran Church. The other claimed that the only rule they had was to have no rules. I asked the members to write an essay on "what freedom means to you," considering freedom in two senses: "(1) as an increase in alternatives or choices . . . and (2) as sacrificing to do something that you want to do" (Hillery, Dudley, and Morrow 1977:687). The respondents (most of whom were college students) were asked to discuss the freedom they had in their commune as compared with that which they had in their families. From their replies, 25 questions were finally constructed, to be answered in a graded response (similar to Likert's method): strongly agree, agree, don't know, disagree, strongly disagree.

After a number of groups had been asked these questions, Charles J. Dudley and I constructed a factor analysis to discover if any patterns existed (Table 2.1). Ego and disciplined freedom emerged rather clearly. However, a third factor appeared, conditional freedom, one I had not predicted, in which one is free to do as one wishes, but other people and things (conditions) must be taken into consideration. (The factor analysis is described in Hillery, Dudley, and Morrow 1977).

These factors correspond closely to the work of Mortimer Adler (1958), who summarized the results of research on freedom by more than 20 scholars over a five-year period. This work also isolated three basic concepts of freedom (the emphasis shows the relation with our research):

Table 2.1
Statements Used for the Factor Scales for the Types of Freedom

Ego Freedom

    I enjoy living here because there is complete freedom from restrictions.

    My freedom is greatest here because I can spend all the time I want doing the things that I want.

    We have little or no rules or regulations to live by.

    This place allows people to do what they want.

    The only real restriction here is not to do anything that would in any way do harm to the community.

    Here I'm on my own unless I really bother others.

Conditional Freedom

    I am free to help the people that I live with.

    Self-discipline is important because there are so many things to do here.

    The only rules here are made for the good of the group.

    In this group, you have the right to do whatever you want as long as you don't hurt anyone else or yourself.

Disciplined Freedom

    Freedom here is closely linked with the idea of sharing and sacrificing.

    Freedom here is disciplined, and each makes concessions to help the others.

    There is freedom here, but to have it, each person must give up something to help the others.

Source: Hillery, Dudley, and Morrow 1977: 690.

1. Circumstantial freedom of self-realization: "a freedom which is possessed by any individual who, *under favorable circumstances*, is able to act as he wishes for his own good as he sees it."
2. Acquired freedom of self-perfection: "a freedom which is possessed only by those

Table 2.2
Statements Used for the Factor Scale for Deprivation of Freedom

---

I used to have more freedom before I came here than I do now.

The people in charge here should be more considerate of the members.

I feel that I do not have the kind of freedom that I should have.

I feel as if some of my freedom has been taken away.

I wish that I could leave here so that I could find a place that would let me do more of the things that I want.

Source: Hillery, Dudley, and Morrow 1977: 687.

men who, *through acquired virtue or wisdom*, are able to will or live as they ought in conformity *to the moral law or an ideal befitting human nature.*"

3. Natural freedom of self-determination: "a freedom which is possessed by all men, in virtue of a power inherent in human nature whereby a man is able to change his own character creatively by *deciding for himself* what he shall do or shall become." (Adler, in Dewey and Gould 1970: 58; see also Hillery, Dudley, and Morrow 1977:699).

Since Adler's three freedoms correspond to our conditional, disciplined, and egoistic freedoms, respectively, we have concluded that the two lines of research essentially tapped the same phenomena, though we were working from entirely different directions: ours from science, his from philosophy.

A word should be said about deprivation of freedom (Table 2.2), an entirely different concept: it concerns freedom that one feels has been taken away. The other types concern that which one feels one has.

Two samples are used for this analysis. The first is designed to establish parameters (Appendices B and C). As many different groups as possible were sampled, though one would not normally want to compare them. For example, monasteries and prisons are different in that one is composed only of voluntary members and the other is composed entirely of people who are forced to enter. The second sample (Table 2.4) is only of voluntary residential organizations.

FINDINGS

Appendix B shows freedom scores for 62 groups, ranging from monasteries to communes, from prisons to fraternities and sororities. (See also

Table 2.3
Mean Freedom Scale Scores for Palisades Abbey, 1972–1985

Year	Disciplined Freedom	Conditional Freedom	Ego Freedom	Deprivation of Freedom	Number of Cases
1972	1. 840	2. 415	3. 700	3. 605	50
1976	1. 885	2. 611	4. 031	3. 620	27
1985	1. 818	2. 511	3. 818	3. 727	22

Table 2.4.) The monks and nuns are one of the most disciplined groups. (A score of 1 is highest; 5 is lowest.) Fraternities and cooperative boarding houses score highest on ego freedom. Monks and nuns felt least deprived of freedom; prisoners, of course, felt most deprived.

The monasteries are most consistent in the way they express attitudes toward freedom. They are among the most free in disciplined freedom and are least concerned with conditional and ego freedom. It is apparent why monks would not be concerned with ego freedom. They are, after all, ascetics. Ego freedom is not a viable option. There is a small plaque in the guest master's office: "Happiness is where you find it, not always where you seek it." Thus, the monk is not opposed to ego freedom. He is willing to accept it when it is offered. Parties are held, for example, at the major feast days. But ego freedom is lowest on his priorities, and it is certainly not the type of freedom around which the monk would construct a lifestyle.

Conditional freedom is more complicated. Whereas disciplined freedom requires commitment and sacrifice and ego freedom seeks simply for freedom to do as one wishes, conditional freedom is equivocal: one says that he or she is free *but* one has to be concerned with other people and things. Such equivocation would not be favored by any group that required strong commitment.

Palisades Abbey falls toward the middle of the range for monasteries for all kinds of freedom. It is one of the few groups for which data on freedom were gathered over time (see Table 2.3). The scores show a general improvement from the perspective of what is desirable for monastic living. Thus, scores show a stronger commitment to disciplined freedom in 1985 than in 1972, feelings of conditional freedom have weakened since 1976, as have scores on ego freedom, and the monks have consistently felt less deprived of their freedom.

What does freedom mean to the monk? We shall look at this question in four ways: What is the monk free from? What is he free to do? What does he sacrifice? What does he gain? Probably most obvious is the monk's freedom from the world and most of its normal obligations. He does not have to concern himself with what he will eat or wear or when he will go to sleep or any of the other numerous things that have to be decided by people in the "outside" world. It also means that he does not have to be concerned with obligations that come from such things as raising a family. It is probably this "freedom" as much as any other that has led some to think that monks avoid responsibility. This charge would be accurate if the monk came to the monastery to avoid these things, but these freedoms are consequences of his coming, not the reasons.

The things that the monk is free to do are rather limited but still important. There are of course numerous minor choices to make, such as what foods to choose from the cafeteria line, what books to read, and so forth. But the most important choices are those concerning "conversion of manners," that is, how the monk will so conduct his daily life that he seeks God and develops agapé.

This freedom to become a "Godly" person is the monk's interpretation of the meaning of disciplined freedom. It is that to which he commits himself, for which he sacrifices. But what is he sacrificing? This depends on the individual monk. What might seem like sacrifice to those outside, such as forgoing a professional career, money, and so forth, may not be so to him. One monk told me, on seeing me with my family, "That's what I miss most in monastic life—having a son of my own." Others quite apparently miss the company of people, as evidenced by frequent appearances in the guest house. In any case, for the monk to gain the freedom to seek a life with God is interpreted to mean that he commit himself to this particular life, and he realizes that it requires sacrifice.

Freedom in the monastery, however, is not an individual affair. The monk is also free because he lives and works in a community with his brothers. This means especially that he is free to pray, undisturbed, and is encouraged by the community to do so. The monks arise at 3:15 in the morning, participate in the religious office, and then are free, from about 4:00 A.M. to 6:30 A.M., to engage in spiritual reading, meditation, or contemplative prayer (see Chapter 10). This period is very important to those who wish to pray contemplatively, since for many if not most, this type of prayer requires intense concentration, and the early morning hours provide opportunity for concentration not possible at any other time. Of course, the world outside has not yet awakened, and so the monk is not apt to be disturbed by calls from visitors. But equally important, the *community* has established this time as one of quiet, and so the monk is not likely to be disturbed by his brothers.

Seven times a day and at Mass, the monks gather for liturgical prayer. Those who sing in choir (and most do) are expected to be there, and this expectation is itself an encouragement. At least one monastery (not Palisades) actually breaks the Night Office midway during the service for half an hour, to encourage monks to engage in contemplative prayer during this time.

The monastery exists for prayer. The monks agree to support one another in their efforts at prayer, they reserve a portion of the monastery where guests are not permitted, so the monks may not be disturbed, and they screen applicants compatible with the life. It is difficult to pray contemplatively in the outside world, because the schedules of others are not geared to such prayer. The monastery provides the maximum opportunity.

The promises made by the monk "of his stability and of the reformation of his life and of obedience" (Doyle 1948: Chapter 58:80), which imply also poverty and chastity (Van Zeller 1959:48), require both sacrifice and commitment. Thus, high scores on disciplined freedom are expected. The organized attempt to realize these promises, together with the provision of subsistence, require sharing. Therefore, the important individual and collective means of life in the monastery are defined by sharing and sacrifice. There are very few other groups that even approach the degree of intensity achieved by the monks on such disciplined freedom.

Further, the monasteries do not score high on other types of freedom. They are among the lowest on ego freedom and fairly low on conditional (most monasteries falling below the median). The commitment to disciplined freedom is very strong, almost to the exclusion of other types. In a sense, disciplined freedom represents the furthest extension in both conditional and ego freedom. We mean by this an extension in either of two morally divergent and contradictory senses: (1) that ego and conditional freedom are both subsumed under discipline (as for example in Nazi Germany), or (2) disciplined freedom is the celebration of one's self (ego) with others (conditional), as with the monks. Nazi ideology required both the submission of self to the discipline of the state and the curtailment of the welfare or elimination of certain groups (such as the Jews). Monastic life in contrast, requires seeking of self through the submission of self with others to a transcendent ideology. The essential difference between the Nazi and the monk is that the monk ultimately seeks self rather than discards it, though this seeking is accomplished in abandonment (surrender through love). This comparison shows that disciplined freedom, in itself, has no moral position. The discipline (commitment, sacrifice) is the important characteristic. Thus, the eventual result of discipline, depending upon what one submits to, can be vastly, even shockingly different.

What are the consequences of disciplined freedom for the monk? To answer that question a sample of groups is taken from those listed in Appendices B and C. Several criteria were used in selecting the groups. First, there had to be more than one group of its kind. Second, the groups had to be relatively homogeneous in group type (thus, the drug rehabilitation center was not included with the cadets). Third, first samples were preferred,

Table 2.4
Mean Likert Scores for Types of Freedom, Cohesion, Alienation, and Deprivation of Freedom for Ten Residential Organizations

	Ego	Condi-tional	Disci-plined	Cohesion	Alien-ation	Depri-vation	Number of Groups
Military Groups	3.970	2.973	3.970	12.538	2.816	1.791	3
Housing Projects	3.237	2.908	3.088	13.053	2.766	2.326	2
Old Age Homes	3.300	2.706	2.257	10.716	2.632	2.678	2
Cadets	4.124	2.659	2.323	9.720	3.171	2.701	2
Boarding Schools	3.502	2.381	2.291	3.013	2.943	2.944	2
University Dormitories	3.146	2.426	2.937	12.289	3.076	3.175	4
Cooperative Boarding Houses	2.610	2.483	2.955	11.909	3.161	3.427	3
Fraternities & Sororities	3.113	1.961	2.117	9.713	3.079	3.584	6
Communes	3.207	2.177	2.161	6.103	3.246	3.607	3
Monasteries	3.896	2.536	1.836	10.603	3.608	3.743	5

since most of the groups were sampled only once (note that only the latest samples are shown in Appendix B). Fourth, only groups were selected where the members voluntarily entered and used the group as a place of residence. Thus, prisons were excluded. The results of this sample are shown in Table 2.4 (where 1 is the highest score, 5 the lowest).

The findings display patterns of low alienation and low deprivation of freedom with high scores on disciplined freedom (see also Table 2.5). The separation of the monasteries from the larger society is intended to increase disciplined freedom. Despite (or perhaps because of) the commitment to poverty and personal sacrifice, the monks show a moderate degree of cohesion. Despite the structured separation from the larger society, the monks exhibit remarkably low scores on sociopsychological alienation. Despite long hours of silence and a regimented existence, they show remarkably

Table 2.5

Standardized Regression Coefficients for the Relation between Scores on Cohesion, Alienation, and Deprivation of Freedom and Types of Freedom, for Monastic and Nonmonastic Groups

Dependent Variables	Independent Variables				
	Disciplined	Ego	Conditional	R	R****
Monasteries (N=72)					
Cohesion	.134	.008	.319*	.381	.100
Alienation	-.147	.247	-.383**	.470	.180
Deprivation	-.207	-.077	.169	.204	-.009
Nonmonastic (N=874)					
Cohesion	.261***	-.121**	.231***	.383	.144
Alienation	.065	.140***	-.037	.139	.016
Deprivation	-.018	-.210***	-.348***	.497	.245

* p < .05
** p < .01
*** p < .001

**** Adjusted R^2

low scores on deprivation of freedom. In short, monastic life, with its focus on personal sacrifice and group sharing, provides an integrative experience in both social and in religious life.

This point needs further comment. Although religious concerns (and in particular, prayer and agapé love) are central to the monastery, this focus does not deny the possibility of developing a social life beyond the religious context (Merton 1966). The monasteries have a social division of labor that provides sustenance for the monks and links them to the outside world. Such a division of labor should, and from observation does, generate normal social relations. Monks exhibit political, economic, and social behaviors and concerns. Yet these experiences do not yield the group fragmentation and personal costs of other groups. The question then arises: Is the concept of freedom related to social organization? Social organization is measured by levels of cohesion, alienation, and deprivation of freedom.

Table 2.5 shows that in the monasteries, conditional freedom is positively related to cohesion and negatively related to alienation. Disciplined freedom among monks shows little significant relation to any of the three dependent variables (cohesion, alienation, or deprivation of freedom) probably because all monasteries score very high on disciplined freedom, and thus there is little variation in these measures from monastery to monastery. Disciplined freedom is more of a condition of monastery life rather than a variable.

The strongest impact of any of the freedoms on the social organization measures is conditional freedom. It is more strongly related to cohesion and (negatively) to alienation than is true of nonmonastic groups. Yet data in the earlier tables (2.2 and 2.4) show that conditional freedom is not the most important type to the monks. At best, the multiple correlations explain only a fraction of the possible variance (never as much as 25 percent). But conditional freedom is still significant enough to have an impact, positively on cohesion and negatively on alienation. Any group probably has to have some amount of conditional freedom to exist (as the data suggest, since all groups register a significant amount—see Appendix B), and monks are no exception. They place more emphasis on conditional than on ego freedom because of the more social involvement that conditional freedom reflects. Of course, disciplined freedom in the monastery is more important than conditional freedom, and the monastery is so structured that much of what would be conditional freedom in the world becomes disciplined freedom.

Of all the types, ego freedom has little relation to monastic life. None of the relationships are statistically significant, whereas all are significant for the nonmonastic groups. Ego freedom does not seem to have much meaning to the monks. Similarly, deprivation of freedom is not related significantly to any of the three freedoms. Apparently, deprivation of freedom also is something with which the monk has little concern. He has made his commitment, and he is able to realize that commitment in his daily life.

Given the uniformly high scores for disciplined freedom and the low relation it has to the three variables of social organization, one could argue that disciplined freedom is the umbrella under which the monks operate. It takes the place of ego freedom, and conditional freedom can operate as it does because disciplined freedom is so important. Though the monk does *not* feel that he can do as he pleases (which is part of the meaning of conditional freedom), he does feel that he must take other people and things into consideration, which is also one of the meanings of disciplined freedom (see Table 2.1: "Freedom here is disciplined, and each makes concessions to help the others").

Monastic life is in a sense an ego-rewarding experience. It is, after all, an attempt to develop a personal form of religious life. Thus, within the setting of disciplined freedom, the need for ego freedom is redefined and satisfied. Conditional freedom refers more to restriction of freedom by the social order; in comparison with the other two types of freedom, it is the most constraining. Though ego freedom is the least demanding, disciplined freedom demands the most, nevertheless there is at least a resulting lifestyle

Table 2.6
Types of Freedom in Monastic Daily Life

Activity	Types of Freedom		
	Disciplined	Conditional	Ego
Office	XX	x	--
Lectio divina	XX	x	x
Labor	XX	x	x
Meals	x	XX	x
Sleep	x	--	x
Hygiene	x	XX	x
Associates (friends)	x	XX	x
Relations to family	x	XX	x
Recreation (as in hobbies)	x	x	XX

Legend   XX = dominant influence
         x = minor influence
         -- = negligible influence

where the monk can find fulfillment. But conditional freedom is constraining and provides little personal reward.

In summary, all of the freedoms may be examined as they are found in the monk's daily life. We may divide the life into three broad areas: First are those things that are most important to the monks, such as the offices, *lectio divina* (solitary prayer and reading), and labor. Next are physical needs, such as meals, hygiene, and sleep. Finally, there are interpersonal relations and recreation. The importance of each of the freedoms in these areas is summarized in Table 2.6.

Note that all the freedoms operate in almost all areas, as Appendix B suggests (since each freedom is shown to have a measurable amount in each group). Table 2.6 indicates further that disciplined freedom is strongly dominant in the three areas the monks consider most important. There is virtually no room for ego freedom when the monk sings in choir. Whatever freedom he has outside of disciplined is conditional: he adjusts to the presence or absence of his fellows. *Lectio divina* is more important egoistically in that the monk reads and prays as he wishes, but this is done within the context of discipline. He will not read newspapers during this period, for example. His freedom again is conditional in that he adjusts to his brothers, as when he goes to his room so he can pray undisturbed. Finally, what he will labor at and when is determined by the monastery.

Conditional freedom is more important in physical matters. The monk takes whatever place in line that comes up at mealtimes, chooses from the items presented to him by the cooks, and eats at his assigned place at the table. In sleep, there is no one to react to (snoring was a problem before the monks had private rooms). Hygienic practices are done in a way that will not offend others.

His relations to friends and relatives are of his own choosing, again within the framework of monastic discipline. Only in hobbies does he have substantial ego freedom, and that, too, must be within the arena of disciplined freedom. The monks encounter discipline even in such matters as sleep (which is allowed between 8:00 P.M. and 3:15 A.M. and after the noon meal).

Monastic discipline is ordered mainly by the Bible, the *Rule*, the customs of the particular monastery, and the abbot. The monk submits to these in order to have freedom to pray. How he will pray, how long, and about what is his choice. His conditional and ego freedom have wider rein only in more unimportant matters, such as the friends he chooses and what he will eat.

UNCONDITIONAL FREEDOM

One more type of freedom remains to be discussed. It differs from the others in that its existence cannot be demonstrated statistically, but it is an important expectation for some. This freedom may be described by relating it to the others, as ideal types.

Egoistic freedom is purely self-centered and oriented to the physical world. Conditional freedom is also oriented toward physical things and in addition emphasizes other people. Disciplined freedom for the monks, like conditional freedom, is oriented to more than self, but it is not as directly concerned with other people as it is with sharing and sacrifice, particularly in reference to a spiritual other. Taking a cue from the very high scores for disciplined freedom of the monks, true disciplined freedom is centered on spiritual truth, which for these monks is revealed by Jesus Christ. The monk disciplines himself so that he may attain the freedom that Christ offers.

These considerations can be expressed in a contingency table (see Figure 2.1). One axis concerns orientation of self; the other concerns orientation to the physical or spiritual worlds. (A minimal definition of "spiritual" is "other than physical" or "physically transcendent." Thus, Nazis may be as spiritual as monks, but it is a contradictory kind of spirituality. A monk told me, even the devil has his disciples.)

The table suggests a fourth type of freedom, unconditional. This type also concerns self, but in a radically different way than is true of egoistic freedom. "Self" has become identified with a spiritual ego, which the monk sees as Christ. The monk no longer follows rules revealed by Christ as much as he

Figure 2.1
Types of Freedom

Assumption that reality is:

Physical   Spiritual

		Physical	Spiritual
	Ego	Egoistic	Unconditional
Orientation of self:			
	Other	Conditional	Disciplined

identifies with Christ personally. This is the freedom of which theologians and mystics speak when they say that he who has the mind of Christ can do as he pleases. (For example, see the reference to Martin Luther in Dewey and Gould 1970: 178; according to one monk, the common source is probably St. Augustine: Love, and do what you will.)

The contingency table provides additional insights concerning the nature of freedom. Egoistic freedom is purely ego oriented and physical. Conditional freedom, though also ego oriented and physical, is in addition concerned with other people. Disciplined freedom is other oriented but from a spiritual perspective. The physical ego becomes irrelevant. Unconditional freedom is ego centered but from a purely spiritual point of view.

Additional information is achieved by shifting perspective. Unconditional freedom is egoistic freedom that has been reoriented to a spiritual world, just as disciplined freedom can be regarded as a spiritualized conditional freedom. Similarly, conditional freedom is egoistic freedom that is also oriented to others, and unconditional freedom is a disciplined freedom in which the spiritual ego of Christ has been completely internalized.

The meaning of unconditional freedom is illustrated by a story told by a monk. Two monks came to a river swollen with spring floods. A beautiful girl was standing by the bank, afraid to cross, and she asked the monks to help her. One of them picked her up and carried her to the other side. The monks walked on for about ten miles. The one who did not carry the girl turned to the one who did and said, "It is not good for a monk to touch a woman." The monk who carried the girl said, "Are you still carrying her? I put her down on the other side of the river."

I have only met one monk that I suspect had unconditional freedom. (He is now "safely" in the monastic graveyard.) This monk was unconcerned about convention. He did not break the rules, but he never seemed anxious about them, for example, by becoming disturbed when the rule could not be followed. He preferred life within the cloister but committed himself wholeheartedly to whatever task was given him. For a while, he was guest master at his abbey, and he related well to all guests with whom I saw him. He was the kind of person who could put anyone at ease, whether the most orthodox Catholic or the most committed atheist. Few monks can follow the monastic life with such apparent ease, but it would seem to be the goal of all.

CONCLUSION

The paradox noted at the start of this chapter should now be explained. Though the monk leads a highly disciplined life, he is still free, precisely because he is disciplined. He realizes that making a choice requires commitment. He has made his commitment and knows that he is free to do so. Further, this commitment extends to many areas of his life.

The key to his disciplined freedom is found in his vows and promises. The monk begins each day in poverty and obedience, and each day he must devote himself to converting his life closer to the Christian ideal. Each day he elects to remain in the monastery. Each day he elects to be chaste. There is nothing holding him except his decision. This is not to deny the pressure to adhere to this commitment. His commitment is after all a set of vows and promises, and he is expected to live up to them by the face-to-face group in which he lives. But no one forces him to keep making it.

There is nothing dramatic in his decisions. On the contrary, one of the most difficult problems a monk has to face is boredom. As one old monk said, "The life is not hard; you just have to keep at it."

Chapter 3

Love and Community

LOVE

The importance of love in monastic life is not readily apparent. Trappist monasteries are isolated, especially by the cloister, where none but monks are usually permitted. Further, a certain type of prayer used by these monks also requires them to be isolated from each other, at least some of the time (see Chapter 10). Yet, as one observes these men, love becomes increasingly evident. Chapter 53 of St. Benedict's *Rule* (Doyle 1948), the blueprint for Trappist-Cistercian monastic life, requires that each guest be treated as Christ, and whereas this is not equivalent to the entry into Jerusalem, it does mean that the guest is given food, shelter, and whatever help is within the monk's means. This help is given with kindness and consideration.

The love in Trappist monasteries is more than just an ideal. In every visit I have made to these monasteries, whether in America, Europe, or Asia, I have been treated with overt expressions of love in the form of hospitality, kindness, warmth, and concern. For those monasteries in which I have spent the most time, this love became more evident. Not that I am always approved. Occasionally some monks, I am convinced, wish I were elsewhere. Even these, however, have always shown me hospitality, kindness, warmth, and concern, which indicates a difference between loving and liking. The point is, such love is not simply a result of natural proclivities. It is a love that is explicitly intentional, an act of disciplined will. Technically, it is known as agapé (pronounced ah-gah-pay).

This love is not apparent in all kinds of groups. I do not expect to meet warmth, hospitality, kindness, and concern when I buy gasoline or groceries,

Parts of this chapter were adapted from George A. Hillery, Jr., "Gemeinschaft Verstehen," *Social Forces* 63, December 1984, 307–34.

meals, or a place for the night. If I am treated kindly, I am pleased. More often, I am satisfied merely with politeness. Such contrasts have convinced me that love is an essential part of monastic life, in behavior as well as principle.

The prompting of the monks themselves led me to investigate this love more closely. I began with the theory of *The Four Loves* by C. S. Lewis (1960). Though the discussion to follow is heavily indebted to Lewis, alterations have been made. First, the types are polarized. Eros need not be constrained to physical love, as is done here, just as affection is not without exclusiveness and friendship has physical contact. (The types of love are essentially defined in Figure 3.1) In reality, the types merge. Polarization is used for clarity (as in ideal types). Second, more variables are added to distinguish the types systematically.

The types in Figure 3.1 are located in such a manner as to suggest that they become more similar as they become more intense. The idealized love of Romeo and Juliet resembles the friendship of David and Jonathan (1 Sam.: Chs. 18ff.), the sacrifice of his life made by Jesus, and the affection of mother and child. However, the loves near the edge of the circle are more superficial; infatuation, acquaintances, love of things, and almsgiving do not have much in common.

One comparison is of a different nature from those in the figure. Eros and agapé are opposites in that at one extreme eros is unintentional whereas agapé at the other extreme is intentional. That is, though one may "fall in love" (erotically) against one's better judgment, agapé is an act of will, extending to one's enemies (Matt. 5:44). Friendship and affection are mixtures of intention and unintention.

All that the monk does is (or should be) a means to achieving love. The monk comes to his community, his monastery, ultimately because of a need for love. This love may at first be ill defined or unrecognized: a desire to serve God, an attraction to the peace and solitude in the monastery. It may even be ill founded: a wish to be noble or to excel religiously. The monk may not at first recognize that the simple objective and the only thing that can sustain him is love. The monk must learn to love his fellow monks and their way of life sufficiently to discipline himself so that they all can work together in their search to realize this love.

Thus the search for love becomes a search in community. The community is markedly different from others in that it does not contain the biosocial family. This condition has both a marked disadvantage and a marked advantage. The disadvantage is that the monastic community cannot reproduce monks. It must rely solely on recruits. Also, the monk must relinquish sexual gratification. This is an advantage more than a disadvantage, however, because it forces the monk to go beyond eros and realize a love that transcends that for any individual. In other words, the monk must develop agapé love.

Figure 3.1
Types of Love

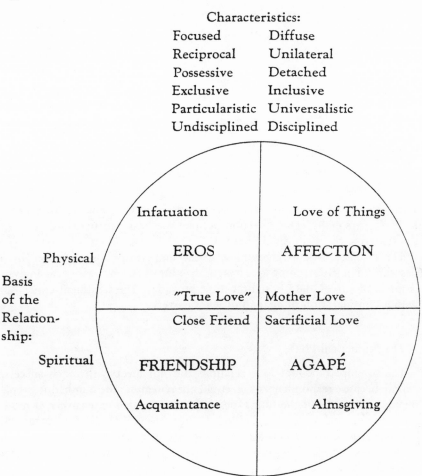

Characteristics:

Focused	Diffuse
Reciprocal	Unilateral
Possessive	Detached
Exclusive	Inclusive
Particularistic	Universalistic
Undisciplined	Disciplined

Basis of the Relationship:

Physical — Spiritual

Infatuation — EROS — "True Love" — Close Friend — FRIENDSHIP — Acquaintance

Love of Things — AFFECTION — Mother Love — Sacrificial Love — AGAPÉ — Almsgiving

My research on love involved three stages. The first was participant observation (see Appendix A), a basic theme in this book. Without this method, the importance of love to the monastery would never have been apparent. The second stage, beginning in 1980, was a statistical effort to operationalize and measure love. Although I had concluded that love is essentially not measurable, in the spirit of science I realized that measurement should be attempted. It is one thing to reach a logical conclusion; it is another to subject this conclusion to systematic empirical scrutiny.

This stage of the research, called the numerical phase, consisted simply of defining the types of love and asking respondents to give the number of persons with whom they had had each type of relationship. Respondents

Table 3.1
Spearman Rank-Order Correlations, Based on Number of Love Involvements

	Friendship	Affection	Agapé
Eros	.333	.365	.170
Friendship		.325	.340
Affection			.403

N = maximum of 132 persons

Source: Hillery 1984: 321.

were also asked to discuss in an open-ended format what the love meant to them personally. This question became the basis for the third stage of the research, the attitudinal phase.

The discussion of love begins with the numerical stage, followed by a description of the meaning love has for the monks. Then a statistical analysis is made of survey data based on these attitudes. The treatment concludes with a consideration of agapé in the monastery.

The Numerical Phase

The attempt to count love relations did not meet with much success, mainly because respondents often could not remember the number of people they had loved.[1] But the four types of love correlated extensively, if moderately, with each other (see Table 3.1). In other words, the data suggested that one type of love may breed other types (Hillery 1981b). However, none of the loves correlated with other variables—not with any of the measures of freedom, violence, cohesion, religious orthodoxy, or anomie.

The numerical phase yielded one other dividend. The open-ended questions allowed the monks to present their own views on love, some of which are reported in the following section.

The Meaning of Love to the Monks

The opinions that are presented here are also those from monasteries other than Palisades Abbey. Since not all Palisades monks offered opinions in the open-ended questions, the larger compass provides a more complete perspective. The responses of monks shall be analyzed with each of the types of love mentioned in the questionnaire, based on Figure 3.1.

Friendship. This type of love was defined as follows: "Friends are chosen because they have something in common with you. Friendship does not, however, need physical contact. Love for a buddy, a pal."

Several words stand out as one reads the replies: sharing, support, help-fulness. In the words of one monk:

Friendships among members of this group have offered sufficient support and love for me to continue as a member of this group. . . . [T]hese friendships offer a most valuable contribution toward my greater fulfillment and vocational choices.

But friendship is something that grows. Another monk explains:

This is a very large community, and each one has his own special personality and temperament, and there are times when the tension is almost unbearable; but God has commanded that we endure all these things, and so with prayer and practice we gradually come to love them as our brothers. This is not an easy thing to come by, and it can only be accomplished when we realize the divine presence in ourselves. It then behooves me to pass it on to all my brothers and especially those that may have an antipathy toward me.

Close friends. The questionnaire distinguished these from friends as fol-lows: "Among your friends, there are some to whom you may feel especially close. These people are important not only because they have something in common with you, but they are important also for their own sake. With how many of your friends have you felt this close?"

Several monks saw no difference between close friends and friends. Many simply referred to their earlier responses on friendship. The same words often appeared in their remarks: help, sharing, support. But also there were terms such as "growth" and "confide."

In contrast, several monks rejected close friendship as nonacceptable, thus harking back to an earlier time when "particular friendships" were prohib-ited. Many have changed from this position:

Though not sanctioned by a large part of the group in view of its unique former behavior of silence, I have experienced, in a relatively short time, a depth of accep-tance of mutual understanding, of unqualified forgiveness among some persons for whom intimacy is not a problem but an enriching dimension of their lives. They have shared this intimacy with me, have shown me my capacity for intimacy and self-acceptance, and I feel myself reciprocating, thus enhancing relationships.

Close friendship is not a common experience. One monk had two such relationships that were especially unique:

My two close friendships are quite different. One is a cause of great joy and comfort; the other is a source of continual pain and sacrifice. Without the joy of the one, I do not know if I could continue the pain of the other. Each has matured

me far more than if I did not have these two close relationships. I am deeply grateful
for the gift.

Romantic love (also known as eros). The questionnaire defined this as
follows: "Sexual love, narrowly considered, and also any love that centers
exclusively on one person and in which you want to possess or be possessed
and physically touch the beloved. Love for a sweetheart."

No other type of love provoked such a wide variety of responses. Many
said this kind of love meant simply "nothing" to them. Some merely said
it did not apply. Others, however, expressed the passion and the hurt.

It should have no place in monastic life as it is a kind of attachment preventing
me from getting close to God. It really tears my heart to pieces and causes much
unhappiness.

There were both positive and negative views. On the positive side:

Romantic love has been a very good experience for me. It has gone into the depths
of me and brought up all my liabilities and assets regarding self and others, intensified
them, and made me come to grip with myself and others. There were many sleepless
nights as well as moments of ecstasy. I have felt confusion between love of God and
love of this other person—was there a difference? I'd experience a move from this
one person into contemplation of God. The "Song of Songs" sings meaning to me.
I hear God say to me "I am sick with love," and I tremble. It helped me to integrate
my sexuality and kept sexual energies flowing that, I feel, are necessary sources if
contemplation is to be achieved and sustained.

And on a more negative note:

It appears to have been a self-interesting thing and spiritually unhealthy. It did
give slight inkling to God's love for me.

An interesting view was expressed tersely: "It isn't good enuf."

Affection. Probably the broadest of the four general types of love, affection
is defined in the questionnaire as follows: "Love of familiar things and
people, especially for someone you have known for a long time. It may or
may not be as intense as friendship, but some kind of physical expression
is often desired (hugs, kisses). There are broadly three types of affectionate
love—love of parents and offspring, love of other relatives and neighbors,
and love of familiar animals, things and places."

Affection merges with friendship on the one hand and with agapé on the
other. Concerning the affinity with friendship, even the same words can be
used: "A strong support, especially in times of stress or feeling down. Also
a source of support in sharing joys, etcetera." The merger with agapé was
often specifically noted:

The affection of others for me has been expressed on occasion and has meant a great deal by way of affirmation and self-confidence. My affection for others, which I would consider an overflow of agapéic love, has enabled me to be patient and to help carry some burdens of others.

Yet, as one monk pointed out, affection is to be distinguished from agapé:

I believe all of them would be included in "agapéic" love, but there is a real dimension of the *affectionate* in the ones I have mentioned. There is what I would call a *conatural* [co-natural; mutual] affection I experience towards me, whereas the other [agapé] is largely *super* natural.

And a historical perspective was provided:

This group is emerging from a past that theoretically espoused such an affection but did not overly encourage its practical manifestation. To see its practical expressions growing in so many small and homey ways is especially encouraging to me to grow likewise.

Charity (also known as agapé and altruism). The questionnaire defined this as follows: "Unselfish love. You give what you have but demand nothing. Though you would like to have the love returned, your first reward is simply being able to love. Charity is an act of will, a devotion that is intentional and deliberate."

There were more replies to this question than any other, perhaps because agapé is so central to monastic life. One detects much idealism in the responses, but idealism is difficult to escape in such a subject. For example: "Ready to die for any of the brothers even if the brother should hate me." Though the answer may border on being trite, it is nonetheless a very accurate rendition of agapé. The next answer is equally idealistic, but one senses a larger measure of realism.

It requires all that I am, plus all that Christ is for us—to achieve this in the nitty-gritty situations. In the last analysis it is a pure gift of total acceptance and surrender and loving response to the whole of the present moment.

A constant (although not unanimous) theme was the difficulty of practicing agapé:

I aim to achieve this every day and, sorry to say, constantly fall short of the achievement. However, I try not to calculate this process of love—I don't think it's healthy for a Christian to "keep score" on his "goodies"—he or she should just do and try their best. Charity here is long suffering and honest!! It is pure and strongly warm.

A related yet clearly distinct theme is that charity or agapé is most clearly perceived in difficult circumstances:

I come closest to it when there is a natural antipathy towards another. Then I'm "forced" to be charity in order to "be." Charity is achieved by desiring to be charitable. It extends to every relationship with every person and thing. It involves both playfulness and dead seriousness.

Agapé is as hard to express as is eros, perhaps partly because of the importance of both to the persons involved. Friendship and affection are either less compelling or less demanding. In the final analysis, anyone who has experienced either eros or agapé knows without doubt that this experience has occurred. But it is easy to think we have experienced these loves when we have not.

Two major conclusions emerge from the survey of the responses: (1) often there is a lack of clear distinction among the four kinds of love in the minds of the monks, and (2) there is a variety of interpretations.

The monks were usually able to work with the basic categories outlined in the questionnaire. In several cases, however, they did not see things that way; friendship merged with close friendship, and both friendship and affection merged with agapé. One monk put it this way:

I find that all four loves mesh into one unified whole experience. Even your love for God loses a differentiating quality. Love is love. Sometimes one could be better served but—love is so demanding yet satisfied with so little. There is one significant other that falls under all these categories while I seek the One Significant Other through all these categories.

The variety in the responses speaks for itself, and in fact, there was even more than has been depicted. For example:

Once I fell in love with a woman who took advantage of my hopeless, almost helpless infatuation. I let myself be compromised. Once a holy woman fell in love with me. And our friendship has grown deeper over the years. There was never compromise. And a rare intimacy and chaste love makes it *the* great friendship of a life. There is love for "females" which can at times share in the characteristics of close friendship, romantic love (without exclusivism), affection and charity. Taking the definition which is given for romantic love, I have answered the questions accordingly, i.e., none of mine had this element of exclusivism. Thus, I find it difficult to answer many of these questions, since the categories given do not match with my own, in some respects.

Accordingly, the merging and the variety of love are related.

The Attitudinal Phase

The question before this section is, Can love be measured statistically? From the evidence, one must reply, some types of love can be measured to some extent, but the measurement is incomplete. Whether love is inherently immeasurable, as I suspect is true, must await further research (but then, measuring the immeasurable is not possible).

Measurement began with the replies from which the comments in the previous section were selected. Brief statements were devised to which monks could respond in a standardized manner. Factor analysis was then applied.[2] The analysis has not been entirely satisfactory, though questions were generated in the same manner as those for freedom (Chapter 2). The only clear factor is for close friendship. That for agapé is weaker. No factor is apparent for eros or affection, and thus statistics for these two types of love are given much less emphasis here (see Hillery 1984 for additional discussion). The questions in the scales for agapé and close friendship are shown in Table 3.2.

Respondents were asked to answer each question if they had "felt this way about anyone in this group."[3] The groups used in the analysis (Table 3.3) were selected to show a variety of communal and formal organizations, so that data on different types of love could be represented. The monks were chosen for agapé, the scouts for friendship (this was a coed college fraternity based on the values of scouting), the trailer park and the suburban community for eros and affection, and the class (on marriage and the family) for eros. The other groups represented populations where the kind of love was problematic, such as the Monastic Center (wherein nonmonks could live the monastic life from four days to a month—see Chapter 4), the football team, and the black students (who were a small enclave at a southern university). In most cases, the sampling consisted only of volunteers. The nuns, however, are the universe of active members. The scouts and the football team members were random samples. Returns for the Monastic Center were based on a mailed questionnaire and represent 55.6 percent of the center's total population.[4]

Analysis of the scale scores in Table 3.3 shows all groups to be loving in having scores for each type of love below middle value (3.0, where 1 is maximum and 5 is minimum), that is, closer to the response that love was experienced "without a doubt." The monks are clearly more involved in agapé than any other group. Only one monastery falls outside of the range of scores of the others, and the abbot of this monastery admitted that many dissatisfied monks took the questionnaire. Only one group falls within the range of scores of the other monasteries, and this is the scouting fraternity. The Monastic Center tends to exhibit less love than any other kind of group, probably because the members did not stay together long enough to form significant relationships.

Table 3.2
Factor Analysis and Reliability of Selected Statements on Love

Definitions of Relations Respondent Experienced Within His or Her group	Factor Loadings* Close Friendship	Agapé	Communalities
Close Friendship:			
A close friend is someone to confide in, to lean on, to be completely honest with.	.76	.23	.63
In moments of crisis, close friends have helped me work through problems.	.72	.29	.61
Close friends are able to share intimate problems.	.71	.20	.54
A close friend is someone who will listen to you and you in turn listen to them, sharing sorrow and joys.	.70	.34	.60
Close friends have helped to get personal feelings out in the open.	.64	.28	.49
Close friends are people in whom we have complete confidence and an ability to communicate at all times.	.61	.12	.39
Agapé:			
It makes me feel good that I can try to help someone.	.29	.75	.64
To put another's welfare above my own has its own reward.	.17	.73	.56
Love is anticipating needs, thinking of others in addition to oneself.	.26	.70	.56
Eigenvalues	4.14	.88	
Variance explained	82.4	17.6	
Reliability			
Chronbach's Alpha	.866	.802	
Number of Cases	282	289	

*Varimax rotation

Source: Hillery 1984: 322.

Table 3.3
Scores for Selected Groups on Agapé and Close Friendship

Groups	Agapé	Rank	Groups	Close Friendship	Rank
Monasteries			Monasteries		
Jericho	1.133	1	Immanuel	1.367	2
Solitude	1.148	2	Bernard	1.444	4
Immanuel	1.267	3	Jericho	1.500	6
Palisades	1.318	4	Palisades	1.621	9
Bernard	1.333	5	Ascension	2.050	17
Ascension	1.818	16.5	Solitude	2.222	18
Nuns	1.476	7	Nuns	1.381	3
Students			Students		
Scouts	1.400	6	Scouts	1.344	1
Blacks	1.545	8	Blacks	1.471	5
Team	1.606	9	Class	1.708	10
Class	1.654	11	Team	1.826	11
Citizens			Citizens		
Suburb	1.608	10	PTA	1.533	7
PTA	1.733	13	Police	1.600	8
Trailer Park	1.800	15	Suburb	1.844	12
Police	1.818	16.5	Trailer Park	1.953	14.5
Center			Center		
Single	1.730	12	Married	1.861	13
Married	1.741	14	Single	1.953	14.5
Clergy	1.894	18	Clergy	1.970	16

Source: Hillery 1984: 324.

The scores on close friendship are more varied. Though the monasteries here, too, tend to rank higher, there is much overlap. The median rank for the monks is, however, higher than that for any other category of groups. These results reflect on the validity of the measures. The monasteries are designed to promote agapé among their members and should rank high. Also, because of agapé, scores should show more friendship. Palisades Abbey tends to be well within the range of scores for both types of love. It is fourth among the seven monasteries (including the monastery of nuns) both for agapé and close friendship. These findings suggest that while social structure can have a marked effect on love, not all love is due exclusively to the type of structure. The data for the Monastic Center suggest that love takes time to develop.

Agapé in the Monastery

Comment is in order concerning the types of love other than agapé in the monastic life. Eros, certainly in its more open expression, is prohibited by commitment to chastity. Never have I witnessed monks touching one another (other than the ritual kiss of peace at Mass). However, affection does exist, noticeable most when monks meet after a long absence. But little or no physical contact occurs, and one would thus conclude that agapé replaces much of affection. Finally, monks do become friends, as the quotations show. Before the Second Vatican Council—1962–65, monks were discouraged from forming "particular" friendships, since agapé was the preferred form of love. This point of view has now been abandoned.

Our primary concern, however, is agapé. We should note that in general agapé is variable in the degree to which it exists. In some situations, some monks are not loving at all. Still, agapé love is an ideal of monastic life, one for which the monastery is purposely structured, and one often attained. In other words, here the community is defined not by what it has done or what it is, but by what it is attempting to achieve, that is, by its primary values. (Cf. the use of goal attainment by Parsons in his AGIL scheme, in Parsons and Smelser 1956). In the following discussion, attention is directed to the diagram on love in Figure 3.1.

First, agapé is diffused. It is not focused on certain people, as is eros or friendship. No one should be excluded, and one who is in agapé is simply a loving person. Cultivation of this love is an objective of the *Rule* of St. Benedict (Chapter 53): "Let all guests who arrive be received as Christ" (Doyle 1948:72). The word "all" is especially important—not only the pious guests, or the attractive ones, or men, or women, but all guests. Of course, affection is diffused also. But affection differs in that it can, and under certain conditions must, involve physical contact: a caress, a hug, a kiss. Agapé is independent of physical involvement.

Agapé is unilateral. One does not love with agapé in order to be loved in return. It is possible also for eros to be one-sided, but such love is not consummated, it is not fulfilled. One who loves with agapé needs no response, though of course a lover always welcomes love and thus wants to be loved. But where erotic love may grow cold if not responded to, one who loves with agapé continues to love even if rejected.

The monks show unilateral love particularly in their care of the sick (Chapter 12). Although the invalid may not acknowledge this care, and may not even be aware of it, he will still be loved. Similarly, though the psychotically hostile monk (I have observed only two such cases in all the monasteries) may become offensive, the monks will continue to care for and love him. The invalid outside, as in a hospital, may be treated impersonally, but this is not probable in the monastery.

Agapé is marked by a certain detachment. Jesus is the classic example.

He knew that he would be killed if he went to Jerusalem (Matt. 16:21–23) and went anyway. When under condemnation, he refused to defend himself (Matt. 27:13–14). Indeed, in some translations this event is called his "passion" (Acts 1:3, KJS and RSV). Eros shows the opposite of detachment in its possessiveness. The lover must possess the beloved, must be physically near, and the loss of the beloved is to some degree always emotionally traumatic. The clearest example of detached love I have seen is at monastic funerals. Those who weep are usually from outside the monastery. The monks feel that the deceased has gone to a better life, and thus why should one mourn? Sadness would be turning one's feelings on oneself and not showing concern for others, to say nothing of in effect doubting the promises of the Gospels.

Of course, eros is qualitatively different from agapé and from all the other types of love in being connected with the sexual act. Alone among the loves, it always requires this physical base, a quality that has led Peck (1976:84) to describe eros as generally not love at all. He qualifies this statement (1976:94), but he is still correct in that the sexual act can be committed without love. In spite of this distinctive quality, eros is always enhanced when combined with other kinds of love.

Agapé is inclusive. Friendship and especially eros tend to exclude others. In its ultimate form, eros is intended only for the beloved. In contrast, agapé is not adulterated by loving others. A monk who openly loved only one person would create a scandal. Thomas Merton provides a particularly lucid example of how a monk may look at inclusive love. "Yesterday," he writes in his journal,

in Louisville, at the corner of 4th and Walnut, [I] suddenly realized that I loved all the people and that none of them were, or could be totally alien to me.... My vocation does not really make me different from the rest of men.... I am still a member of the human race—and what more glorious destiny is there for man, since the Word was made flesh and became, too, a member of the Human Race! (Mott 1984:311)

Agapé is universalistic in that love is offered not only unilaterally and inclusively but to everyone. "There is neither Jew nor Greek, there is neither slave nor free, there is neither male nor female; for you are all one in Christ Jesus" (Gal. 3:28). The person who loves with agapé may have special friends, but she or he will still be able to love everyone, including enemies. Probably the most penetrating description of the universalistic nature of agapé appears in Paul's first letter to the Corinthians (13:4–7):

[Agapé] is patient and kind; [agapé] is not jealous or boastful; it is not arrogant or rude. [Agapé] does not insist on its own way; it is not irritable or resentful; it does not rejoice at wrong, but rejoices in the right. [Agapé] bears all things, believes all things, hopes all things, endures all things.

Paul contrasts a particularistic love with the universalism of agapé. He points the way beyond our immediate situations, with their hurts and limitations, to a universal love that includes not only all people but all conditions.

Agapé is disciplined. One speaks of "falling in love" erotically, with the implication of a lack of self-control. Agapé, however, is an act of will; it is intentional. In the Sermon on the Mount, Jesus tells his disciples to love their enemies (Matt. 5:43–48), and he means that such a love is something we can choose to do ourselves, in spite of formidable obstacles.

The way of life in the monastery is organized to encourage agapé. Such things as the coming together of the monks for prayers in the liturgy and in the Mass and gathering for the common meal at noon all strengthen the love of the monk for his brothers. The monks are provided time for spiritual reading and prayer, where they can retire and strengthen their resolve through replenishing at the source of their love, their God. Further, they are taught that only through contact with a loving God can they love adequately (in agapé) at all. This teaching forms the bulk of their formation as novices in the first six years. Separation from the world also has its place. Some monks say that they are not strong enough to live a Christian (read "loving") life outside the monastery.

Since agapé is intentional and disciplined, one would conclude that it comes through disciplined freedom. As shown in the previous chapter, monks have developed such freedom far beyond that of any group yet measured. It is discipline through prayer that enables the monk to become committed to loving other people.

To be sure, the monasteries carefully choose those who would be monks (a process that should be considered an aspect of the organization) in that loving men are probably more often selected. But the monk is also encouraged and taught to love, and in the most successful cases, believes that love is the reason for his presence in the monastery. The remaining chapters deal with agapé (and sometimes its lack) in the monastic life.

THE COMMUNITY

In this book, the monastery is considered a community or, more precisely, a communal organization. The reasons for this position are given in the theory of communal organizations presented in the following section. After this background, the way in which the monastery specifically operates as a communal organization is introduced.

Community is one of those terms, like freedom and love, that has almost a different definition for each person using the word. Cecil Willis and I have identified over two hundred definitions (Hillery 1955; Willi 1977). According to the Oxford Universal Dictionary, "community" has two meanings: it is a sentiment, and it is a form of social organization or group. One may interpret "community sentiment" in several ways: (1) as sentiments *about* community, that is, the way people feel about a specific community (Hummon 1990), (2) as a sentiment *of* community, that is, as those peculiar sentiments, if any, arising from a particular type of community (Zablocki 1971), and (3) as morale, cohesion, commitment, or love (Toennies 1957; Kanter 1972). In the last two senses, "community sentiment" is a potential property of any human group, and this will be the perspective used here. The discussion begins by examining community as an organization.

A Theory of Communal Organizations

The most important thing about the theory to be outlined here is not its logic. There are numerous theories of community that appear to be quite logical. More important is the method used to formulate the theory, for it is the results of that method that have encouraged me to develop this theory for more than 30 years (see Hillery 1968, 1982, and 1985 for more detail).

My research on community commenced with a survey of definitions (Hillery 1955), but no criteria were available that would allow me to select the definitions that were most adequate. I decided that in order to understand this phenomenon. I had to examine the things that had been called community rather than try to make sense of the definitions. I began by assuming that the agricultural village (later called the folk village) was a community, because none of the definitions I examined denied it. I also assumed that other communities would differ from the folk village only in degree. Ten villages from ten cultures were found to have 19 components in common, including mutual aid as a type of cooperation, the family, and some kind of spatial pattern. All traits were integrated by these three, and thus they are called focal components. Five cities in four cultures were then analyzed and had all the traits of the folk village in some form. The principal difference was that in the village, most traits were integrated by the family; in the city, most traits were integrated by contracts. According to the two basic assumptions, the city was a community.

Since the prison and mental asylum had also been called communities, five of these were also examined. They conformed to Goffman's (1961) model of the total institution: a system in which a bureaucratic staff compels a localized collectivity to act for certain specific ends. In the case of prisons and asylums, these goals were treatment or custody, which are quite specific. Thus, total institutions differed qualitatively from villages and cities and accordingly were not communities. To understand total institutions, a model of community is not appropriate. Most relevant are formal organizations, which Parsons (1960) defines as heavily institutionalized systems that give primacy to specific goals. Therefore, villages and cities should be defined in contrast to total institutions and other formal organizations. The logical conclusion was that villages and cities were heavily institutionalized systems

Figure 3.2
A General Taxonomy of Human Groups

ENDS: SPECIFIC GOALS

		Primary	Not Primary
INSTITUTIONALIZATION	High	FORMAL ORGANIZATIONS Political State Corporation Small Business	COMMUNAL ORGANIZATIONS National Culture Vill (Village or City) Family
	Low	COLLECTIVE BEHAVIOR Social Movement Crowd	INFORMAL GROUPS Ethnic Group Clique

Means

Source: Hillery. *Communal Organizations: A Study of Local Societies.* Copyright ©1968 by
The University of Chicago Press.

that did *not* give primacy to specific goals. These I call communal organizations, because "community" has so many definitions.

Two other conclusions followed: (1) the two dimensions of institutionalization and primacy of specific goals can be used to classify all human groups (see Figure 3.2), and (2) villages and cities are only one kind of communal organization. These I have called the "vill" (Hillery 1968). Other kinds of communal organizations are household families, neighborhoods, nations (as opposed to states, which give primacy to making and enforcing laws), and, of course, monasteries.

The dimension of goal orientation given in Figure 3.2 has two distinct components: primacy and specificity. Primacy means placing more value on certain tasks or things than on others; specificity gives things more importance than people. Specific goals have three qualities: (1) the goal is readily identified, (2) it is an output that can be used as an input for other groups, and (3) it can be contracted for (for example, it can be bought and sold—Hillery 1985; Parsons 1960).

These qualities can be summarized by saying that the success in attaining specific goals can be measured. In other words, some groups are set up to make a profit, to cure people, to make laws, or the like—that is, they are designed to attain goals that are identifiable, and the success of attaining these goals is measurable. One thinks of businesses, hospitals, jails, and governments, in other words, formal organizations. In contrast, groups such as families, cities, villages, monasteries, and nations are not set up primarily to attain specific ends. They may strive for specific goals temporarily, but such things as making profit or laws is not their primary reason for existing. These are communal organizations.

Thus, communal organizations are defined in part negatively: highly institutionalized groups that do not give primacy to specific goals. This negative definition is intended to reflect an important difference in the ends or purposes of both formal and communal organizations: formal organizations have more narrowly defined goals. For this reason, the number of primary goals is limited: one does not ordinarily make automobiles in a hospital. And if goals are combined, as in so-called private schools, special care must be taken as to which goal is more important (primary).

Communal organizations permit a vastly wider range of goal achievement; such groups include those concerned with various industries, child rearing, religious activities—in fact, the entire range of institutionalized human behavior. Briefly, then, we may say that communal organizations refer to types of local arrangements that are set up to enable people voluntarily to live together. They are not developed primarily to accomplish anything specific or measurable. They *may* do such things, but other activities always compete and often supersede them. Communal organizations always have openended kinds of goals: raising families, worship, recreation, and general welfare of the group, as well as more measurable kinds of activities like raising crops, gathering food, and so forth.

The monastery fits into the broader category of human groups that we have called communal organizations. The closest that monasteries come to being organized primarily for specific goals is in their prayers. Prayers, however, are not as much goals as means. In any case, prayers are not identifiable (how does one know when someone else is praying?) and one cannot usually measure the success of prayer. Thus prayers are not specific goals. The ultimate goal of monasteries is creating agapé love. If love is so important to communal organizations, as is maintained in this book, then we should be able to show its existence in all of them, especially in the vill as the normal type and in the monastery as the most radical deviation.

The importance of love in the monastery stems from the exclusion of the biosocial family. If the family is central to the normal vill, how, then, is the monastery able to function? In answer, I have suggested the compensatory hypothesis: if a communal organization does not contain the family or its own spatial territory, then it compensates by emphasizing something else. Evidence for absence or relative lack of these two foci has been obtained only for monasteries, communes, and gypsy bands.

According to Kanter (1972:282), research suggests that where communal ideology is emphasized, the nuclear family is weak or nonexistent. Communes, however, are fragile structures. Most communes do not last. Monasteries are a type of commune (Hillery and Morrow 1976), and they constitute the dominant exception. The monastery compensates for the lack of the family by emphasis on agapé love. This emphasis requires intense dedication (90 percent of those who apply to be Trappist-Cistercian monks do not make final vows) and an elaborate organization and ideological structure to support it.

When communes cease to be committed to an alternative life-style, they usually take three courses: (1) they disband completely, (2) they become an ethnic enclave (as the Amana colonies did in Iowa), or (3) they become a normal vill (as the Oneida community did when it became Kenwood, New York—Carden 1969). The family is a powerful institution, and it is easier to build a communal organization around the family than otherwise. To ignore or even subordinate the family requires intense dedication.

Gypsy bands also conform to the compensatory hypothesis. The type of group being discussed is the *kumpania*, a band of gypsies (*Rom*—a group of gypsies divided into four or five nations) traveling or living together. The territory inhabited by the *kumpania* contains both gypsies and nongypsies (*gaje*). Thus, the territory is not exclusively their own. In compensation, gypsies place heavy emphasis on kinship. Blood relationship is stressed; even in-laws are suspect, considered almost as *gaje* (Sutherland 1975:166). Strict morality and separation between the sexes is practiced, and there is pervasive respect for elders. Regardless of the amorality that gypsies may practice toward *gaje*, they are highly moral regarding their own kin (see also Pippin 1978; Hillery 1985).

In eliminating the biosocial family and requiring chastity of its members, the monastery also eliminates the integrative power of erotic love. According to the compensatory hypothesis, it should compensate. It does so by means of a religious ideology that places great emphasis on another kind of love, agapé.

Summary. The foregoing discussion may be summarized by three statements:

1. The kind of communal organization most frequently found in the world is the vill, a model including villages and cities, based on *families cooperating in a localized setting*. The three traits of family structure, cooperation, and local setting are known as the *foci* of the vill.

2. There are many kinds of communal organizations. They are all *highly institutionalized* and *none give most importance to specific goals*. This last quality permits a high degree of flexibility and freedom.

3. A communal organization may *modify or eliminate a focus of the vill if it compensates* in some way for this change. This statement is known as the *compensatory hypothesis*. Thus, monasteries substitute agapé love for the family.

It is not possible in this study to prove this hypothesis. What I wish to do is examine the monastery as a supporting case. Therefore, the monastery is one datum, one bit of evidence. We want to look at this group carefully and to present the evidence as completely as possible, since it has not been fully recorded elsewhere.

The Monastery as a Communal Organization

The analysis of the monastery as a communal organization is accomplished in each of the chapters in Part II. The remainder of this chapter gives an overview. Each of the components is examined to show the nature of its relation (or lack of relation) to the central or main purpose of the monastery.

As a communal organization, the monastery has a wide range of goal-oriented activities, since it does not give primacy to specific goals. Instead of centering on families cooperating in a given space (as in the normal community), monastic activities revolve around a religious ideology. Being Christian, the ideology is based on freedom and agapé love. In spite of the perversions experienced throughout history, especially in religious persecutions, Christian ideology nevertheless places a premium on love and freedom. The greatest commandments are those concerned with love (Matt. 22:34–40; Mark 12:28–31; Luke 10:25–28). Further, the choice to become a Christian is a free one. The Christian is *invited* to accept salvation (Rev. 3:20; Matt. 11:28–29); no one can force it. Accordingly, the religious ideology, revolving around freedom and love, penetrates the monastic community in a multitude of ways.

The ethnographic analysis begins with the guest house, the institution of monastic hospitality (Chapter 4), which is also usually the first contact an aspiring monk (a novice) will have with the community. Since virtually all monastic activities are acted out within a particular space, and since the religious ideology has a large hand in determining the use of this space, we examine the physical aspect of the monastery (Chapter 5). The normative patterns of interaction are considered next, primarily as set forth in the *Rule* of Benedict. Attention then shifts to the patterns of interaction actually found in the monastery in cooperation and conflict (also in Chapter 5).

The analysis of specific institutions begins with the family: the monks' relations to their families of orientation and to their own celibate commitment. Celibacy is important not only because it precludes eros but also in that it makes recruitment from outside a necessity (Chapter 6). The monks must earn a living, and that topic (Chapter 7) shows how the religious ideology influences this most secular of tasks. Similarly, the political institution (Chapter 8) rests largely on the abbot and his leadership. In spite of his power, there is a decided inclination toward egalitarianism (Chapter 9), to be expected in a free society. There are no permanent classes or status layers in the monastery. Though status differences appear, they depend on individual characteristics and are nontransferable. This phenomenon is also in keeping with the religious ideology: the last will be first and the first last (Matt. 20:16). In other words, such a position as priest has no necessary bearing on monastic status.

Prayer is at the heart of monastic life (Chapter 10). Prayer in the liturgy reinforces the monk's group ties and thus his love for his brothers. Prayer in his closet (silent and contemplative prayer) reinforces his love of God. But though the monk ideally should be single-minded in his search for God, in reality, the ascetic demands are mitigated by celebration; fasts are punctuated by feasts (Chapter 11). The last ritual in which the monk will be involved is his death. This final rite of passage reminds the monk that the purpose of his life is not the maintenance of the community or self-fulfillment but unity with his God (Chapter 12). Lest we forget that the monks are still human, a study of their life shows that they too have patterns of deviance. Even among a collection of saints there are sinners (Chapter 13). However, the nature of the sin and the degree of its severity are determined by the religious ideology. What is a sin for a saint may be innocence for the sinner.

Thus, the monastery as a communal organization is composed of many things, but without the religious ideology and its emphasis on agapé, it loses not only its distinctiveness but its reason for being. The ideology is powerful precisely because it operates in a communal organization. Since it is not confined to specific goals, the ideology is able to extend to all areas of monastic life.

NOTES

Parts of this chapter are adapted from George A. Hillery, Jr., "Gemeinschaft Verstehen," *Social Forces* 63, December 1984, 307–34 and from Hillery, "Love and the Monastic Community," in Austin B. Creel and Vasudha Narayanan, *Monastic Life in the Christian and Hindu Traditions* (Lewiston, N.Y.: Edwin Mellen, 1990), 361–91.

1. Nine groups were studied: the children and the staff of a foster home, the staff of an elementary school, a random sample of married couples, four monasteries for men, and a monastery for women. All monasteries practiced contemplative prayer.

2. I am indebted to Charles J. Dudley for major assistance in preparing the factor analysis.

3. Five choices were possible: (1) Without a doubt, (2) Yes, I think so, (3) Don't know, (4) I don't think so, and (5) Definitely not. Scale scores were obtained by computing the means of the responses for each of the two sets of questions, where 1 is high and 5 is low.

4. Analysis of variance for the four major populations (monks, the center, students, and citizens) showed that all populations were significantly different from each other at the 0.5 level for all types of love except agapé (which was significant at .126). With "Monk 2" removed from the analysis (since it was markedly different from the other monasteries), all types of love were significantly different at the .05 level. Of course, this is a hypothetical analysis, since the populations were not randomly selected.

Part II

An Ethnographic Analysis

Chapter 4

The Guest House and the Novitiate

Let all guests who arrive be received like Christ.
—*Rule for Monasteries*, Chapter 53

The novitiate is not part of the guest house. But the novice enters by way of the guest house, and thus, in the experience of the monk, the two have at least an initial connection.

THE GUEST HOUSE

The guest house is the gateway of the monastery to the world. It is the place to which almost all visitors come, the place where those who are on retreat live, and the first place a future monk will see. In the year beginning July 1, 1984, 1,225 persons signed the guest book, and not all visitors did so (many were just passing by). It is significant that the guest house is connected with the church, for the church is the spiritual meeting place of the monastery with the world, as the guest house is the secular meeting place.

Many kinds of people come to the guest house: (1) retreatants, (2) monastic associates, and (3) candidates are the primary interest of this chapter. There are also (4) those attending church, (5) business contacts, (6) clientele, (7) relatives, (8) friends, (9) former monks, (10) visiting dignitaries, (11) neighbors, and (12) researchers. These categories often overlap. Some visitors also attend daily Mass (which includes a small but faithful congregation). Business contacts are mainly to the monastery's farm and garage, but there are others, such as tax officials and repair men (for those occasional tasks that the monks cannot handle). Clientele come to see certain monks, particularly for spiritual counselling. Three or four monks are most often involved. Visiting dignitaries may be church officials (archbishops, bishops, abbots); priests, monks, or nuns; Protestant clergy; authors; singers; and lecturers.

A potential monk makes his first visit usually as a retreatant—one who comes for a few days of prayer and meditation. Should he find monastery life attractive, he contacts one of the monks, generally the guest master. After being interviewed and undergoing a screening process, he may be invited to come to the monastery for four to six weeks as a candidate (formerly called an observer), where he lives the life of the monks. (This position was instituted at Palisades Abbey. It is explained in more detail later in this chapter.)

The guest house is the first experience the potential monk will have with the monastery, both as a retreatant and as a candidate. One of the first things he will probably do is have a meal or a cup of coffee. There are several dining rooms and a kitchen. Ten or twenty persons can usually be expected for meals, though holidays increase that number significantly. Guests serve themselves, cafeteria style. The menu is similar to the monks', except that meat is included on the menu and eggs are served more frequently. Coffee is available 24 hours a day in a separate room.

One complete wing of the monastery is occupied by the guest house. It contains three floors; 26 rooms are sleeping quarters and 11 are speaking parlors. Most rooms have a private bath; the others were built earlier and have communal baths. The dining rooms, conference rooms, and kitchen are in the basement.

Guests are awakened at 6:10 A.M. by a monk who walks through the halls ringing a set of chimes. Some guests will probably have been up earlier, attending the Office of Vigils at 3:30, but this is optional. A typical weekend retreat consists of conferences held with groups or individuals and lasts from Friday evening until after the noon meal on Sunday. Mealtimes are usually times for talking, though some prefer to sit alone. It is possible to get a "subculture" of conversation started that will continue as various guests come and go. I saw such a subculture emerge once as I struck up an acquaintance with a newly graduated student from a Catholic college. We were joined the next day by a priest from the Franciscans. The following day, a layman from the West Coast became a part of our group. He was replaced in a day or two by a diocesan priest who worked with mental patients. Then all left except the college student and me. We were then joined briefly by a chainsmoking ex-marine and a member of Dorothy Day's Catholic Workers. The ex-marine dropped out, then the college student, leaving only the Catholic Worker and me. From time to time we were also visited by one of the monks. In all, this group had been composed of a total of eight people, though no more than four ever interacted at one time.

Conversations ranged over widely varying topics: Jesus, the devil, Bible memorization, seminary life, monastic life, the impact of Vatican II on various orders, the problems of different Catholic Worker houses, and the "addictive" power of Trappist retreats. Usually, the conversation was stimulating, but occasionally one of those who sat with us somehow lacked something in social skills and that particular group would be rather abruptly terminated. None of us participated in the normal conferences or lectures given by the retreat master. Those who did so usually ate together. The members of our group ordinarily read or prayed alone.

Of course, not all or even most retreatants form such subcultures. Most either participate in a conference or take their retreat by themselves. There usually is not time to do more.

In 1977 and 1978, a sample of the retreatants at the abbey was surveyed. Almost all were male; most were over 30, single, and from middle-class backgrounds. They came from small towns and large metropolitan areas, mainly from adjacent states. On the average, they had attended college and had upper-middle-class occupations. Retreatants were overwhelmingly religious in orientation, with only an occasional agnostic appearing in the sample. They felt also well adjusted to their society. Almost all were Roman Catholic; about one-third were priests and two-fifths seculars. Most had made more than one visit to Palisades Abbey; most knew one or more of the monks and had contact with two or more during their stay. They learned of the monastery from friends, mostly, but also from relatives and priests.

There were 34 clergy and 37 nonclergy. Since they sometimes replied to the questions in the survey differently, separate accounts have been prepared. In assessing the differences, the statistical concept of significance is employed. When a statistician says that differences are significant, it means that the differences are not likely to occur by chance.

Clergy and nonclergy differed significantly in the number of visits. Though an equal number were on their first visit, nonclergy had been to Palisades more often and knew significantly more monks than clergy. One explanation for this difference is that laymen find any contact with a monk to be something strange and new, and they seek to cultivate a relationship if only for that reason. Simmel (1950) has pointed out the stimulation such contact gives to social interaction. There was, however, no significant difference in the number of monks actually contacted.

Differences in reasons for coming to the monastery are more apparent than real. Thus, clergy came to the monastery primarily for spiritual values, to be on retreat, and for spiritual or psychological change, whereas nonclergy came mostly because of a desire for spiritual or psychological change, for spiritual values, and to be in touch with God.

Similarly, "The most important thing that happened on this visit" was expressed somewhat differently by clergy and nonclergy, but the meaning is the same. Clergy felt that spiritual values (especially prayer and peace) were most important, whereas nonclergy included being in touch with God.

Both groups are satisfied with silence (though some want more) and believe that both solitude and social contact are equally valuable. When desire for social contact is expressed, it usually concerns something to do with solitude or silence, and is not always regarded as a good in itself. With few exceptions, the retreatants do not come to the monastery to meet people.

The overall impression one gets from these data is one of a relatively homogeneous body of religious men who have learned that the monastery can be for them a place of peace and spiritual value. The retreatants seem generally satisfied, which is not surprising. Over the years, they have become largely self-selected. They would not keep returning if they were not to some degree content.

THE MONASTIC CENTER

The retreatant is still part of the outside. He comes to the monastery as an outsider and almost all expect to return to the world in a few days. His attitudes may range from intense devotion to regarding the monastery as simply a place to get some rest. Some, however, desire a deeper experience, and for these, the Monastic Center was created. Known also as the Associate Program, it is a unique venture in monasticism. In most monasteries heretofore there were only retreatants and monks. A retreatant who wishes to become a monk applies to become a candidate and begins the process of monasticism. But there has been little place for the man who wishes to share the life more than simply being on retreat and yet does not wish to be a monk. A few monasteries have allowed some to live in the community for a few months or even a year. But only the Monastic Center provided a program where men could participate in the monastic life and make no commitment. (Variants on this program have since been adopted by other monasteries.) The hope is that some will make the complete step into monasticism, but no coercion or suggestion is made. In the first years of its existence (beginning in January 1980), very few from the center had applied to become candidates.

The associate rises, prays, works, eats, and retires when the monks do. Like them, he spends free time in prayer, meditation, and sacred reading in the solitude of his cell. He has his own robe (a light brown pullover garment which comes below the waist with a hood) and sings in choir with the monks. Residence in the center may last from four days minimum up to a month. No fee is charged, and the applicant must be at least 18 years old.

Though the associate lives as a monk, he eats and sleeps separately. A third floor of the guest house has been portioned off for that purpose. It has monastic cells and contains a collection of books on contemplative and monastic spirituality. The associates eat together.

During the first 13 months, 114 associates participated in the center. Twenty-nine were married, 63 were single (lay) persons, and the remainder (22) were priests or religious. The average (mean) age was 34.2 years, with

Table 4.1

Comparison of Associates of the Monastic Center (1981) with Palisades Monks (1980), in Percent

	Palisades Monks (1980)	Associates			
		Single Laymen	Married Laymen	Clergy and Seminarians	Total
Per cent from farms	23	26	29	17	25
--from cities of 10,000 or more	68	61	64	83	67
--from cities of 100,000 or more	45	21	25	39	27
High school graduates	91	100	96	100	99
College graduates	50	53	75	91	69
Born in U.S.	86	91	93	100	94
Born in this state	9	19	21	17	19
Consider themselves members	95	67	75	74	71
Believe in God	100	91	93	100	94
Orthodox*	92	78	77	83	79
Anomic*	20	31	32	23	29
Number of cases	22	43	28	23	94

*Scores are the percent who agreed to the items on the respective scales.

slightly less than half (45 percent) under 30 years old. The largest number came from an adjacent state (25 percent) with the next largest from the state containing the abbey (24 percent). Twenty-eight percent expressed interest in monastic life as a possible vocation; 12 made at least one return visit; and 11 were non-Catholic.

In October 1981, I distributed a questionnaire to 169 former associates, of which 56 percent were returned. Of these, 46 percent were single laymen, 30 percent were married, and 25 percent were clergy, religious, or seminary students. Thus, single persons number fewer in the sample than in the first year of operation, and the married and priests are slightly more numerous (see Table 4.1) compared with the monks. Associates come from farms about as frequently as monks and are more often college graduates. More monks are foreign-born and fewer are from the state containing their abbey. Associates do not consider themselves as much a part of the center as the monks consider themselves a part of their monastery. The center laymen do not believe in God as much as monks and the clergy in the center. Monks are more orthodox and less anomic.

During my own stay (four days), there were five of us, and we developed a substantial cohesion. Some of it, if not all, was probably there before I came. Although we did not see each other all of the time, there were numerous contacts: at the offices, at Mass, during morning recreation, at the noon meal, before going to work at 2:00 P.M., at the evening meal (which was supposedly a time of silence but really turned out to be a "recreation"), and at Conference at 6:30 P.M.

One of my work assignments was picking beets under the supervision of Father Tom. He was very kind. I was going at a pace which I thought was somewhat slow, and when he came up to see how I was doing, I told him, "I don't think I'd win any prizes." He asked, "What do you mean, 'prizes'?"

"I'm afraid I'm going rather slowly," I said. My back and my arthritic knee were hurting. He said, "It's not monastic to try to go fast."

I cannot say that there was glory in picking beets. It was dirty, tiresome, and insects were bothersome. But it was still good. Not only did the physical activity break the otherwise sedentary life, but I was out in the sunshine and fresh air and had a sense of contributing to the life.

One afternoon, the monk in charge held a question-and-answer session with the associates:

Q: Why do you reject applicants to the center?

A: Because of disability, physical or mental; if a person is just simply curious; if he has no religious preference. One person was rejected for that reason.

Q: What if he was a Unitarian?

A: I would probably accept him. There has been one non-Christian: a Ba'Hai.

Q: What is the longest an associate can stay?

A: One has been in six weeks, two more than a month, at most. One of the problems with a longer stay is that the conferences get repetitious. There is also an emotional drain as people with shorter stays come and go. You get to know them; then you have to break off the relation. Those who stay longer are neither a member of the center nor of the community. They tend to look for sociability in the community. If they want to have a longer stay, they should make arrangements with the abbot.

There was a community meeting on the center after one year of its existence, he continued. Of course, some who didn't like it could have stayed away, but there was overwhelming support. The value the monks saw in the program was (1) a source of vocations, (2) sharing the monastic life, and (3) a sign of support from the outside world. As one monk put it, "We're not wasting our time." People seem to be looking for something.

Q: Why isn't contact permitted between the associates and the monks?

A: First, there is the value of the enclosure. There is a difference in solitude and loneliness. Loneliness tempts monks to reach out, such as constantly being in the guest house. Such contact is not real. The monk is not facing up to the interactional problems he has in the monastery. Second, it's a question of not blurring the line between monasticism and the outside. Like a married man not keeping his vows.

The monk summed up the major differences and similarities between the center and the monastery: (1) there is no difference in horarium (schedule of activities); (2) the intention one has of joining varies (the center is a temporary group); (3) the day-to-day, year-to-year living the life is different for each.

To these could also be added the difference in background. In the group that I joined there was a Methodist, a Nazarene, a Presbyterian, and two Roman Catholics. The monks, of course, are all Roman Catholics.

THE NOVITIATE

The first concrete step one makes in becoming a monk at Palisades is to apply for candidacy. The candidate participates fully in the life of the community, except that he does not wear a habit. After four to six weeks, he leaves the monastery for a month and decides whether he wishes to join. If he decides not to, the matter is ended. No one will contact him. If he still wishes to become a monk, he informs the monastery, and the Formation Council (consisting of the abbot, the novice master, and two other monks) tells him if he is acceptable. If accepted, he enters the monastery as a postulant.

The new monk stays as a postulant from six weeks to six months. He resides in the novitiate and participates fully in the life of the novices. Then he becomes a novice for two years. During these stages, his habit is completely white. He next takes simple vows and becomes a junior, receiving the black scapular and leather belt. His cloak, however, which he wears over the habit, has no sleeves, only slits for the arms. The stage of simple vows may last from three to nine years, depending on the amount of additional formation the abbot and the novice master may feel is needed.

During these stages, the monk may leave at any time, in that his vows are for one year only. At the end of his temporary vows, he is voted on by the community and, if accepted, makes his solemn profession, becoming a full member of the community.

The usual method for instructing the novice is to place him under the supervision of a novice master. In September 1968, a new approach was instituted that lasted five years. Instead of a novice master, a formation team was used, consisting of the abbot and three monks. The change was probably influenced by the interpersonal revolutions occurring in the nation at that time. In 1979, one of the monks who had been on the team told me the community was "going through a phase of no structure. We all understand this implicitly, now, because we let the focus drop, and we know what we missed. We were caught up in the sixties and seventies, with all the talk of openness and so on. Their life of prayer went along smoothly before because of the structure they had. Of course, the novice had to realize that prayer had to come from within. But then it can't come from within without the structure. It's not going to be done unless I start again fresh each day. But we haven't got the structure quite back again."

The team approach was conceded to be a failure, for two main reasons. First, there was not enough discipline, especially in daily affairs. Novices would be allowed to make decisions virtually on their own—decisions such as going to a daughter house. "It was almost as if he was telling us rather than asking," according to a former member of the team. Second, the novice had to relate to four people as spiritual directors. This arrangement created problems. "For example:" said a team member, "Imagine a novice sitting in a room with four others, all his seniors and superiors, talking about his life. Imagine if you can. It is almost as if he is appearing before a court. It is awkward, very unbalanced, even excruciating." Another monk said: "Four people can't get that intimate with one person."

At times opinions were divided. The team might come to a unanimous position, but when one person talked to the novice privately, that person's own opinions came out, whether he agreed with the others or not. Also, there would at times be advice from too many sources, which would only increase the novice's uncertainty. In contrast, a person could play the team members against each other.

The chief advantage was that one had four opinions about someone. This was especially helpful during the period of transition following Vatican II.

In 1973, the formation team was abandoned and a novice master was appointed. I interviewed him after he had held this position for approximately two years: What follows is the interview largely as he edited it:

Q: Is the month-long period of observership in part a test of celibacy?

A: Indirectly. Actually, we need some assurance that one can live the celibate life before he comes here. One can live as a celibate because he has received the gift from God. Part of discerning whether the person has a vocation to the monastic life is the inquiry: Are you living a chaste life in the secular world? (Of course, one need not be a virgin. Thomas Merton was not. There could have been objectionable practices in the past. The important question is the observer's present condition.)

Much attention is paid to screening. Four interviews are involved; they are extensive and private, concerning motivation, spiritual condition, psychological condition, and social, moral, and sexual dimensions. The novice master stresses that he is asking the questions to help the applicant. "If he can't speak honestly, he should just bluntly say so. It is usually obvious when he's lying."

If a person is conscious that his former overt sexual acts (such as masturbation or homosexuality) constitute a moral issue, if he is trying to overcome them, is making some progress, and if everything else looks good, then there should be no problem in letting him start as a candidate. Once he has entered, the matter has to be approached in its deepest aspect. All human sexuality has to be put in the service of human loving. A married person does this by committing his sexuality to one other person. The monk is called to integrate—not repress—his sexuality into his way of living, and this is done through prayer. Prayer is the monk's primary act of loving. He seeks a prayerful intimacy with God, first; then he seeks a respectful, celibate, nonpossessive love for his brothers.

Prayerful intimacy with God must be focused. St. Bernard expressed it as a "carnal love for Christ" (Latin: *Amor carnalis Christi*; a distinction is made between genital and existential sexuality, realizing that all humans are sexual in one way or another). The more the whole of a person is taken up in Christ and the transforming love of His spirit, the more his sex life takes care of itself.

The novice master gives conferences on celibacy. He goes into all problems as explicitly as possible. This is not usually done until the novice has been in the monastery a year or two. Otherwise, he would not really understand.

Q: What does freedom mean to you, and how do you work this concept into the novitiate?

A: Freedom is the ability to love. What most hinders my freedom to love is self-gratification. St. Bernard says: Man is created in the image and likeness of God. The image of God in man is his freedom to love. The likeness of God occurs if man is actually loving. Through sin, man has lost this likeness. He retains still his image of God, his freedom to love. The monastery is a school of love, a place where we recover our lost likeness to God. The whole idea of discipline comes in the practice of doing this. Discipline comes from the Latin word *disciplina*, meaning a learning. It correlates with the English word "disciple." The early Cistercians looked upon the monk as a disciple who learns the art of love from Christ in the monastery.

In the first two years, "you are learning an art, and the only way to teach art is by constant repetition," repeated emphasis on fundamentals of spiritual living. Spiritual direction involves a one-on-one situation, novice master and novice. He meets with each, once a week for an hour.

There is a Formation Council composed of the abbot, the vocation director, his assistant, and the novice master. Its function is the admission and selection of candidates. To admit a candidate, the council has to be unanimous. The same council decides if a candidate is to be admitted to postulancy. The next step is the novitiate, and here the Abbot's Council votes on a candidate's entrance. The vocation director is responsible for the initial contact—correspondence, initial interviews. He can block it there, without either the abbot or the novice master seeing the man. The abbot and the novice master together must decide if a postulant or novice must leave.

During the candidateship, the vocational director(s) gives the conference, explaining to the candidates the meaning of the life, contemplative prayer, liturgy, *lectio divina*, manual work, and so forth. The novice master talks to candidates about their personal life.

In the novitiate, there is no council. The abbot has all authority, and he delegates. The novice master assumes control over the novices. Someone other than the novice master should assign work duties. Novices read too much into the novice master's acts otherwise. A submaster assigns work, teaches music and the sign language. The novice master also invites members of the community to give special lectures and conferences.

The novice master stressed that "it is important that I work with them. I observe such things as thoughtfulness, how the novice speaks: is he always speaking of himself? You observe the little everyday things. It comes with living with a person. Sometimes the [novices are] so psychologically debilitated that they aren't free— their problems are so deep-seated that you don't catch them at first. The question here: where is their center? You also find out about their ego through their attitudes toward obedience. Does he do what he's supposed to do? Is he sneaky about his mistakes?"

The monks used to admit candidates who wanted to "try" the life and "see" whether they had a vocation. That does not work. None of such candidates stayed, and they caused difficulties while they were there. A postulant will not be accepted unless he really seems to have a vocation.

Novices may only write home once a month and are permitted one other letter. They may see only immediate family, not friends; this occurs one to four times a year, depending on distance. It is not that family is bad. Novices must be free to attach themselves to what they came here for: prayer. If the attachment is to the monastic community, in order to have it, a person can't remain attached to his family. When one says yes to one thing, he says no to another.

Q: Do you have any criteria for rejection?

A: Not on paper, but there are some. One: inability to obey. Here, we do not play around. A man can't stay with serious and persistent problems in this regard. Two: if he can't follow the horarium. Occasional slips are not what I'm talking about; it's more a general sloppiness. It's not slavish conformity that we are looking for but good will. Three: psychological problems, such as prolonged depression. Four: inability to live chastely. Five: inability to get along with others, such as being demanding, possessive, bitter. Discerning these things takes time. Six: tendency to "workism," overemphasis on work. Some come, fit in, but do not have the grace to seek God directly in prayer. They then may get overinvolved with others. Even though they conform, they would be asked to leave.

In all of these matters, the abbot and I must come to a consensus. I cannot dismiss someone on my own.

Q: How do you handle discipline?

A: For a long time we did nothing. In this sense, it is good to have had a "past," so we can see the things we've gotten rid of. The standard practice is to warn a novice about a fault twice, and if he won't listen, to bring it before the Conference (which consists of other novices). I might bring a problem up in the group first if I thought the novice could take it better that way and if it might help the group.

Thus, a novice master's task is to a large degree a personal matter, differing from master to master and from abbey to abbey. The formation of novices takes place in each monastery. The intention of the novitiate is to have the candidate learn to be a monk by living like a monk under close supervision. The novices have conferences at Palisades Abbey five times a week. It is obligatory for them to have two extra offices each day, Terce and None (which are not obligatory for the solemnly professed). The novices have more common work (they are mostly responsible for the garden). Silence is more structured, to initiate them into it. Spiritual growth is watched more closely. There is a more intense common life.

Though screening is used extensively, including psychological examinations, there is no way to tell if a candidate will become a monk. Ninety percent do not. At times, obvious problems will surface during the candidacy, as when a candidate turned out to be an alcoholic, became drunk, and gave an impromptu speech to the community at dinner (which the monks are supposed to eat in silence). Others may seem exceedingly promising and still leave. I asked a monk who had been involved with novices for many years how one could tell if a person would make a good monk, and he answered, "Most of the time you don't know until they are ten minutes in the grave."

CONCLUSION

The guest house exists in accordance with Chapter 3 of the *Rule*: "Let all guests...be received like Christ." (Doyle 1948: 72) The responses of various people show a gradation in experiencing love in the monastery, beginning most superficially with the visitor, and becoming stronger respectively with the guest, retreatant, monastic associate, novice, and solemnly professed monk.

One of the manifestations of agapé most clearly sensed by visitors and guests is the presence of a deep peace. The retreatant will perhaps be more aware of this peace, and the candidate may feel an attraction of sufficient strength to do something about it (that is, he joins). Indeed, accommodations and the reception of guests exist in the monastery because of a love for Christ and a love for people (though the strength of that love varies). Separation from the world is not a rejection of it. The monks separate from the world partly in order to pray for it.

The monastic associate participates more fully in the life and experiences some of the cohesion and commitment of the monk. He begins to have a larger share in the agapé form of love.

Postulants and novices feel the attraction even more strongly. The monk's own response is through teaching and selection. Agapé is a process, not a state. One must be taught to love with agapé. Not all can do so sufficiently, and thus there is a process of selection—much of it self-selection. The novice master's role in particular constitutes an act of love. He receives no special privileges for his work. He does it out of an act of obedience and because he feels this way of life is important.

One cannot perceive the full development of agapé in the monastery on one visit. Appreciation of that love becomes significant only after years of involvement, after having lived the life day by day, through the prayers, the different kinds of behavior, through living together with one's brothers, and in the continuing effort of drawing closer to God. The process is seldom dramatic. It is slow and unobtrusive, much of it growing from simply living as a monk. It is with this life that the rest of this book is concerned.

Chapter 5

Space and Interaction

Although monks have social contacts that are worldwide, they still live in a localized system, a territorial setting that contains most of their interaction. We shall discuss the integrative qualities of space, spatial patterning, and spatial boundaries.

Interaction is the basic process of any human group. In this chapter, the standards of interaction are outlined as they are set forth in Benedict's *Rule*; then patterns of personal contact are described as they actually take place, including the social processes of conflict and cooperation.

SPACE

> If it can be done, the monastery should be so established that all the necessary things, such as water, mill, garden and various workshops, may be within the enclosure, so that there is no necessity for the monks to go about outside of it, since that is not at all profitable for their souls.
> —*Rule for Monasteries*, Chapter 66

Spatial Integration

The territory occupied by the monastery is integrated above all by the values of the monks. The parts to this territory or space may be roughly divided as follows: (1) the abbey building, (2) the guest house, (3) the grounds where the guests are free to walk, (4) the enclosure, and (5) the farm. There is overlap—part of the enclosure is the farm, as is part of the abbey. But as one approaches the monastery building, the line between the outside world and the monastery becomes ever more conspicuous, until finally one sees it in signs marked Private, Monastic Enclosure, No Women Permitted, No One Permitted Beyond This Point unless Accompanied by a

Brother. These signs mark the enclosure. No physical or natural boundaries separate the monastery from the rest of the world.

The justification and cause of the enclosure is the value the monks place on separation from the world. A part of their abbey is open to outsiders, especially the church. Another part is marked off from the world, to permit the monks peace in following their call. Even with this demarcation, the monastery and its grounds are looked on by the monks as a unit. Whether he speaks of the lawn where the guests are permitted, the lawn within the enclosure, or the farm, the monk refers to it as "our land," "our place," "our monastery."

No monk owns the land. The monastery as a group does so, in that it is incorporated according to the laws of its state. The monks—all monks, including the abbot—have surrendered all property; thus questions that arise in other communities are not relevant here. There is no common ownership, since no monk owns anything. To be accurate, there is a kind of political authority over the territory, and one may consider the abbot a mayor. But if so, he is a mayor only as one small part of his job. He is to some monks a father confessor and advisor; to all he is the president of the corporation, occasionally the officiating priest, a fellow worker, and a pilgrim brother. Thus, the monks have political authority over their territory, but it is not political in the customary narrower sense.

So the space is not integrated by common ownership. The political authority is not enforced by a specialized population (such as police or guards). Rather, authority, and hence unity and integration, come mainly from the values of the monks. This is the place where they have renounced everything for their God. It is *their* place of renunciation. It is theirs because they have surrendered it to a cause that is common to them all.

Spatial Patterning

The monastery occupies some 3,600 acres, of which 1,800 are in cultivation, 300 in pasture, 1,000 in timber, and 100 occupied by lawns, gardens, and the abbey building.

The abbey is not in the center of the farm but to one side (see Figure 5.1), ranging from a quarter of a mile to a mile away from the farm buildings. The monastery is not constructed for economic efficiency. Not that work is unimportant, for labor is part of the Trappist ethos, balanced with liturgy and *lectio divina*. However, work is *only a part* of the spiritual call and labor must be subordinate to that call. (The *Rule* says specifically [Chapter 43: 62]: "Let nothing, therefore, be put before the Work of God," in other words, the Divine Office, which is performed in church.) Thus, the work buildings are placed out of the way. When the monk does go to work, his arrangement is as efficient as he can make it, with relevant buildings in easy access.

Figure 5.1
Map of the Principal Monastic Buildings

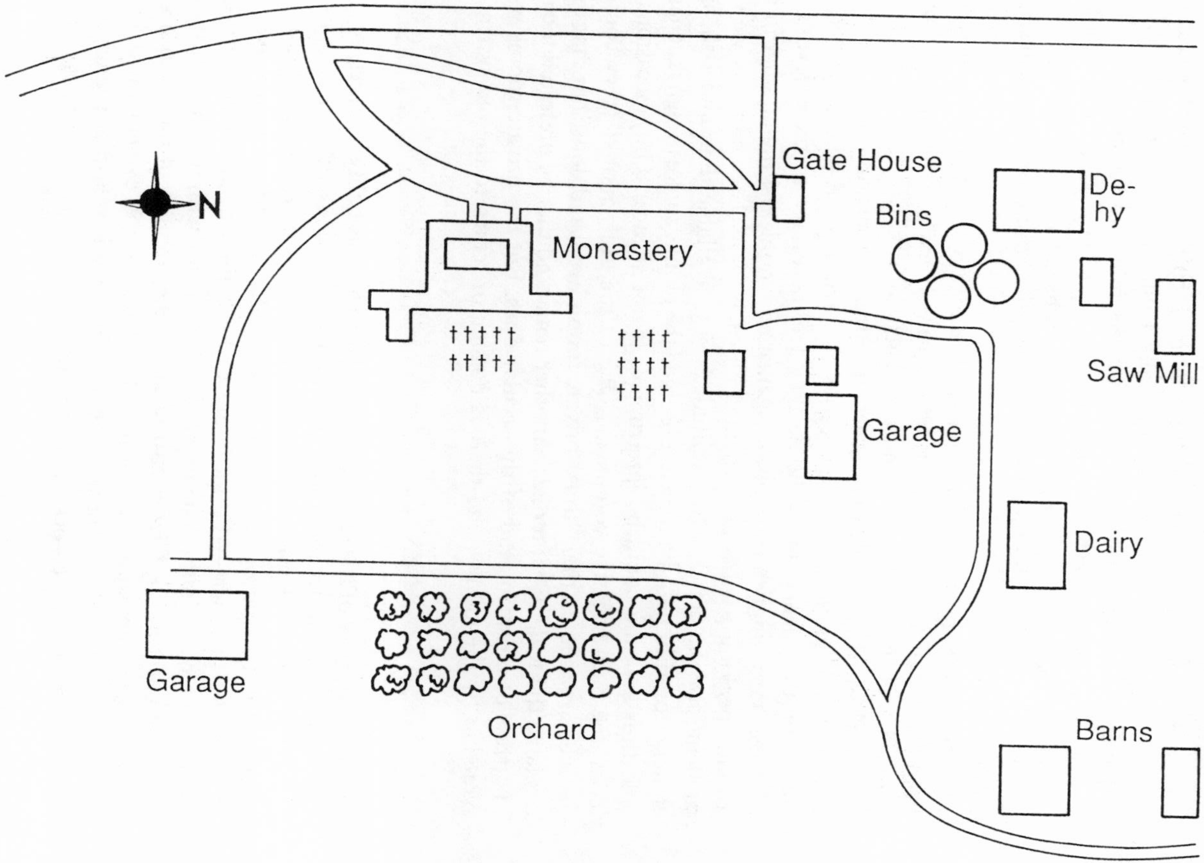

Equally important is the use of space within the monastic building proper. There are five levels of activity; subbasement, basement, and the first, second, and third floors. The most important of these are shown in Figure 5.2. The church occupies the second and third floors such that it is most accessible both to the guests and monks, especially from the monastic cells. Most activity within the monastery occurs on the first and second floors. The third floor is almost solely occupied by dwelling rooms. Much activity takes place in the basement, but it is mainly of a transient kind—washing, changing clothes, storage. The subbasement houses the print shop, electrical shop, and boiler room.

Probably the most significant physical change within the monastery has been the installation of private rooms. Formerly each monk slept in a partitioned stall in a common dormitory. The stall was roughly five by seven feet, and its only door was a curtain. After the custom of silence was modified, the monks felt it imperative to have a place where they could retire for the silence and solitude they feel necessary to their devotions. There is accordingly a prohibition against any monk visiting another in his room. Speaking parlors are provided on each floor. The change is viewed as being for the better. More solitude is now available than under the old system (for although silence was observed the monks spoke in sign language, and thus solitude could be interrupted, if not silence). Only occasionally does one hear negative comments. One of the older monks (very conservative) commented that "those private rooms are scandalous," in that they violated the *Rule* (Chapter 22). Another remarked that he preferred the old mattress of straw instead of the secular ones. But the private rooms were voted in by the monks, and there is no sign of return to the old system.

Boundaries

The sharpness of the enclosure boundaries has probably been responsible for leading some to think of monasteries as prisons. It is true that the canonical boundary known as the monastic enclosure is carefully preserved. But it is not based on force. The locks could be readily broken. Nor are the monks prisoners—the locks are to keep the outside world out. One source of tension in the monastery is the frequency with which some monks visit the guest house.* Each visit weakens the strength of the enclosure.

Another point should be noted: The enclosure is evident on only the southern side of the monastery, where the outside world approaches. Although the enclosure does surround the monastery on other sides, it is not

---

*Five monks work in the guest house as part of their expected labor. Twelve are frequently in the guest house, either for visits or conducting retreats or prayer meetings. In contrast, 20 monks seldom leave the cloister.

Figure 5.2
Plan of the Abbey

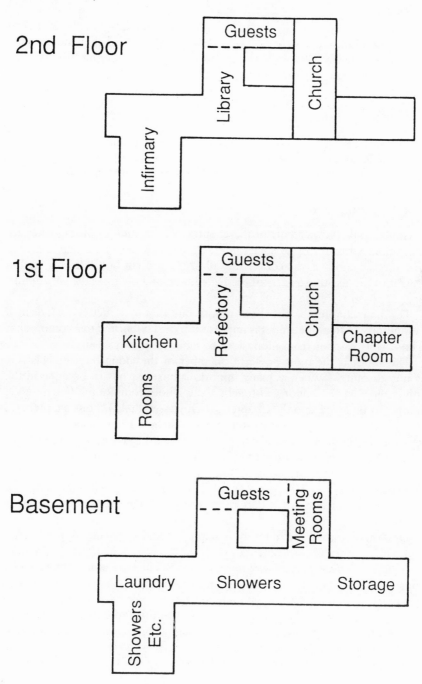

always apparent. Finally, all locks operate on the "night latch" principle—a single key fits them all (each monk has one) and is not needed inside the enclosure.

Another measure of the importance of the boundaries is the extent to which the monks cross them. Twenty-six percent stated that they usually spent part of each day out of the group, for intervals varying from 4 to 24 hours. Obviously, the boundaries are for the monk's convenience.

INTERACTION

> In all things, therefore, let all follow the Rule as guide, and let no one be so rash as to deviate from it.
> —*Rule for Monasteries*, Chapter 2

Rules for Interaction

Almost half (47 percent) of the chapters in the *Rule* of St. Benedict are concerned with norms of social interaction. Such norms of course are, in one way or another, the concern of all of the present book. In this section I want to discuss those parts of the *Rule* that explicitly treat the way monks are supposed to relate to one another.

The first chapter of the *Rule* points out that it is better to live in a community than alone, and it is important to be *committed* to a community. Those who wander from monastery to monastery are censured.

The abbot is the most powerful member of the monastery. But his rule is not absolute. "Whenever any important business has to be done in the monastery, let the abbot call together the whole community and state the matter to be acted upon" (Chapter 3—Doyle 1948: 12). Four chapters (5, 23, 64, and 71) stress the importance of obedience. The monks should obey all superiors immediately and completely, even if the task appears impossible (Chapter 68). Failure to obey raises the threat of excommunication (Chapter 23). A hierarchical structure of administration is useful, especially if the monastery is large (Chapter 21). Each monk is assigned a place in the monastery according to the date of his entry, though the abbot can change this ranking (Chapter 63).

One should strive for humility (Chapter 7) and never attempt to defend himself (Chapter 28) or someone else (Chapter 69). Punishment is predominant in the *Rule*, especially excommunication. The term as used by Benedict means exclusion from meals and the liturgical office. It is not equivalent to the usage in modern canon law, where excommunication means exclusion from the sacraments. Six chapters are given to this topic (Chapters 23–26, 28, 44). Excommunication is a matter of degree. For lighter faults, the monk is "excluded from the common table" (Doyle 1948: 44) and cannot sing in choir (Chapter 24). For weightier faults, he is excluded from all interaction.

If one attempts to communicate with him, he suffers the same punishment. The ultimate excommunication is to be sent away. Lack of obedience is the main reason for excommunication, though tardiness to the Divine Office or to the table are also grounds (Chapter 43).

Contact with the outside is limited. No gifts are to be received without permission from the abbot (Chapter 54). Brothers who are working far from the monastery should say the Divine Office where they are (Chapter 50). But brothers on a journey less than a day away are not supposed to eat until they return (Chapter 51). No one who has been sent away on a journey should tell anyone "whatever he may have seen or heard outside of the monastery" (Chapter 67—Doyle 1948: 95). If one leaves the monastery of his own volition ("through his own fault"), he can be received back no more than three times (Chapter 29).

Several chapters treat special cases: care of the sick (Chapter 36), of old men and children (37), of guests (Chapter 53), of pilgrim monks (61), and of priests, both those applying to be monks (60) and those ordained in the monastery (62). Two chapters (58 and 60) discuss the manner in which beginners move from postulant through various degrees of the novitiate. Even sleeping habits are regulated: each monk is to have his own bed, and dormitory living is the norm (Chapter 22).

The spirit of silence is important: "permission to speak should rarely be granted even to perfect disciples" (Chapter 6—Doyle 1948: 20). No one should speak after Compline, the last office of the day (Chapter 42).

Finally, Chapters 4 and 72 specifically treat love. Chapter 4 begins with the two great commandments, to love the Lord with the whole heart, soul, and strength, and then, to love one's neighbor as oneself. From this point, 70 verses describe how this love is to be manifested: one shall not murder (and so through the rest of the commandments), one should visit the sick, console the sorrowing, not be proud, hate no one, and so on.

Although it is dedicated to the Strict Observance of the *Rule*, the monastery does not scrupulously follow all of it today. Excommunication is not as pervasive (probably because it is now a much harsher penalty), brothers who are away from the monastery for less than a day do in fact eat outside, and speaking is permitted from Mass until Compline. But with such exceptions, the *Rule* provides a set of limits and prescriptions that indicate how the monks are supposed to respond to one another.

Personal Contacts

Interaction in the monastery is pervasive. Everyone knows who comes to choir and who does not. Everyone knows who are isolates, who is closer to whom. Everyone knows what not to say to whom because he may be friendly with someone else and such a thing should not be said in that context. Yet one of the basic values of the monastery is solitude, and it is prized highly. Most of the monks (92 percent) approved of hermitages, although hermitages had earlier been discouraged by the order. Those available to the monks are extensively used, at least by some. (However, the monastery has only one full-time hermit.) Even the abbot has his day of retreat (Wednesday), on which he withdraws from the monastery completely and goes to one of the hermitages. The purpose of this retreat is to provide spiritual and psychological relaxation. In this way, the abbot, as the leader of the monastery, is kept in harmony with one of the most fundamental monastic values, solitude. The solitude, in turn, is interpreted as a means to an end, that of prayer and being with God.

So all of the monks know much about each other. Yet, as one monk said, "The monastery is a pretty big place. It is possible to go for weeks without seeing some of the people, and thus it is pretty easy to stay away from people that you do not particularly care for." Though some monks would challenge such a statement, the principle is used by others.

The knowledge that the monks have of each other is probably greater than it was a few decades ago. In 1967, the Trappists sharply modified the custom of silence—one that had been maintained for more than 800 years. Around it had developed an elaborate sign language. The purpose of the silence was not just to prohibit communication (needless communication was sacrificed as an ascetic practice). Silence was important for promoting a condition that would enable the monk better to confront his God. There seems to have been less contact under the old rules, when a monk was supposed to speak to no one except his superior and his confessor. I recall vividly in 1967 talking in the gift shop of one monastery to a brother who was quite upset that a monk had recently left. "After 18 years," he said, "and we never knew that he was intending to leave." Today, communication is more open, and lively speculation occurs concerning those most likely to resign.

The rapidity of communication can be startling. A person can be anonymous in the guest house and the chapel, but his presence will be observed within the enclosure almost immediately. I have felt this from the first moments that I walked through the monastery in the company of another monk, even during the period of silence (laymen are normally not allowed in the enclosure—I was given special permission to be there for this research). Nor was my presence known simply because I did not wear the habit, or because my head was unshaven, for monks quite often dress in laymen's clothes, and not all shave their heads. The monastery is a place where everyone knows everyone else.

Contacts with the Outside

At the entrance to the abbey church there stands the following inscription on a bronze plaque:

The American Institute of Architects
has selected this project for
1977 honor award.

The plaque stands as an interesting if not ironic index to the association of the abbey with the rest of society. For though these monks are committed to separation from the world, the world beats a very determined path to its doors, and the response is not negative (Lawrence and Hillery n.d.).

Regardless of what St. Benedict may have wished, the monastery has always been both separated from the world and in active relation with it. The extent of contact is not large. For example, the average suburban housewife will drive her car on most days during a month. Trips taken by the monks outside their home, however, are dramatically fewer, for during a month, most make less than two trips. In each case, we are speaking of a base of operations; for the housewife, it is her home, and for the monk, it is his monastery. During one sample period, only three monks made more than ten trips per month out of the abbey: the procurator (business agent), the farm boss, and the manager of the garage. Most of the trips (excluding those of the farm boss and the garage manager) were to the nearby city (41.7 percent). The main reasons for leaving the monastery had to do with religion, business, and government. Other reasons range over a wide expanse: medical, educational, charitable, and even recreational purposes.

Religion. The most frequent contacts of the monastery with the outside are through the guest house, especially through the abbey church and with retreatants (see Chapter 4). A newsletter is sent out twice a year to 16,000 persons. It contains some information on the monastery (number of novices, visitors, a chronicle of happenings) but also an assortment of news taken from other monasteries, various religious happenings, poems, and religious essays. It is now in its fourth decade. Other contacts concerning religion are with the nearby city (where the bishop has the offices of his diocese), with Rome, with the nearby Trappistine monastery (for women), with the daughter houses, and with the mother house in France.

The bishop has final authority on liturgical matters. He has no other jurisdiction over the abbey. The affairs of the abbey are otherwise controlled by the abbot. Contact with Rome is mostly by mail, except for the meetings of the General Chapter of the order every three years. The abbot attends with one delegate from the monastery. During the 1960s, eight monks studied in Rome.

A Trappistine monastery is located about 13 miles from the abbey and relies on it for a priest (to hear confessions and to say Mass) and one other monk to help with manual labor. The priest returns to the abbey once a month; the brother once a week. They live at the convent while visiting. The monks use the Trappistines as a place of retreat. The novices of the two houses also meet to discuss spiritual matters, under the direction of their novice master and novice mistress.

Meetings with the abbot and the abbess are very sporadic—every two or three months. The abbot is the Father Immediate for the convent, but there is little for him to do. Relations are more friendly than official. The abbess virtually never comes to the abbey. She has to obtain permission from the bishop, since he has more control over the Trappistines, and he is conservative concerning such matters. The monks do much of the Trappistines' interaction with the outside and provide extra help occasionally in such matters as repairs.

The abbey has had three daughter houses: (1) An annex was started as an experimental community of four monks in the late 1960s. It never became a foundation in the full sense of the word and was closed by 1987. To avoid having the annex spending most of its time in work and not enough in prayer, the abbey supported the monks there in part, as needed. (2) A monastery was founded in 1950. It still needs assistance, both in money and personnel. Visits are made by the abbot as the Father Immediate every 18 months. He usually is accompanied by two or three monks. (3) Palisades also has a daughter house in England assigned by the General Chapter. The abbot of Palisades has been there only a few times since 1974. The daughter house sends a sort of day-by-day diary each month. The abbot would like to take one of his monks to visit, but the cost is prohibitive.

Palisades Abbey has been assigned (again by the General Chapter) to a mother house in France. The original mother house of Palisades had too many daughter houses, and the General Chapter made the assignment to keep the original Father Immediate from being overworked. The purpose of visits from the Father Immediate is twofold: (1) to support the abbot, and (2) to promote interhouse contact and thus strengthen the order. This last was probably the original reason for instituting the custom of abbatial visits in the Charter of Charity (see Chapter 1). Interhouse contact is especially important because the order has become international in the last century.

The abbey also assists monasteries in other countries by sending them some of its own monks, though this has happened only a few times. All of the monks have now returned. One of the countries was as far away as Indonesia.

Economics. Whether there is more outside interaction through economics than through religion is difficult to say. Probably more people *come* to the monastery for religious reasons, and economic concerns are concentrated in the hands of fewer people. In both cases, contacts are usually made in the guest house, though the gate house is also used. This is the entrance to the farm, approximately 200 yards from the guest house (see Figure 5.1). Generally, contacts occur less often on Sunday and Holy Days of Obligation when neither the gate house nor the gift shop is open. The gift shop is in the guest house and is operated by one of the monks. A small but steady stream of customers purchases various kinds of religious articles: Bibles, candles, incense, rosaries, and so forth. The gift shop is also an outlet for candy made in the Trappistine monastery.

Outside sources supply many basic needs. Electric power, gas, telephone service, and food all come from the nearby city, as is true of shoes, much of the nonmonastic clothing, and hardware generally. Some monks go to the city for mail. As one monk observed, the old rule of St. Benedict about having everything in the monastery could be followed more stringently, but it is not. Things could be obtained by mail order, for example, and thus many outside connections would be curtailed. But some enjoy the liberty of purchasing on their own. It is an unusual experience for monks to buy things. One monk remembers when he did not go out at all. When this account was written (1976), there were two regular shopping trips a week.

There was once a heavy involvement in cattle, but they have now been sold. Contacts at that time were almost nationwide because of advertising, public relations, and sales (for which the monks went out of the monastery at times). At one sale on the monastery grounds about 400 persons came, including men and women. Their presence, however, was mainly at one of the barns on the farm, and other monks hardly knew they were there. One hired hand helped, but one or two neighbors also volunteered occasional labor.

Government. The involvement in government is pervasive in that most monks are affected, but the involvement is not heavy. The monastery retains the services of a lawyer on a contingency basis. He is used several times a month.

Most of the monks vote, though not so much in the primaries. Approximately the same number vote in local as in presidential elections. Most are Democrats, but they do not talk about it much. According to one, they vote partly from habit. Voting was one of the few reasons a monk could get out of the monastery in the old days.

Miscellaneous. The monastery has its own infirmary but no physician. Often the monks choose their doctor in the nearby town and make their own appointments. The monastery has medical insurance for the monks. A dentist in town gives the monks a free hour once a week, at noon. He can accommodate four monks on each trip.

Blood donation is of course voluntary. Some monks go at the maximum rate, which is every three months. They make appointments. Blood types of the monks are on file, and the blood bank calls when they have a need.

In the vicinity are several colleges from which the monks take courses, usually in religion. Some have taken correspondence courses. From time to time, special needs arise, such as nursing training for the infirmarian, liturgy courses for the liturgist, and counselling for the novice master. Universities in other states are used, for example, Catholic University in Washington,

D.C., which is some distance away. Occasionally, monks attend workshops on topics such as mechanics, taxes, medicine, and religion.

A few regularly stop by the public library in the city. For some it is a form of recreation, though the abbey has a library of 15,000 volumes, including local and religious newspapers, the *Wall Street Journal*, and a popular news magazine. There used to be two news magazines, but one monk has a private subscription to the one that was stopped, and it circulates "underground."

One of the older monks, in commenting on outside contacts, observed that some monks are foolish enough to leave themselves open for invitations, and then the people invite them to visit. It would be better simply to tell everyone that the rules don't allow social visits. "Then you would settle the whole thing. But you can't accept an invitation to a birthday party from one person and not do the same for another. Some people from town want to come out and pal around a bit, but you've got to watch that. They'll devour you."

Neighbors, family, and charitable donations. With several thousand acres of farmland, the monks have many neighbors. Seventeen farms border on the abbey. Relations seem good. For the few neighbors that I was able to interview, Palisades is more than a neighbor; it is a special kind of place. Several families are more closely involved than others. Some help with the work, but this depends to a large extent on the monk involved. The farm boss, for example, does not use neighbors for help. Others do. There is not as much sharing through mutual aid as formerly. One monk observed that the older men know much more about neighbors than the younger ones.

A Catholic church which used to be operated by the monastery is within walking distance of the abbey. In town, it is sometimes still called the Palisades Church. One of the priests who died only a few decades ago was formerly a monk at the abbey. The property still belongs to the monastery (though the church or the graveyard do not). If the priest gets sick, the abbey will help, but there has been no pressure to do this. The church has respected the monastic vocation.

Most and probably all of the monks have visits from their families, as discussed in Chapter 6. When visiting, relatives stay at a small motel a few miles away. It is operated by a retired policeman, and "to help [the motel] get some business, we pick up the tab for any member of the immediate family of the resident monks," one monk said. "If these same relatives want to stay at any other motel, they pay their own way. We can use it because it's close and because they are kind. They are willing to drive people over if we get caught in a bind. This relation started in the late sixties."

Charitable relations are often conducted on a personal basis with neighbors. The manager of the beef department gives meat to some poor persons in town. Sometimes he sells cattle at a lower price than he would normally if he knows the person cannot afford it. The abbey gives away much garden produce. Much of the help is spontaneous. The abbey has a particularly deep well, and sometimes if there is a fire, the county fire truck will use it.

The informality of the charity is shown best from an interview: "Some people were burned out and we sent them a check. Another neighbor got in an automobile wreck and didn't pay his bills. We cancelled their bill [with us] as a Christmas present. Another man died, and his family had tough sledding. We cancelled their account [with us] and sent them a check. One farmer was running his corn chopper, and his little boy walked into it and got all cut in pieces. We sat up with the family that night. No one else came. We thought someone else would show up but they didn't. We don't do that sort of thing as an apostolate. We try to figure out if help is really needed. We have a policy to give away as much as we get, and something extra."

I checked to make sure: "You give away as much as you get?"

"Yes. If someone gives us a few thousand dollars, then we give away that much. But we've got to be careful. We're not mendicants. We have to pay our own way, and so we have got to have some security. We have a committee to decide about the giving of ordinary alms. It doesn't have to be a Catholic institution."

Social Processes

Conflict and cooperation. The two major forms of social interaction are conflict and cooperation. Conflict, as used here, is a broad concept, referring to any kind of disagreement, ranging in intensity from arguments to murder. Although no one has given a completely satisfactory reason for why it is so, conflict is pandemic to humanity. Whether Adam or Jesus, murderer or monks, humans disagree. The monks have ranged over the spectrum, though they tend to be much more disputatious than violent. Dialogue, as one type of conflict, is institutionalized. Whenever any monk can obtain 15 signatures on a topic, a special meeting is called to discuss it. At the other extreme, although no monk has reported the use of a weapon against another monk, a weapon was used against an animal in the year of the survey. More interesting, however, is the pattern of conflict.

The measure of conflict developed for this research consists of a seven-item scale (see Chart 5.1). The respondent is asked whether he or she has been personally involved in any of the types of conflict mentioned. The question is asked for the respondent's activities during the past week and the past year. The results are then averaged.

The scale of conflict is divided into two parts: *Disputes*, or conflicts of lower intensity, refer to the first three items of the scale (conflict with disagreement, tension, or antagonism—see Bales, 1950), and *violence*, or conflict of higher intensity (shouting, use of force, inflicting physical harm, and use of weapons).

Chart 5.1
Questions Asked for the Conflict Scale

The following questions describe only the contacts you may have had within this group during the past WEEK. We are interested only in situations in which you were actually involved, as for example, speaking with at least one of the persons involved when the action occurred.
Has this occurred to you this week?

1. A discussion in which some <u>disagreement</u>   yes _____ 1
   occurred (include rejecting someone's   no _____ 2
   ideas). EXAMPLE: arguing over a   uncertain _____ 3
   difference of opinion:

2. A discussion in which some <u>tension</u>   yes _____ 1
   occurred (include refusing to give   no _____ 2
   information or withdrawal of help).   uncertain _____ 3
   EXAMPLE: being obviously upset, even
   if you did not say anything.

3. A discussion in which some <u>antagonism</u>   yes _____ 1
   occurred (include deflating someone's   no _____ 2
   status, or aggressively asserting oneself).   uncertain _____ 3
   EXAMPLE: being in an open quarrel.

4. A disagreement in which <u>shouting</u>   yes _____ 1
   occurred.   no _____ 2
                                            uncertain _____ 3

5. A situation in which some physical   yes _____ 1
   <u>force</u> was used on someone (include pushing,   no _____ 2
   shoving, etc., do <u>not</u> include physically   uncertain _____ 3
   harming someone or use of weapons).

6. A situation in which some physical <u>harm</u>   yes _____ 1
   was done to someone (such as cutting,   no _____ 2
   punching, bruising--do <u>not</u> include use of uncertain _____ 3
   weapons or killing).

7. A situation in which <u>weapons</u> were used   yes _____ 1
   or where someone was killed (include   no _____ 2
   threatening with weapons, such as rocks, uncertain _____ 3
   guns, knives).

(The questions are repeated, but instructions change the time frame to a year).

Disputes during the week of the survey involved approximately half of the monks. During the preceding year, approximately seven or eight out of every ten monks claimed that they were so involved. It is interesting that the proportion was not higher. Violence, as might be expected, is much lower. No more than one or two monks reported that he had been involved in violent conflict during the week of the survey, and during the entire year, no more than ten or eleven (of 49) so reported. Of course, the question arises, What do the monks mean by violent conflict? One monk, when asked whether he had been personally involved in "a situation in which shouting or some physical force was used," said, "Yes, someone pushed me when I was standing in line in the refectory once." Such an incident would probably not be remembered by most.

The point is that conflict operates within relative limits. Although no one could normally confuse a "discussion in which some disagreement occurred" with a "situation in which some physical harm was done to someone," there are grounds for blurring the distinctions. And grudges are held. For example, a few of the more conservative monks still resent, and deeply, the fact that the abbot removed many religious statues when he came into office. This was a move in keeping with the Cistercian ideal of simplicity, but it ran counter to another Catholic tradition which emphasizes religious statuary.

Comparative data for selected groups are shown in Table 5.1. Since the measures of conflict were developed especially for this study, the reader must be aware of the extremes in various forms of groups if one is to understand what is meant by high and low levels. Thus, data for prisons are provided because they represent high degrees of conflict (if the levels were not high, the measure would be in question), and boarding schools are included because they had the highest levels. The other groups were chosen mainly for comparative purposes, and all selected groups contained members that spend large amounts of time in physical proximity to each other.

The table shows little relation between disputes and violence. Disputes may be high simply because issues are openly discussed, and this was the case at Palisades. Violence was somewhat higher at Palisades than at other monasteries, but it was not at the highest level for monasteries. Violence for monasteries tends to be low, in general.

Conflict is often assumed to be the opposite of cooperation. Sometimes this is the case. But conflict and cooperation can occur at the same time, as when someone disagrees because he or she does not understand and because of the disagreement obtains enough information to attain greater cooperation. Palisades Abbey occupies the median position for both disputes and violence among 25 groups. None of the eight Trappist monasteries have the most extreme scores for either measure. Boarding schools score higher in disputes, as do two of the college dorms and a commune. Old age homes have lower dispute scores, as does one of the communes.

Twelve groups have higher violence scores, including such disparate groups as a commune, the college dorms, old age homes, boarding schools, and prisons. Only the nuns are lower. Even with their emphasis on prayer and solitude, the monks interact with a frequency comparable to a range of other groups. Monks are by no means isolated from one another.

Serious friction is rare. According to one informant, only about 15 persons are so involved out of all 70 monks, and only 7 persons are at the heart of these frictions.

Table 5.1
**Conflict in Selected Types of Groups, According to Percentage of
Persons Involved***

Group	Disputes	Violence
Palisades Abbey, 1970	66	**
1972	55	5
1976	59	4
1980	61	6
Monastery 2	43	2
Monastery 3	44	2
Monastery 4	56	4
Monastery 5	63	7
Monastery 6	72	10
Monastery 7	70	7
Monastery 8	57	10
Nuns 1	48	1
Nuns 2	50	4
Religious commune	54	3
Secular commune	69	12
Women's college dorm 1	57	7
Women's college dorm 2	68	11
Men's college dorm 1	64	15
Men's college dorm 2	74	13
Old age home 1	40	14
Old age home 2	54	18
Boarding school students	56	16
Boarding school delinquents	67	42
Boarding school staff	85	21
Boarding school delinquent staff	83	43
Women's prison	58	34
Men's prison	62	38

*Scores are the mean of conflict reported for the week and the year prior to
when the questionnaire was completed.
**Data not complete.

Competition is also rare, because there is little if anything to be competitive about. The monks are not vying with each other to be the best monk. If this *were* true, then one of the traits to strive for would be humility, the antithesis of competition. One could strive to be humble, but to boast of humility is to negate it. Not that competition is entirely absent. For example, one monk was proud that his department made more money during the Great Depression than others. Also, the beef department, when it was in existence, had prize-winning bulls, but this is competition outside the monastery.

Cooperation is given considerable attention in later chapters. Of course, much of it goes on unobtrusively through the institutionalized division of labor, and the monks have worked out their system so that seldom does one have to ask for unusual help. Yet opportunities for special assistance do occur. For example, one monk must exercise regularly, and another accompanies him on his walks. A monk put the wrong kind of fuel in a machine, and another monk left his work and spent an hour or more helping him undo the damage. The point behind such episodes is that these monks were not necessarily close friends. In fact, similar cooperative incidents have occurred between people who were involved in mutually recognized frictions. After one such event, one of the monks remarked to me rather wistfully, "How can you stay mad with a guy like that?"

The monks are usually sensitive and empathic. I have experienced varying crises while doing field work at the monastery (personal illness, robbery at home, the death of a friend), and in each case a monk extended sympathy and comfort. In fact, the monks have so much empathy that it sometimes becomes a problem in their vocation. Many continually reach out to help guests and neighbors to such a degree that this activity becomes a temptation that violates the purpose of the monastery, which is separation from the world for the sake of prayer for the world.

Cohesion. The monastery is a highly cohesive group, and the monks are highly committed to it and its ideals. Kanter (1972:69–74) provides a model that is useful in analyzing the structural basis for this commitment. (See also Roberts 1990:103–10). She identifies three basic kinds of commitment, each operating through two processes. Instrumental commitment is calculated cost and reward. The process of sacrifice is realized by the monks in giving up everything they possess, material wealth, career, and to some degree family and friends. The positive process is investment: all of the monk's labor is offered to the monastery and through the monastery to God. His investment is thus maximized.

Affective commitment means that the monk is emotionally dependent on the monastery. Negatively, he renounces all other ties for the process of communion with his brother monks. Communion, however, is not simply affection. Practically all of the monk's social ties are with other monks in the monastery, and these are the ties that bind him in communion.

Moral commitment involves commitment to the values and norms of the monastery. Kanter (1972) sees this as brought forth by the processes of mortification and transcendence. Mortification is extensive. It is accomplished by asceticism, separation from the world, poverty, chastity, and obedience, to name only the more important. Trascendence, however, is not directed to the group as much as it is to God. (For a case of group transcendence, see Zablocki:1971.)

Not all groups use all of these commitment mechanisms. The monastery does, in greater or lesser degrees, which helps explain why the monks have deep commitment and why they have lasted as a movement.

The monks do not purposely use these processes to enhance commitment. Further, several processes may be served by the same practice. Separation from the world, for example, is sacrifice, renunciation, and mortification. Liturgy serves as investment, communion, and transcendence. Though the monks were probably not fully aware of the sociological implications, a study of monastic cohesion, with its emphasis on group support and separation from the world, makes one better able to appreciate the abbot's concern over monks frequenting the guest house or St. Benedict's emphasis on liturgy.

Conclusion. The importance of love is seen first in the norms of interaction in Benedict's *Rule*. Early in his *Rule* (Chapter 4) and toward the end (Chapter 70), Benedict makes the importance of love explicit. But one can argue that all of the *Rule* is dedicated to love, that the *Rule* is a blueprint for achieving agapé.

Love is found in the contacts of the monastery with the outside world mainly in the relation with guests, neighbors, and the families of the monks. In other areas, particularly in economics and government, love is not as clearly displayed. The principal explanation is found in personal relationships. Love is always personal, and when formal (impersonal) contacts are considered, such as in legal processes, voting, purchases of machinery, education, blood donations, dentist visits, and so forth, there is little room for love. This condition speaks directly to the place the monastery has in the world today. Contact between groups in modern society is usually formal and impersonal. The monastery's contacts with other groups seem to be no exception.

Paradoxically, conflict does show love, as when "enemies" cooperate. The absence of love is indifference, not anger. We can be much more angry at those we love than at strangers. Of course, anger is one thing, hurtfulness and destruction another. ("Be angry, but sin not"—Psalm 4:4.) Thus violence scores of the monks are very low.

The monastery church with a view of the choir stalls.

A sign marking the enclosure.

One of the cemeteries.

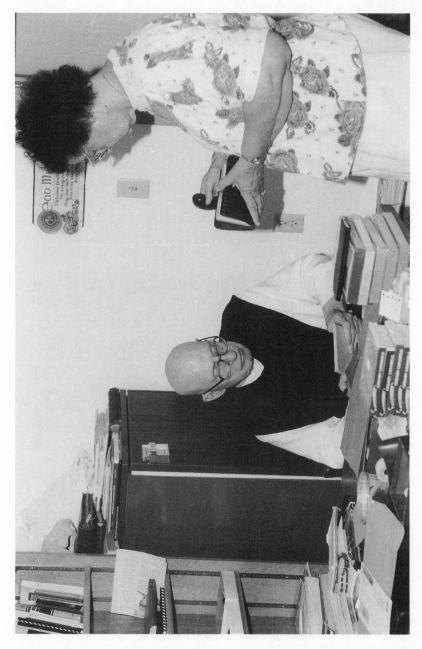

The manager of the gift shop with a customer.

Spraying herbicide.

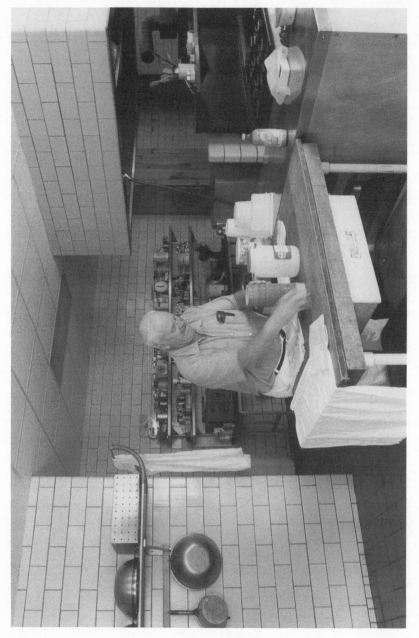

The monastery kitchen.

The refectory (dining hall).

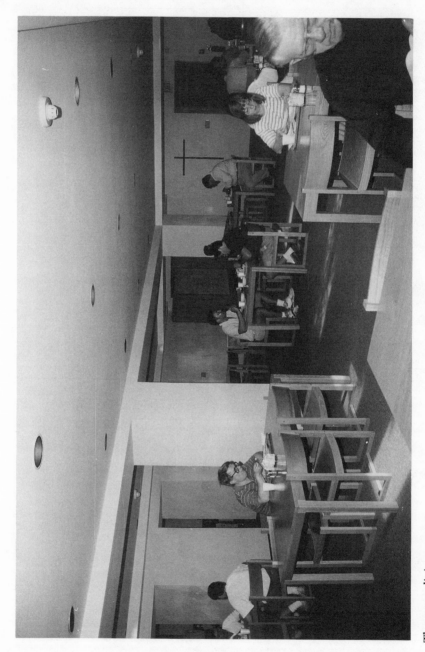

The guest dining room.

The library.

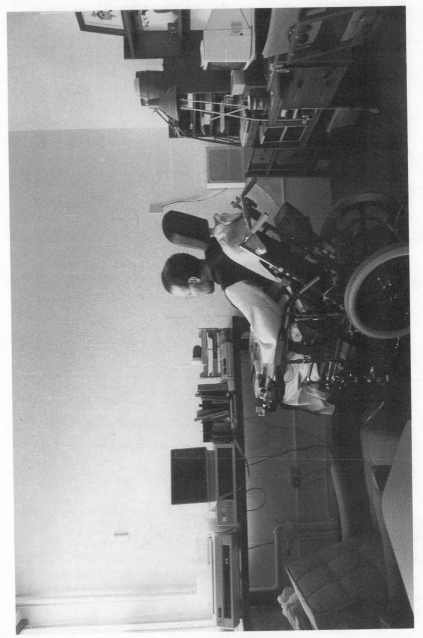

A patient in the infirmary.

A bust of Christ, carved by one of the monks.

Chapter 6

Family and Celibacy

> Care must be taken that no monk presume on any ground to defend
> another monk in the monastery . . . even though they be united by some
> tie of blood-relationship.
>
> —*Rule for Monasteries*, Chapter 69

The monk can never escape the family. It impinges on him in several ways.
First, the monk was born in his family of orientation. Second, the monastery
uses kinship models in its social structure. Third, because the biosocial family
is absent from the communal organization of the monastery, certain institutions must be substituted, called here the "institutions of maintenance."
Finally, the reasons for these institutions are directly attributable to the vow
of chastity. Each of these topics is discussed in this chapter.*

THE FAMILY OF ORIENTATION

The family into which the monk is born is of vital consequence to his
monasticism. Most important, his family was largely responsible for his
present religious background. Second, most monks are in close contact with
their families. One can hardly enter a guest house of a large monastery
without learning of some monk whose family is visiting. Family members
are housed at the expense of the monastery. Some monasteries have specific
family houses on the property. Palisades uses a nearby motel.

Slightly more than three-fourths of the monks were from American-born

---

*Unless otherwise specified, all data are from the contemplative survey of 1968 (Research
Committee of CMSW 1969).

families. Over 90 percent of both parents were Roman Catholics, and most of the monks consider the religious life of their family "good" while they were growing up. Most of the heads of the families were blue-collar workers: craftsmen, foremen and related workers, laborers and operatives, or farmers (see Table 6.1). Slightly more than half of the parents did not complete high school. Most of the monks assign themselves either to the middle or to the working class.

In the sample I took in 1970, the monks' families were large in comparison to average American families: 2.3 brothers and 2.3 sisters, totaling approximately 6 children (including the monk himself) in the average family. Most monks were neither the oldest nor the youngest child, though more were youngest than oldest (30.6 percent as compared with 18.4 percent). The monastery seems to have a relatively strong attraction for the youngest child. Only one monk listed himself as an only child, a significant figure when one considers that these men are living in a fairly close-knit community. There may be an association between growing up with other siblings and a willingness to adjust to the demands of communal living.

Most of the mothers are still alive; most of the fathers are not (51 percent had died as of 1970). Ties to the mother are still close for most (70 percent). Slightly more than half (56 percent) feel close to their fathers. Monks at Palisades and among Trappists generally felt closer to their mothers than to their fathers.

More than half of the monks consider themselves very well informed about the needs of their family. In 1968, almost half of the monks felt there should be more home visits to relatives. Thus, although the monk has left family and friends to join the monastery, home ties are still close—paradoxically, perhaps closer than ever.

Although some monks have few or no family ties, the ties for most are numerous. Visits from family are virtually always festive occasions, attesting to the affection family members have for each other. Of course, such observations have an inherent bias, because visits would not be frequent if they were unpleasant. But the monks plan for the visits and enjoy them. Apparently the relatives do, too. At times only one or two may visit—a mother or a sibling. Often what resembles an extended family arrives, and the solemn peace of the abbey is temporarily suspended, at least in the guest house. When a prospective candidate for monasticism first announces his decision to be a Trappist, the reaction from the family is often one of shock, disbelief, and disappointment. But such wounds usually heal, and families come from great distances to see their kin, at times even from Europe and Australia.

IS THE MONASTERY ITSELF A FAMILY?

Whether the monastery can be considered a family depends largely on definition. I have heard strong arguments raised on both sides of the ques-

Table 6.1
Occupational Categories for the Heads of the Monks' Families while the Monks Were Growing Up, Palisades Abbey, 1968

Occupational Category	Percent
Clerical and related workers (bookkeepers, stenographers, ticket agents, counter clerks, railroad conductors, etc.).	11
Craftsmen and related workers, such as: bakers, carpenters, electricians, jewelers, etc., and all skilled workers requiring a long apprenticeship--including foremen.	30
Laborers and operatives: garage workers, stevedoers, gardeners, unskilled helpers in construction, farm laborers, chauffeurs, semi- and unskilled workers in manufacturing, delivery men.	15
Farmers.	15
Private household workers such as: servants, laundresses, employed housekeepers.	--
Professional, technical, and similar workers, such as: teachers, editors, dentists, clergymen, professors, architects, librarians, etc.	9
Proprietors, managers, and officials such as: public officials, company officials and managers, army personnel.	12
Sales workers such as: salesmen, insurance and real estate agents, stock and bond salesmen, etc.	3
Service workers, except domestic, such as: firemen, police, beauticians, practical nurses, porters, professional soldiers.	5
Total	100
Number of cases	66

Source: Research Committee of CMSW 1969, Table 188.

tion. A nun once suggested to me that the convent was a family of mutual adoption (see Hillery 1969: 147). Her position has some basis. On the one hand, there are the titles of "Father" and "Brother." Primary group ties abound. Consider the statement by Merton (1953:40): "I am a part of

Gethsemani. I belong to the family.... I am glad to belong to this community, not another, and to be bred flesh and bone into the same body as these brothers and not other ones."

However, when I asked a Trappist monk at another monastery whether he felt that the monastery could be described as a "family of mutual adoption," he replied: "I feel that there is something to it. The abbot is a kind of father. But this is not exactly a family life. What keeps us here is a spiritual commitment. The big thing here is our commitment to God." I asked whether that was one of the major differences between a monastery and a family; in the monastery, the allegiance of the monks is not to each other but to God. He answered, "Ah, precisely!" and continued: "God's mercy comes to us both directly and through the community. We have a formula when we take the habit: 'What do you seek?' And the answer is: 'The mercy of God and the order.' At first, you do not really realize what that means. As you are here longer, you become very aware of the mercy of the community. You have been able to live here fifteen years and grow through the cooperation of others. One cannot do that without having to forgive others many things—and without experiencing the forgiveness and forbearance of others.

"Our relations are less emotional here in the monastery. We do make real friends, but it is not just on emotional ties but on our common mission. Certainly the ties are personal, but they are not as affective as in a family. Also, we have an obligation not to be dependent and to be solitary in a very real sense. This does not exclude friendship but it does limit the scope of friendship."

A monk in Our Lady of the Palisades, on reading the above, commented that commitment was not an either-or situation: the monk was committed both to God and to the monastery. And on closer reading, there is room for such an interpretation in the quotation.

It is probably significant that a nun first suggested the concept of a "family of mutual adoption." There may be a greater tendency among women than among men in American society to interpret primary group ties in terms of kinship. This was suggested by Giallombardo (1966) in her study of a prison for women. Most of the prisoners formed groups, using terms such as mother, father, son, daughter, uncle, niece, grandmother, and so on (Giallombardo 1966: 210).

The evidence for this difference is at once both meager and vague. On the one hand, monks more often than nuns "think it would be better for community life if we dispensed with titles like Mother Superior, Father Abbot, etc." (Table 6.2). Palisades monks were more willing to discard the title Father Abbot, perhaps because they had only recently selected what for an abbot would be a young monk (approximately 40 years of age). Whatever one may feel about the relation to the superior, whether he (or she) is a substitute parent, most of the monks and nuns do not "think the

Table 6.2
Attitudes toward Dispensing with Titles

Do you think it would be better for community life if we dispensed
with titles like Mother Superior, Father Abbot, etc.?

	Total sample of Contemplatives (81.1% nuns)	Total sample of Trappists	Palisades Trappists
Yes	49.4%	59.1%	72.7%
Number	1349	235	66

Source: Research Committee of CMSW 1969, Question 466.

obedience of religious life is similar to the obedience children owe their
parents" (Research Committee of CMSW 1969, Q. 486).

Whether the monastery is one of men or women, and whether the terms
used are kinship terms, certain roles are almost always found in families
the world over that are absent from the monastery: the biosocial role of
husband and wife and the relation between an immature human (child) and
its parents. The monastery may approach the family in the preponderance
of primary group ties, but even then, as the monk noted, the relationships
are not quite as intense. My own conclusion is that the monastery is not a
family, though the family is used as a model. It is the absence of the family
that promotes agapé and other institutions, as the next section will show.

INSTITUTIONS OF MAINTENANCE

Because there is no family, the monastery must be involved in some system
of recruitment. This is not only because the family is absent but because
the monk has taken a vow of chastity, which for him means celibacy. And
if the monastery is to remain a communal organization, it must have pro-
visions for allowing the monks to leave. Otherwise, the monastery becomes
a prison. These three institutions are termed "institutions of maintenance"

(Hillery 1968). They are discussed in the following order: celibacy, recruitment, and discharge. (Note that unlike Goffman's (1961) total institution, the monastery today has no institutions of custody or treatment.)

Celibacy is one of the most basic aspects of monastic life. It makes possible the meaning of the word "monk." (The word is from a Greek word, *monachus*, which translates as "single" or "solitary.") It rules out the biosocial family. Celibacy may be one reason for the extended longevity of monasteries as social systems—perhaps communes can generally be handled no other way. (In the West, the only intentional community that has lasted even approximately one-fourth the time of monasteries has been the Hutterites—see Hostetler 1974). And yet celibacy is one of the values which the noncelibate finds most difficult to understand.

There is a gulf between the celibate and the married that is probably greater than either is aware. This gulf has been no bar to either telling the other what is "good" for them. One monk said that for him celibacy was a supernatural gift, something that "I couldn't attain naturally. I really can't say, I have no guarantee, that I can do this the rest of my life." (I have heard very similar statements more than once.) The monk then went to another and (curiously) closely related aspect of monastic life, stability. He noted that the vow of stability is very much like that of marriage. "My commitment to the community is for better or for worse. You find out things about marriage that you didn't know of first, and the same way here. You get to the point that 'this is no longer the community that I joined.' Your ideals evolve with the community."

None could disagree that there are important similarities between the vow of stability and that of marriage. But it should not be forgotten that two processes in a marriage are absent in a monastery. The first is that of heterosexual adjustment and the problems, satisfactions, and growing involvement of learning to live with one person who in certain ways is fundamentally and unalterably different from oneself. The second is the children: their entry into the life of the married pair, their first years of tumultuous change, the gradual maturing, the problems of adolescence, and then the ultimate break for which they were born and toward which much has been directed (at least in the United States).

The monk's commitment is different in two ways: First, he has committed his life to God through Jesus Christ, and second, through this commitment he is committed to others, and especially to his brothers in the monastery. Celibacy thus makes possible the expression of agapé love. It is probably impossible to say whether the monk's emotional attachment is as deep or intense as that in marriage, because the attachments are so different—as different as agapé and eros can be. But his emotional attachments certainly are more extensive. His celibate commitment permits him greater latitude.

The monk today does not necessarily regard celibacy as the better way, though this was the counsel of St. Paul. Instead, he looks on celibacy as *his* call and hopes that married couples consider marriage as *their* call. Nor does the monk necessarily feel that all priests should be celibate. An older priest (who probably would never relinquish his vow of celibacy) expressed much displeasure that the Pope had said that all priests had to be celibate. He did not think that such a thing ought to be compulsory.

The opinions of the monks gathered in 1968 bear out these observations (Appendix D). One is not surprised to find the monk deeply committed to celibacy. Yet the monk does not see his vow as an excuse for running away from marriage or people.[1] For him, celibacy is consecrated, a way of expressing love—both human and religious.[2] His main objections are to the traditional way that chastity is presented, particularly in his training to be a monk,[3] and he objects to any invidious comparison with marriage.[4]

Virtually all of the monks agreed that celibacy makes it possible to act out love rather than simply feel it.[5] The love in question is, of course, agapé (see Chapter 3), and it shares with all love the necessity of being vulnerable.[6] Celibacy is not simply a denial. It provides a structure within which love can operate.[7] These three statements were agreed on by more than 80 percent of the monks.

The monk is quite concrete in his views. Celibacy is not "an angelic life on earth."[8] It does not consist of avoiding others.[9] And the monks do not feel it was adequately treated in their education ("formation") when they were novices.[10]

We have no survey questions concerning sexual involvement or temptations. However, from extended personal conversations with at least six monks, it can be said that celibacy does present problems. Some still feel the strength of sexual drives and are reminded of this, especially by nuns on retreat at the monastery (see Chapter 13). Many undoubtedly never realize a call to monastic living partly in consequence. Apparently, each monk starts his novitiate having already worked out some solution, though not always is it adequate. Many have left and married for these reasons.

Contact with women is a different situation. Celibacy in and of itself does not mean isolation. Whatever may have been the case in the past, the modern Trappist at Palisades tends to have at least one friend who is a nun, and almost one-third have "quite a few." Palisades is more open in this regard than other Trappist monasteries: almost twice as many monks at Palisades as those in the remaining sample of Trappists have "quite a few nuns" as friends.

The problem of women in the guest house has manifested itself in several forms. (At the time of this study, there was no provision to house women in the monastery.) Only a few monks seemed involved, and never was the contact any threat to the monk's chastity. At least one monk felt strongly that he had worked out an important part of his vocation as a monk by having counselling relations of a spiritual nature with women, but another would prefer as little evidence of women in the monastery as possible. These are the extremes. Many monks perceive no problems at all, probably in part because they are seldom involved in the guest house.

At any rate, celibacy is an essential part of monasticism. To pursue a life of prayer, the monk requires solitude and simplicity. Solitude means that he must not become overly involved with others. He must maintain a significant degree of detachment. Simplicity means he must turn his full attention to God and not seek other diversions. He is "wedded to the Word made flesh" (Appendix D, Q. 62). Under such conditions, marriage becomes most difficult.

Recruitment, the second institution of maintenance, is another problem. Although candidates come, very few stay. There were only two or three novices in 1970 (though the number has sharply increased and declined since). Some monks are deeply concerned and wonder whether the monastery should do something about recruiting, such as maintain a school. Probably the most mature statement came from one of the older monks, who had been a teacher of the novices.

"I'm not too worried about attacks on monastic life. God will always raise up people ... who want a life of prayer. They might be not like this [monastery] or be as open about it, but He'll see to it that they float to the surface. I'm really not too worried about Palisades. I am loyal to it, and I love it. But even though the devil might attack it, while he's busy trying to destroy it, something else is going to be springing up behind him."

The point is that these men are called to lead a life of prayer—not of recruitment or teaching or anything else. Their first mission is to attempt to stand alone before God. As one monk said: "If we really center our life on prayer, everything else will take care of itself." This statement is an ideal, and not all monks hold it. But much more important, some monks do.

The discharge (or the leaving) of a monk, the third institution of maintenance, seems to vary with the person and ranges over a wide extreme. Of four cases known fairly well to the writer, one novice left with the best will of all concerned. Although he was in the monastery only a few months, all felt that the relationship had been "healthy" for everyone concerned. A priest left in an atmosphere of general goodwill, though there was still concern. As one of the monks (himself a priest) said to the departing priest, "Brother, my heart goes out to you, but you are breaking my heart." And another: "He sure has got guts; takes it all in his stride."

A third monk, a priest, left with feelings of tension. I noticed that when he returned for a visit, the monks seemed more open to me, a visitor, than to him. When this monk left the monastery, he had held important administrative positions (though he was not the abbot). That there was a tension in his leaving was not fully evident until his return visit. He brought his wife, a former nun, dressed in extremely brief shorts. She seemed embarrassed. I gave no other interpretation to this act than that he was trying to make obvious to his former brothers the extent to which he had rejected their life.

Finally, one of the monks under temporary promise had been in the monastery for several years, and his leaving caused quite a furor. Although he was voted out, and although several people said that there had been "signs" that he should have read, his leaving caused more repercussions in the monastery than anyone else's that I have witnessed. I never learned the full explanation, but some felt that the abbot did not exercise sufficiently strong leadership.

In contrast, Palisades has started reunion meetings with monks who have left. Twenty-five former members of the monastery attended the first one. Wives and children brought the total number to "around 75." The abbey newsletter observed: "The meeting was a deeply moving experience for the participants. The outcome was the scheduling of a second reunion, with the opportunity of visiting the monastery and renewing old memories and acquaintances." Other reunions have followed.

Thus, a monk may leave with hardly a ripple in the monastery and with the goodwill of all concerned; or he may leave with bitterness at least in some.

Finally, some monks are in the process of leaving and no one else knows (except perhaps the abbot). They go off on leave and the leave never ends. When the break comes, many have expected it, and contact has ceased long enough not to do much apparent damage.

CONCLUSION

The monk leaves his family of orientation, but he does not abandon it. The affection he knew as a part of a relatively large family (almost eight persons, on the average) still remains part of his life, though contact is limited to occasional visits. He adds to this affectionate love a different kind, agapé, which is more encompassing and is enhanced through celibacy. His new group, the monastery, is not a family, particularly since eros, so important to the family, is ruled out. Because the monks are celibate, new members must be recruited. No one can be born into a monastery. Since the monastery does not actively recruit, monastery growth is slow and even nullified by monks leaving the community. Though some friction is caused by leaving, many monks who leave remain on good terms with the monastery.

Thus, two kinds of love in particular have been treated in this chapter: affection and agapé. Affection is part of a well-developed family, and its appearance through family visits is often a celebration. Agapé is developed through celibacy. Though ideally agapé should take the place of the other loves, this is not always the case (compare Question 61, App. D). Affection remains, as witnessed in the emotional intensity of family visits. Love also appears in the friendship monks have for one another. In this sense, celibacy is more than simply a relinquishing of sexual contact. Celibacy, as a means of achieving agapé, involves a wide-ranging sacrifice of all forms of love directed at particular people and having a physical basis. That agapé is not the only form of love in the monastery is simply evidence of the monks' humanity.

NOTES

1. App. D, Q. 64.
2. App. D, Qs. 61, 66, 70.
3. App. D, Qs. 69, 492.
4. App. D, Q. 68.
5. App. D, Q. 66.
6. App. D, Q. 70.
7. App. D, Q. 61.
8. App. D, Q. 67.
9. App. D, Q. 64.
10. App. D, Qs. 69, 492.

Chapter 7

Earning a Living

For then they are truly monks when they live by the labor of their hands,
as did our Fathers and the Apostles.

—*Rule for Monasteries*, Chapter 48

Trappists are required to earn their living. They cannot beg. Economic
concerns are thus as important to the monastery as they are to any community. Accordingly, some monks are greatly concerned over economic
matters, and the economy occasionally has been a very divisive issue. As is
true of communities, generally, economic matters are pervasive. The monk
looks upon labor as part of the natural balance of monastic life, together
with prayer and liturgy (see Chapter 10). Further, poverty is central to his
conception of asceticism (see Chapter 11). The monastery is incorporated
as a business, and the abbot is its president. He is also the monastery's
political leader (see Chapter 8), and of course its spiritual shepherd.

In fact, the pervasiveness of the economy makes it a difficult topic to
discuss. Not only is it involved with government, but it also impacts on the
guest house, stratification, and the infirmary, to mention only the more
apparent. Another difficulty is that when data for this chapter were gathered,
three different accounting systems were employed, and the picture of the
material condition depends largely on which system one uses. I have not
attempted here to reconcile all systems. My major concern is to present an
overall view.

There are three objectives for this chapter. First, I want to describe the

Parts of this chapter are adapted from George A. Hillery, Jr., "Monastic Occupations: A
Study in Values" in Richard L. Simpson and Ida H. Simpson, eds. *Research in the Sociology
of Work: Peripheral Workers* Vol. 2 (Greenwich, Conn.: JAI Press, 1983), 191–210.

monastery's economy. Then the attitudes of the monks toward the economy are examined. Finally, the interaction of the religious ideology and the economy produces important problems for the monastery, and these are considered.

A MONASTIC ECONOMY

In attempting to make sense of monastic economics, the most comparable model is the family. Like the monastery, the family is not simply a profit-making organization, although there must be money to pay the bills. In both, somebody must be boss if an appreciable degree of efficiency is to be realized. In both, not everyone is always competent to know the economic picture, even if he or she would like to. And then, many of the decisions of a financial nature must be made on an emotional and even a spiritual basis.

There are differences, of course. (1) Probably most important is the matter of scale: the monastery is from ten to twenty times larger than most families. (2) The lines of authority are much more clearly institutionalized than in many families. (3) The division of labor is more complicated. (4) There is no danger posed by the death of a major breadwinner, as there is in the normal family. (5) Unlike the case with urban families, most economic activity takes place inside the land owned by the monastery. (6) The goal is not maximizing profits or even well-being but determining the correct relation between profit and security. (7) The concern with charitable do-nations is greater than that in the average family, and the monastery differs from almost all families in the extent to which it relies on contributions from the outside. Yet as much as the monks give to charity (see the later discussion), many are concerned that they should be giving more. (8) Despite clear avenues of economic authority, and because of the factor of scale, it is easier for disparity to result between spenders and earners. Certain monks can legitimately spend what they want, if it does not become obvious. The same applies to family members, of course. The wife buys a new pair of shoes, the husband has drinks at a bar, the children spend allowances on candy. The factor of scale, however, means that what is small in the mon-astery is much larger than in the family. Thus the disparity in spending between spender and earner can become greater.

Economic matters have always seemed to be one of the most volatile problems in the monastery. Many of the personal concerns of the monks rise out of things to do with work and income, and the monastery's ad-ministrative affairs essentially revolve around the economy. This is especially true, according to one brother, of a monastery that has been struggling for some time. He remarked, "A lot of time the things we do [here] are not just working for efficiency, and a study of these decisions brings out the value structure. We have a paradox. Ideally, the most important thing is to be as little concerned about mundane affairs as possible and [to be] living in the eschatological affairs of Christ." Yet, economics occupies many if not most of their problems.

The initial question to be answered in this section is, How do the monks make their living? That question inevitably leads to others, such as the emotional interplay between economics and prayer, economics and authority, contact with the outside, and so forth. The answer to this question will thus have to be interpreted through the attitudes of the monks and the problems they face in areas other than economic ones.

Of the methods that could be used to discuss the economics of the abbey, the cash basis (income and expenses) was selected, primarily because it is simple. The year selected for detailed examination is 1975. This was not a typical year—no year is. But it had the twin virtues of not being exceptionally unusual and of being one of the years I was personally involved in the monastery as a participant observer.

The monastery's economics may be categorized into production departments and other sources of income, on the one hand, and expenses on the other. Of the production departments, the farm produced by far the most income in 1975, as is shown in Table 7.1. The miscellaneous departments were not readily distinguishable in 1975, though in past years the gift shop and incense departments produced almost three-fourths of the miscellaneous income. The names of the other miscellaneous departments designate the kind of income they produce: sawmill, orchard, garden, crafts, and honey.

Production activity revolves primarily around agriculture. The farm department mainly sells corn; the beef department sells purebred Angus cattle. The alfalfa dehydration department (dehy) produces pellets from alfalfa obtained from the farm department. The service department is not shown in Table 7.1 because the abbey does not account for the income it produces. It primarily services various machines operated by the monastery, including tractors and automobiles. Its functions are electrical maintenance, carpentry, plumbing, painting, and operating the garage. The expense of this department is averaged among the others. Next to farming, income from interest, the dehy, and Mass stipends (gifts made by persons in order to have one or more Masses said for someone or some purpose) were most important. Income from the guest house department should not rightly be termed "fees" or "payments," since retreatants contribute no fixed amount, and many who visit the monastery pay nothing, even for meals. The food bill for the guests and retreatants is almost half that for the monks themselves.

The meaning of contributions varies. Some regard the guest house department as producing acceptable income (even in the same class as production departments). Others would rather see no charges at all, with all retreatants treated as guests (i.e., making no payments). Similarly, some regard Mass stipends as legitimate offerings. Others do not approve of them in principle.

Table 7.1
Income and Expenses for Palisades Abbey, 1975

	Income			Expenses	
	Amount (1,000s)	Per-cent		Amount (1,000s)	Per-cent
PRODUCTION DEPARTMENTS			COMMUNITY LIVING EXPENSES		
			Recurring:		
Farm	$241.0	53.8	Food	$ 26.3	12.4
Dehy	26.2	6.5	Medical	19.9	9.3
Bakery	9.7	2.4	Heat, Power	9.1	4.3
Beef	2.4	0.6	Housekeeping	3.1	1.5
Guest house	14.1	3.5	Maintenance	8.8	4.1
Other departments	13.9	3.5	Travel	3.6	1.7
	$307.3	76.3			
OTHER SOURCES OF INCOME			Telephone	5.0	2.3
			Wardrobe/laundry	7.6	3.6
Interest	65.8	16.3	Insurance	6.5	3.1
Mass Stipends	20.1	5.0	Gasoline	5.7	2.7
Social Security	4.0	1.0	Prof. services	5.6	2.6
Contributions	5.6	1.4			
	$ 95.5	23.7	Liturgy	3.2	1.5
			Library	2.8	1.3
			Miscellaneous	10.6	5.0
			Depreciation	13.8	6.5
			Service dept.	6.7	3.1
			Community cost of living	$ 138.3	65.0
			Other:		
			Capital expenses	4.6	2.2
			Donations	56.2	26.4
			Absent brothers and tuition	11.9	5.6
			Miscellaneous	1.8	0.8
Total all income	$ 402.8	100.0	Total all expenses	$ 212.8	100.0
NET INCOME FOR 1975				$ 190.0	

Expenses diverge widely. Only food amounted to more than 10 percent of the recurring expenses. Medicine was clearly second. Donations was the largest item among all kinds of expenses, though the amount of money donated varies from year to year. Though not shown separately in Table 7.1 (since the expense is divided among the various departments), the monastery pays approximately $13,000 each year in property taxes alone. This is important when one considers that the monks send no children to school, no people to old age homes, and contribute no deviants to asylums or jails. The monastery produces its own drinking water. The monks do have county police and fire protection. At times, however, county services can be a disadvantage, as in the case of the highway that reduces their solitude.

How, then, do the monks make their living? Even with this vastly simplified presentation, the question is difficult (and whatever the answer, the result depends to some extent on the accounting system used). In a crude and brief fashion, three activities figure most prominently in the monastery's economic picture: agriculture (including the dehy), interest, and Mass stipends.

Interest was more important than any of the production departments other than agriculture in 1975. The source of interest at that time was money market funds: treasury bills, notes, certificates of deposit, and checking accounts. About 10 percent of cash and securities was in stocks. Contributions were important both as income and expense. For example, money given by guests for room and board is a form of income. Contributions of the monastery to various charities (donations) is an expense. Donations given were ten times larger than contributions received. The significance of contributions is probably greater than that indicated by the statistics, since much monastic hospitality is credited against the guest house department. In other words, what the monks spend on the guest house (for food, heat, power, housekeeping) beyond what they take in, is in effect a donation.

Even with mechanization, industrialization, and urbanization, the monks are still mainly farmers. But they are supported to a large extent by the financial accumulations of past years (that is, income through interest). They are also heavily concerned with charitable donations, especially giving.

Whether the monastery is economically viable is uncertain. The monks are not primarily concerned with profits. Their more important economic objective is in establishing sufficient security so they will not be overburdened with financial cares. Cash income over expenses in 1975 reflects this— approximately $190,000 (for a community of 70 persons). But on a profit and loss computation (figured differently from a cash basis computation), the monastery showed a net loss during the four years from 1968 to 1972.

Some monks are concerned about economic security. Some prefer fewer investments and less reliance on contributions in any form. And some are concerned (if naively) only that, regardless of the economic complexities, somehow money continues to find its way into the abbey's bank deposits.

Discussion of decision making in the economic sphere also merges into discussion of monastic government. Thus, this chapter will prepare the ground for the next (Chapter 8). The structure of the decision-making bodies in the monastery is presented in Chart 7.1. It shows six kinds of roles: the abbot, the treasurer, the accountant, the business council, the department heads, and the community. Authority is discussed in terms of levels. Each level has more authority than the one beneath it. Thus, the abbot has final

Chart 7.1
Levels of Economic Authority

Level 1:	Elected by community:	Abbot
Level 2A:	Elected by community & appointed by abbot:	Business Council
Level 2B:	Appointed by abbot:	Treasurer, accountant
Level 3:	Appointed by abbot:	Department heads
Level 4:		Community

authority in all matters. However, the levels do not form a chain of command. For example, the Business Council does not have authority over the lower levels; it just has more authority in that it makes decisions that will affect them. Major decisions are made by both the abbot and the Business Council, which in turn consists of three members appointed by the abbot and three elected. The treasurer and the accountant act as resources for the abbot and the council. The involvement of the community will also become apparent; given the culture from which these monks come, it would be difficult for a communal organization as small and as closely integrated as this to be run by anything even approaching a dictatorship. As is suggested by the *Rule*, "Whenever any important business has to be done in the monastery, let the Abbot call together the whole community and state the matter to be acted upon" (Doyle 1948, Chapter 3: 12).

The *Rule* goes on to specify a stronger position than that taken by the abbot at that time (Fr. Daniel). For the *Rule*, the abbot is ultimately accountable only to God, "knowing that beyond a doubt he will have to render an account of all his decisions to God, the most just Judge" (*Rule*, Chapter 3: 18). In fact, the abbot did not go against the best-intentioned desires of the monks. He preferred to rule by indirection and sought the will of the community as often as possible. Questionnaire data are not available, but from speaking with some of the monks, I found that there was by the early 1970s a mixture of respect and dissatisfaction about the abbot's use of authority. On the one hand, these monks felt that Fr. Daniel was not at home in economic matters, that the direction of his decisions was unclear, and that he was not consistent in following his own policies. On the other hand, with almost no exceptions, the monks showed him genuine fondness and respect.

Historically, the Business Council was preceded by a Permanent Economic Committee (PEC). The committee was dissatisfied because it had no authority. A monk from another monastery was consulted, and he recommended a Business Council. The PEC was subsequently dissolved.

The abbot then brought before the community the possibility of a Business Council. The community elected the members of a selecting board, composed of ten monks who would themselves choose the council. Their problem was as much one of selecting a group that could work together and was knowledgeable as it was one of selecting those who would represent different concerns of the community, concerns that were not necessarily economic. The final selection included the following:

A brother who was the subprior, a member of the formation team, and who worked with the heating equipment and the septic tank.
A brother who was the infirmarian.
A brother who worked in the beef department and was studying for the priesthood.
A priest who worked at the gatehouse and was the buyer for the monastery.
A priest who was the head of the farm department.
A priest who was the head of the beef department.

The abbot is not a member of the Business Council but "shares his authority in matters of temporal administration with the Business Council." These remarks were described by one monk as "the magic words." Some matters are initiated by the abbot and on some he seeks advice. Sometimes the Business Council takes the initiative. For example, an expensive machine was available at a bargain, and one monk was anxious to have it purchased. The council decided against it mainly because they felt that the equipment would not be in the best spiritual interests of that monk. (They felt that he would use it as a play toy.) Usually the Business Council does not take this much initiative.

The treasurer and accountant occupy fairly autonomous positions. They are not members of the Business Council. The Business Council also assigns monks who are not part of a permanent work force. The subprior has the main responsibility in this matter. Formerly, the abbot would appoint a monk for each job at the start of each day. This would take at least five minutes. Some people would be given the same job day after day but still it would be "called out" by the abbot in the morning.

The monks view work as something valuable in its own right and as a break from routine. In a series of 17 interviews held at Palisades Abbey in 1980 (Hillery 1983), most of the monks felt that work contributed positively to the monastic vocation. For some, such as the cantor or the novice master, work and vocation merge. For others, such as farmers, the work is not monastic in itself (hoeing beets is not more monastic than driving a tractor), but one can certainly pray during work, and many do. Finally, particularly for the abbot, it is difficult to find the simplicity and solitude that are the hallmarks of monasticism, and a day of retreat is provided for him each week.

The monks worked 4 to 6 hours per day in 1972. Before 1969, they worked considerably more, and in fact this monastery had a reputation among the others for being a work-oriented house. Thirty-six monks worked between 4 and 6 hours per day, though they wanted fewer hours. Twenty monks felt that they worked from 1 to 5 hours more than they felt responsible for. Only two monks said that they were working less than they should, but 20 monks felt that their responsibilities matched the amount of time they were spending in labor.

The monastery employs four outside laborers in the service, farm, and beef departments. The service department has the highest payroll expenditures; the beef department the least. During 1970 (data are unavailable for 1975), a total of more than $26,000 was paid out in wages by these three departments.

Admittedly, these wages appear low. Several factors must be considered. There are additional benefits and perquisites, such as meals and use of the monastery's registered bull. The farm economy at that time was quite depressed. As the monastery's income increased, so did wages, almost doubling in four years. Also, farm wages are not as high as those of industrial workers.

Most of the monks (54 percent) have only one job, but 46 percent have two or more. Some of these other jobs are really extra assignments, such as being a student for the priesthood (although some are full-time students), working in the garden, and conducting retreats.

ATTITUDES

The following discussion concerns information gathered during the monastery's self-study of 1969 (see Table 7.2). The first question in the table shows strong agreement with one of the basic Trappist values, self-support. The second question reveals a minority who feel there is not enough communication between the rest of the community and those concerned with economic affairs. It was this dissatisfaction that led to the creation of the Business Council. The fifth question in the table reflects a continuing type of behavior expressed by the monks: an economic activity is not necessarily followed because it is efficient or profitable. The dehy (when these data were gathered) was noisy, demanded time, and produced a distinct and unpopular odor. Most preferred that it be terminated, and it was. However, there was a decided minority (seven) who felt strongly otherwise, and thus the dehy became a point of contention. The important consideration, however, is that this problem was acted on, rather than avoided or subjected to unilateral decision.

Monks took opposing positions on two questions: the fourth and the sixth. They are divided on the question of poverty and the permissibility of excess work. Neither question, however, is seriously polarized (only two persons are found at one extreme, and five or six at the other). In other words, there are not two camps, each strongly opposed to the other.

The last question shows that the monk is not dissatisfied with what he

Table 7.2
Attitudes Concerning the Economy, March 1969

Question	Percent				
	Strongly agree	Agree	Neither agree nor disagree	Disagree	Strongly disagree
1. We should strive to be fully self-supporting.	33	46	4	4	5
2. I can now obtain as much information regarding our economy. as I need.	12	40	13	17	12
3. I feel that work time taken for individual projects is hindering community work.	12	40	27	12	2
4. The practice of poverty in our community is generally satisfactory.	4	44	5	31	12
5. I feel that, if possible, the dehy should be discontinued.	25	15	23	17	13
6. Each monk should be free to work as much as he cares to, over and above what is assigned.	4	35	15	35	10
7. If I had my choice, I'd prefer to do work other than that which I do now.	8	6	35	37	4

NOTE: A total of 52 replies were obtained. However, some monks did not respond to all questions. Percentages were computed with 52 as the base. The remainder is thus composed of those who did not answer.

Source: Hillery 1983: 202.

is doing. Approximately one-third do not care, which is in keeping with monastic values, and another 40 percent did not want other kinds of work. A monk does not take a job. He follows a call to prayer.

The monks are divided over whether each should be allowed to work as much as he wants, but a majority feel that time taken for individual projects is hindering the community (Question 3). Though work was seen as important and individual needs worth consideration, some monks were felt to be carrying their projects too far.

The monks' values on poverty are shown in several questions. When asked to state the class to which their present standard of living compared, half checked "lower middle class," and a third checked "upper middle class" (10 percent checked "wealthy"). But when asked to state the class to which the monks *should* compare, a fourth said "poor" and almost two-thirds said "lower middle class." (None said "wealthy.") Thus, there is a discrepancy between where the monks think they are and where they think they should be. Poverty is a positive value.

Most at the time of the self-study felt that their overall financial position was "fairly secure" or better (77 percent). There was some dissatisfaction. Half felt that the production departments were not producing all that was needed, but most felt that the monastery's income was sufficient or more than this. Not all were satisfied with the financial situation. Some were worried and were (and still are) quite vocal about it, but most were not concerned, which of course served only to increase the anxiety of those who were worried.

The contemplative survey, taken six months earlier than the self-study, generally shows the same picture. Other than providing more depth, the chief advantage of the contemplative survey (Research Committee of CMSW 1969) is that it permits a comparison with all 232 Trappists who took the 600-plus-item questionnaire (i.e., the 166 other monks). (See Table 7.3.)

Question 502 gives additional explanation for the dissatisfaction about insufficient communication in economic matters. Palisades monks *expect* more communication than the rest of the Trappists. However, Palisades monks are more satisfied with their own jobs. More than three-fourths so responded to questions 351, 352, 354, 356, and 357. Though none of these differences are statistically significant, Palisades monks are consistently more satisfied.

More than is true of other Trappists, these monks are dissatisfied with the practice of poverty in the order, though they admit that conditions in the order could permit a level of "poverty" that would allow for a standard of living "according to the middle-class society." (See Table 7.4) There is an incongruity in this response: the middle class in America does not have a standard of living of poverty.

The practice of poverty is pervasive. The monk has one extra set of clothes, and a stain or slight tear is not sufficient reason to get new ones. The monks' use of material goods means such things as two telephone lines and three automobiles for 40 persons. Though this conception of poverty does not mean destitution, neither does it mean wealth, at least by U.S. standards.

PROBLEMS

What problems do the monks face in the economic realm? This is an extremely important question, because the economy of the monastery affects

Table 7.3

Attitudes Concerning Occupation and Other Economic Matters in the Monastery, from the Contemplative Survey, 1968

		Percent Responding "True of my Work" or "Yes"	
	Other Questions	Trappists	Palisades
351.	My work is frequently changed when I am in the middle of it and I never get anything completed.	8	5
352.	I am not given the necessary independence of judgment and responsibility in carrying out the work assigned.	13	9
354.	The location of my work is bad for my health.	2	--
356.	My work is detrimental to my religious life.	4	8
357.	I just don't like this kind of work.	9	9
502.	Is it customary in your order to keep the religious informed about finances?	52	67
518.	Would you say that poverty in your order allows for a standard of living according to the middle-class society?	63	71

Source: Research Committee of CMSW 1969.

virtually all other spheres of activity, no matter how transcendental. Fasting is one thing, famine another.

First, on the positive side, many of the problems noted during the self-study seem to have been worked out. The Business Council apparently is regulating work more satisfactorily. The monks work fewer hours, and they appreciate the added time for prayer and study. The council is handling the problem of communication in a much more satisfactory manner. Yet five problems that the self-study brought out remain: (1) the history of mistrust, (2) the question of abbatial authority, (3) the need to clarify monastic purposes, (4) the "infection" of the world, particularly for some positions, and (5) constraints induced by property. These problems overlap.

One of the most severe problems of this monastery is the heterogeneity in the ideology of its membership. In a sense, much of the difference is

Table 7.4
Satisfaction with the Practice of Poverty in the Order, for Trappist Monks

Responses	Palisades	Other Trappists
Satisfied	9	12
Somewhat satisfied	32	49
Mildly dissatisfied	47	31
Quite dissatisfied	11	7
No answer	1	1
	100	100
Number of cases	66	232

Chisquare = 7.77, with 3 degrees and freedom, .10> p> .05

Source: Research Committee of CMSW 1969 (Question 595).

illusory, because as is noted in Chapter 8, there is an extensive basis of agreement. Yet, it is a sociological principle that if people believe a thing is real, then it is real in its consequences. Some monks believe there are basic differences among them (or they believed so in 1969–70), and this belief caused significant dissension. A minority report by three monks on the study group on economy continually demonstrated this in the problems it isolated. Phrases that had similar themes reoccurred: The monks perceived a "lack of consensus" concerning the ideals of poverty and simplicity of life, they noted that the economic aspect of the community "lacks cohesiveness and unity of direction," they saw "a need for improved communication on all levels of our economic structure," they mentioned "the problems of mistrust" behind many of the communication problems identified in the report, and they noted that the system of departments was "in some respects divisive of the community."

One is confronted with two somewhat contradictory facts. First, mistrust exists. Second, there is an undeniable base of cohesion and emotional security. As is shown in Chapter 8, there is a large area of common values, and the most extreme disagreements are not directly concerned with the monastery.

Additional evidence more directly challenges the idea of mistrust. The measure used is technically known as "anomie" (roughly translated as "normlessness"). In surveying 16 other groups, only one had a lower anomie score, and this was a commune of young people that had just begun. They were idealistic and highly motivated, as is not surprising, since they were on a new adventure. All other groups had anomie scores higher than Palisades (showing greater feelings of disorganization), and this included other communes (some religious), college dormitories, sororities and fraternities, and also prisons and boarding schools, where one would expect higher scores. However, anomie had been slightly higher in the past, as shown in data gathered in June 1968 by the contemplative survey (Research Committee of CMSW 1969).

Two interpretations of the feelings of mistrust can be made: First, the monks were reacting to a situation that was in the process of change. Undoubtedly, the very fact that the monks were alerted to change through the recommendations had some effect itself in producing this change. Probably also important were sessions in group dynamics held in the monastery during the two-year period between measurements. Second, the scores were still low even in the 1968 measures. The persons who were mistrustful were apparently quite few but quite vocal. No negative judgment is intended. If the mistrustful monks were vocal, it is good that their mistrust was aired. Because the monks are concerned for each other, feelings of mistrust by a few are of concern for the others. The important point is that tension has decreased. But the history of mistrust (by a few) should be recognized for what it is: history. Mistrust in the monastery by the 1980s was negligible. It is important now only in the memories of those concerned.

The question of abbatial authority was also basic to the first problem. The Business Council was instituted to deal with it, but the problem remained to some degree throughout Fr. Daniel's tenure. The difficulty is that some monks wanted more direct authority, whereas others wanted more collegiality. No one could please everyone, and Fr. Daniel was probably the best man for the job.

The third problem, the need to clarify monastic purposes, is difficult to substantiate and merges into the fourth problem, the infection of the world. It is my opinion that the minority report was correct in that the monks lacked cohesiveness and unity of direction, at least relatively. Of course, there is a common body of beliefs. But something more is needed.

Data from the contemplative survey can help (see Table 7.5). In every comparison except one, answers by the Palisades monks lean away from a strictly Trappist answer. (The exception is Question 48, where the "yes" answers are equal.) Not that Palisades monks are not Trappists (the differences are not statistically significant). Rather, the intensity of dedication is not always the same.

Visits to other monasteries strengthen the impression of more uncertainty about traditional Cistercian values in Palisades than in the other monasteries. Admittedly, the differences are not extensive. We are, after all, dealing with minor fluctuations in the same population, but it is a type of life that requires more than average dedication. With up to one-fourth or one-fifth of the monks uncertain about crucial aspects of their vocation, it is not

Table 7.5
Attitudes Concerning Vocations, from the Contemplative Survey, 1968

| | Percent "Yes" | | Percent "No" | |
Questions	Other Trappists	Pali-sades	Other Trappists	Pali-sades
42. Because contact with the world can be a danger to salvation, Christians should be careful about getting too involved in such things as politics, social movements, and leisure activities	19	12	50	76
45. The best contribution contemplative religious can make to world problems is to pray about them	66	56	15	20
48. Religious should be occupied with spiritual things leaving laymen to take care of secular matters	14	14	50	76
92. My apostolate is contemplative prayer	64	61	14	15
Number	169	66	169	66

Source: Research Committee of CMSW 1969.

surprising that the monks sensed a lack of cohesiveness and direction. There is cohesiveness and there is direction. But the cry is for more clarity, more certainty.

The fourth economic problem in the monastery is the infection of the world to which certain monastic jobs are exposed. The Abbot General of the Trappist order put the matter clearly in his Christmas letter to the monks in 1956. "Experience proves, alas, that the danger of like contacts with the outside is only too real. It has been verified that the monks who are unfaithful to the vocation in a great proportion were religious whose charge put them in frequent relations with the exterior: cellarers, guestmasters, chaplains."

No monastery is an insulated capsule. There must be dealings with the "exterior." But the problem is then to make certain that monks in such roles maintain their central allegiance. Granted the temptation, is the abbot sending a monk to a sort of monastic doom by appointing him cellarer, guest master, or chaplain?

There are two alternatives: First is the old monastic custom of changing jobs each year. Since there are few if any records, there is no way of knowing whether one is exposing people to temptation for only a short period or whether he is ultimately draining the monastery of good monks. Palisades tends to keep some monks in certain jobs year after year.This means that one is either particularly immune from temptation or that he will be infected. If infected, he may develop a modus vivendi (as several have) by more or less permanent affiliation with the guest house or with the role of cellarer. This way, he has one foot in the monastery and one in the world. But what does this do to his monastic vocation, especially contemplation?

Finally, there is the problem arising from poverty. The value of the fixed assets (land, buildings, machinery, furniture, dehy, and library) in 1975 amounted to almost two million dollars. This is one set of facts. Another is that the monks are called to a life apart from the world, yet the nearby city has expanded, year after year, until it is increasingly more accessible. The situation has been aggravated (the word is carefully chosen) by the county's building a hard-surfaced road directly to the monastery. So the world, with its noise and temptations, is increasingly thrust onto the monks. What are they to do? It might be advisable to move. The monks have mentioned this. But though it be a "leaky Gothic monastery" as one monk put it, it is paid for. So the economic consideration weighs heavily on the spiritual.

Is there any common thread to these problems? There is a general economic uneasiness in the monastery, and in fact one of the monks traces this uneasiness directly to the history of economic difficulties. Thus, the first two problems, that is, the history of mistrust and the question of abbatial authority, may be linked directly with the past. Further, the abbot remains the person best suited to direct the divided situation he inherited. And finally, the constraints exerted by the fixed assets are a cumulation of past labors. The only thing that is not a product of the particular history of Our Lady of the Palisades is the infection from the world—cellarers, guest masters, and chaplains are and have been universally vulnerable.

But there is a particular heritage that seems to be involved most pointedly with the need for clarification of purpose. In earlier times, Palisades seemed to have wandered somewhat from the Trappist path, though its course is now going toward it again. Exactly when or how it happened is unknown. It could have been a product of incomplete novitiate training or an earlier overemphasis on making economic ends meet or on climbing out of debt. It could have been a heterogeneity resulting from the sudden surge of veterans after World War II. But the problem for the monks of a lack of clarity in monastic purpose seems involved in all the other problems, without exception.

Undoubtedly, some monks cannot change—even those now responsible for the lack of consensus. (Of course, complete consensus is not necessarily the goal; the problem is reducing the uncertainty.) What to do about them? Almost all, if not all, are solemnly professed. The general kindness of the monks precludes "kicking them out." Until they change or the composition of this monastic population changes, the problem will remain.

AFTERWORD

The monastery's economic picture has changed drastically over the last 20 years. The dehydration machine is gone, at considerable economic expense. The Angus herd has been sold. Greater emphasis is placed on soy beans and corn. The gift shop used to have more goods, including a thriving business in selling the bread used by the monks. Gift shop and bread sales have both been drastically reduced.

The monks also change as the world changes, for they must interact with the world as well as be separate from it. They no longer attempt to keep their monastery a self-sustaining unit. They, like the world in which they live, have become part of a society that is intricately specialized. So they do not weave their own cloth, make their own shoes, generate their own electricity, and so on, as they once did. In this sense, they have become part of the world. They change their way of making a living to some extent to conform to the world. They also change as the population of the monastery declines and they simply lack the manpower to do what they used to. But they change, too, to protect themselves from the world, as in the case of the dehydration machine.

For there are limits beyond which the monks will not go. They still do not own anything personally. What they use, they use frugally. They tend toward poverty rather than wealth. And if any economic activity interferes with their prayer life or their liturgy, it is avoided. In this sense, economy still conforms to religion.

CONCLUSION

For many religions, and especially for Christianity, there is a contradiction between religious concerns and making money. Jesus said, "Do not lay up for yourselves treasures on earth, where moth and rust consume and where thieves break in and steal, but lay up for yourselves treasures in heaven, where neither moth nor rust consumes and where thieves do not break in and steal" (Matt. 6:19–20). The monastery is set up precisely to follow such teachings, and such teachings are the way to agapé. Thus, since the Cistercian monks do not permit themselves to beg (though they cannot refuse a contribution), they must work, and since work produces money, or earthly treasure, they have a problem. They must earn a living, but they must do so within two constraints: (1) keeping the economic concerns always subordinate to the demands of their faith, and (2) operating in the best interest of the individual monk. Since the faith requires that they love one another (that is, that they do what is best for one another), the two constraints become one.

Concerning the faith, numerous instances were shown where economic behavior was modified because of religious considerations. Charitable donations, working fewer hours to have more time for prayer, abandonment of the dehy machine, and the general positive value placed on poverty all operate contrary to maximizing economic benefit and are motivated by constraints of the faith. More directly related to love is the operation of the guest house department (see Chapter 4), and the high value on trust (see Chapter 8). But Palisades Abbey has experienced problems in working within these constraints. Contact with the world has a compromising effect on faith, and so does the fact that so much is invested in the monastic buildings, making it difficult for the monks to move if they felt the nearby city was encroaching too much on their solitude. Such compromises are bound to have an inhibiting effect on love, and the compromises may be part of the reason for the feeling of uneasiness among some.

Chapter 8

Authority and Government

The first degree of humility is obedience without delay. This is the virtue
of those who hold nothing dearer to them than Christ.
—Rule for Monasteries, Chapter 5

The monks have been democratic longer than the societies in which they
live, in that they have elected their abbots (except during the debilitating
time of *commendum*). Yet their government is pre-Hobbesian, based more
on consensus than contract. The monks consent to be governed by a rule,
and they individually petition the abbot for their grievances. The abbot is
as constrained by the rule as the monks. His role is to help them find
consensus with the *Rule* and the monastery. The vows and promises are
thus more than nice things said during ordination. They become the base
on which the monastery is built. Despite their religious convictions, monks
require a rule of law as much as anyone, and they are similarly political.

AUTHORITY

Authority is centered in the abbot. He appoints all offices (see Chart 7.1).
When the monk takes his vows, he pledges to the abbot complete obedience.
The abbot does not rule over the monastery as much as he interacts with
the monks. The councils, committees, and offices he appoints become his
advisors. He is always available for consultation with any monk, and this
becomes a major part of his job. The monastery, governed by consensus,
is comparable to the governmental and power structure of a small town
(Domhoff 1978; Dahl 1961).

The monks consent to be obedient because they are not so concerned
with political matters as people on the outside are. They are practitioners

of solitude in community, and this juxtaposition produces many political constraints. They have little or no involvement in the external political world. Though many are registered voters, only one monk spontaneously revealed his political affiliation. In introducing me to some visitors, he remarked, with an approving smile, "Here is my friend Dr. Hillery. He's a Democrat." (I do not recall ever telling him this, though he was correct.)

Members of other religious orders are quite often political. One thinks of the Berrigan brothers and the Latin American priests. Though occasionally Trappist monks express political concern—Thomas Merton (1948, 1966) is an example—the only external political act I heard of in the monastery consisted of going out to vote. I saw no monks in political demonstrations and I know of none who held political office in the "world." Thus, this chapter discusses only the internal politics of the monastery.

LOYALTY

There is a paradox about the loyalty of the monks. On the one hand, they are supposed to love their neighbor, and they show this love to both their immediate neighbors—their brothers in the monastery—and more conventional neighbors. On the other hand, their loyalty is not to this world. They gave up the world to come to Palisades to find God, or through a call from God. Thus, how could one expect them to place group above supernatural loyalties?

Attitudes reflect this sentiment. The monk is highly committed to his monastery. Thus, when asked, "How important is it to you personally to have this group [the monks] meet regularly for religious services?" almost all (92 percent) said it was either important or very important. Scores like these are very high, though some groups score higher. Other attitudes similarly show a strong commitment to the local house. For example, the monks at Palisades feel their morale is better than that at the other houses and is getting better (see Table 8.1). These men do not hesitate to be critical of their house, their order, or their Church. They are emotionally attached—even ethnocentric—about these things. But they view them all from the perspective that something else is prior.

HOMOGENEITY AND CONSENSUS

To understand any political body, one must also know the nature of its belief system. In this section, we explore the kinds of beliefs for which the monks are in almost total agreement. The next section treats the nature and extent of disagreement. Chart 8.1 concerns the areas of agreement that were abstracted from the results of two surveys. Approximately seven-hundred questions were asked. Each statement refers to those questions to which approximately 90 percent or more agreement was given. Thus, about nine

Table 8.1
Assessment of Morale, in Percent

Question & Answer	Other Trappists	Palisades
Q. 288. What is your impression of your local house in renewal? A. It seems to be improving rapidly.	8	55
Q. 289. How would you relate the morale of your community/cloister right now? A. Morale is very high.	9	18
Morale is higher than average.	27	51
Morale is average.	5	21
Q. 290. Would you say that the morale of your house now is lower or higher than the morale of the house five years ago? A. Higher.	56	76
Lower.	23	14
Number	169	66

Source: Research Committee of CMSW 1969.

out of ten monks who took the survey will correspond to the description in Chart 8.1 (although they would not necessarily agree with every item in the description).

The chart shows that values important to the monk are those concerned with his religion, prayer, an afterlife, celibacy, and love. However, as important as these beliefs are, he is quite flexible in his interpretation of God, the Bible, and the Church. Similarly, though the Mass is essential to his life, he is not overly concerned about recent changes stemming from Vatican II. He is open to experimentation in a wide range of behavior, and he wants more democracy in monastic life. But his idea of freedom still depends on discipline (that is, it requires sharing and sacrifice), both for himself and for his abbot. His view of the Church extends beyond the monastery, and though he is concerned with secular events, he looks on life with hope.

The monk feels that tensions and frustrations inherent in life at Palisades are not significantly greater than those experienced in other religious vocations. He is opposed to the monastery operating a boarding school for high-school-age boys for the sake of vocations (it once did so as a form of recruitment). But he is not opposed to education. He feels that outside professors may be engaged for part or all of the teaching at the monastery,

Chart 8.1

Statements to Which Approximately 90 Percent or More of the Monks at Palisades Abbey Agree

Chart 8.1
Statements to which Approximately 90 Percent
or More of the Monks Agree.

The Palisades monk was born an American[1] and was raised in a Roman Catholic family.[2] He believes deeply in his religion.[3] At one time or the other, he has practiced contemplative prayer.[4] Essential to his contemplative way of life is commitment to a life of worship, defined as an interior attitude before God.[5] Prayer is thus more than a psychological thing in his life.[6] He believes in a divine plan and a life after death.[7] The afterlife will in some manner retain everything which has value in human life.[8] Celibacy is important as a means for coming to know the meaning of love, especially love in Christ and the deepening of this love in bringing it to others.[9]

He thus has certain absolute values[10]--he is by no means a complete relativist.[11] He is quite open in his beliefs. He views concepts of God to some degree historically and culturally conditioned.[12] The monk agrees that God speaks always in diverse ways through events and other persons, through the Bible and the Church.[13] Further, the charismatic gifts of the Spirit working in the laity are as necessary for the good of the Church as is the authoritative power of the clergy.[14] The Mass, with the Eucharist at its heart, is still basic to his life,[15] and especially is it basic to his community,[16] sociologically and religiously. The recent liturgical changes do not strike him as a radical departure from the true tradition of the Church.[17] But he does feel that both the pilgrim condition of the Church and its servant character should be clearly manifested in its style of life.[18]

He is committed to his monastery, especially to the religious services and the group discussions.[19] He believes, however, that he is living in a situation where the community wants (or wanted) experimentation,[20] such as wearing secular clothing for particular kinds of activities[21] and home visits in times of sickness and death.[22] He expects to see a greater voice of religious in planning.[23] He believes in discussion. He wants consultation from delegates before they go to to religious meetings,[24] open and free communication among contemplatives of different monasteries,[25] and consultation before assignment of duties.[26] He believes that such things as community discussion in renewal[27] and psychological screening of candidates are helpful to the monastery.[28] He also wants opportunities for a temporary eremetical (hermit) life.[29]

Freedom of the monk is linked closely with sharing and sacrificing,[30] that is, with discipline.[31] He does not think that it is hard for him to decide which are the right rules.[32] Although the Abbot has an authority role, the monk feels that the Abbot is very much a part of the community and shares in the give and take of community life.[33] The monk's freedom also means having a consideration for others.[34] He believes in the dignity and worth of the individual human being,[35] and he is convinced that there are dependable ties that can be made with other people.[36]

As important as his monastery is for him, he does not see the concerns of the Church as limited to his enclosure--they extend to all of human life.[37] He is positive in his attitudes toward civil rights,[38] and he thinks Catholic organizations should be so engaged.[39] He avoids the use of force in achieving his ends.[40] But he is a realist: he knows he is under restrictions and has made sacrifices.[41] Still, he is relatively free from tension.[42] He also knows that there is loneliness and injustice in the world.[43] Life, however, has hope, not only for him but also for children yet to be born.[44]

Chart 8.1 (Continued)

Note: In the references to follow, "C.S." refers to the contemplative
survey (Research Committee of CMSW, 1969), and "H" refers to a sample of
Palisades Abbey taken in 1970 by George Hillery. The numbers cited for
C.S. refer to the table numbers, whereas the numbers cited for "H" refer
to the question numbers in the questionnaire.
1.   H 73.   2.   C.S. 209-11, H 64.   3.   H 141-43.   4.   C.S. 386.   5.   C.S.
307.   6.   H 143.   7.   H 141, 142.   8.   C.S. 57.   9.   C.S. 66.   10.   H 119.
11.   H 110.   12.   C.S. 1.   13.   C.S. 6.   14.   C.S. 26.   15.   C.S. 37.   16.
C.S. 326.   17.   C.S. 35.   18.   C.S. 29.   19.   H 50, 51.   20.   C.S. 362.
21.   C.S. 494.   22.   C.S. 527.   23.   C.S. 394.   24.   C.S. 483.   25.   C.S.
561.   26.   C.S. 566.   27.   C.S. 515.   28.   C.S. 567, 546.   29.   C.S. 542.
30.   H 77.   31.   H 100.   32.   H 150.   33.   C.S. 574.   34.   H 97, C.S. 647.
35.   H 121.   36.   H 117.   37.   C.S. 41.   38.   C.S. 126, 132.   39.   C.S.
135.   40.   H 128-137.   41.   H 86, 84.   42.   H 115, 116.   43.   H 105, C.S.
126-32.   44.   H 121, 153.

and he is willing to participate to some degree in carefully planned and
spaced programs, lectures, workshops, and seminars conducted at the abbey
for his community.

It is a paradox that all of the monks are committed to one interpretation
of the Christian belief, the Roman Catholic faith, and yet they differ personally from one another to a marked degree (see Appendix E). Perhaps
this paradox can be illustrated by a remark made by one monk concerning
the habit. This is the uniform worn by all professed monks: abbot, priest,
and lay brother. It consists of a white, long-sleeved, long-skirted garment
(the robe), over which is placed a black scapular and hood. The scapular
is draped only over the front and back of the monk, leaving the sides,
sleeves, and most of the white robe exposed. The scapular is secured to the
robe by a leather belt.

The habit, of course, produces a striking uniformity. But the monk in
question explained the other side of the paradox: It is precisely through the
sameness of the habit that the difference of the faces are emphasized (the
monk used the word "persona"). Though the immediate purpose of the
habit (particularly in its uniformity) is one of submerging individual differences as a part of renunciation, an unintended consequence is that individual
differences are emphasized.

DISAGREEMENTS

The abbot does not govern an undifferentiated mass. Though there is a
core of generally undisputed belief, the monks have their differences. In
comparing the questions on which the monks disagree, the problem is more
difficult than discussing homogeneity. How much disagreement is important? Somewhat arbitrarily, the criterion was placed at 40 percent or more
for each of two opposing positions. In other words, to qualify as an area
for disagreement, 40 percent or more of the monks had to agree (including

"strongly agree") with a statement *and* 40 percent or more had to disagree (including "strongly disagree"). (See Appendix E.)

Religious disagreements are of particular interest.[1] For example, some are willing to trust everything to God, as opposed to those who are not.[2] But it is in opinions about prayer that opposing attitudes are especially interesting, for prayer is the center of monastic life. The attitudes dichotomize into those who consider prayer the end and the justification of everything and those who disagree.[3] Authoritarian attitudes can be detected in attitudes about the order.[4] Similar attitudes can be uncovered also in the opinions about the local house and in personal opinions.[5]

However, a discussion of disagreements is misleading unless four points are kept in view: (1) There is an extensive agreement on fundamentals (see Chart 8.1). (2) There is a willingness to discuss differences, though some wonder whether important differences are overlooked because it would be an unkind thing to bring them up (Smith 1990: pp. 22–38). (3) Most things about which the monks feel intensely are somewhat removed from daily behavior. These differences can be expressed with less chance of overt friction than the intensely held differences involving the local monastery. (4) The monks can leave if they diverge too widely from the beliefs of their fellows. Thus, there are mechanisms for working with the differences (if not solving them), and it is perhaps because of these mechanisms that the most pressing differences—those that involve the local house—are kept to a minimum.

CLIQUES

I have not made a sociometric diagram of the monastery, but I did investigate various "camps." Although it is extremely difficult to type these monks, in a rough way it is possible to say that certain people are more often seen with certain others. Sometimes this clustering results from work or similar duties. For example, the cook is often seen in the company of other monks in the kitchen, those in the garage tend to associate together, as do those in the library, and the infirmarian is thrown into close association with the invalid monks. But work association does not imply friendship. Certain brothers, for example, are never seen together out of choir, and some who work daily in the company of others are otherwise regarded as usually solitary.

Thus, the monastery is interlocked with cliques of varying degrees of attachment. From six to ten monks could be called "loners," but even they are not necessarily completely so. One of the most isolated monks at community Mass is well integrated into the community clique structure—and the Mass is central to the monastic life.

It is possible to characterize the monks in four camps roughly according to their monastic values. The largest group of 25 men I will call the "old guard." They are primarily comprised of elderly monks (although some of the older ones are at the opposite pole: the "radicals.") They prefer the older customs (pre-Vatican II) of complete silence, eating no fish or eggs, and having more penance and asceticism. Some are older not in years but by training: they feel rules to be valuable in and of themselves. They justify the rules by saying, "They keep us in contact with our forebears." The slightest change is anathema, and at least some were much opposed to the abbot for his sweeping reforms. Others, the "neoconservatives," are Cistercians who do not place rules first. They believe in a complete dedication of self to the will of the Holy Spirit, and the rules of asceticism, silence, and so forth, are important means to such a dedication. They have intensified this dedication under the new system. Although they do not approve of all changes, they manifest a deep respect for the abbot. They number about 15 monks.

This group includes monks of all ages as well as the abbot. The position of the abbot is known to all and can be described publicly: A Cistercian of the Strict Observance, he believes that the *Rule* of St. Benedict should be internalized simply because it represents one interpretation of the Gospels. The *Rule* is important for that reason rather than because some holy person promulgated it. He would rather see rules abandoned if they were followed for the rules' sake—and that is the reason for much of his action. He puts rules second because he is a monk first, and the person takes priority. He believes he has been called by God to this monastery, and he is abbot only because he feels that this monastery wants him to be. He is a monk, then, who has sacrificed to become an abbot.

The "liberals," claiming eight men, feel called to the monastic life, but the *Rule* is not as important to them as it is to the old guard and the neoconservatives. Their orientation is to the guest house. They are concerned with guests and cultivate their friendship. The "radicals" are composed of 15 monks. They carry the ideas of the liberals to greater extremes. Radicals are oriented more to the outside world, liberals more to the monastery.

Camps are not now effective in monastic politics. The old guard, for example, is not a political party. Clique members tend to talk with one another rather than become political cells. Each monk approaches the abbot with his problems individually. Under such a condition, conservatism is to be expected. Further, this individuation tends to keep each monk relatively equal to the others, avoiding much of the problem of power structure inherent in other communities that have more developed stratification systems (Gilbert and Kahl 1987; see also Chapter 9).

THE ABBOT

Government is complicated in that it is much more than merely the visible structure. The monastery's government extends further than the abbot and his prior. Ultimately the government is found within each monk, or there could be no monastery. The monks select candidates to the life who can "govern themselves." The abbot becomes primarily a coordinator, an adjudicator in matters about which the monks cannot agree, and the person who provides the outside perspective where the monk is too personally involved. Even if the abbot wanted to, he cannot make many rules, since there are so many that the monk already follows (whether from his culture, his religion, or his own commitment to Trappist ideals). There is little deviance to administer (see Chapter 13). The abbot's main task is in dealing with the externals of behavior, especially for the more marginal members (also called "singulars" in monastic custom). His job is not so much being a leader as being a shepherd. The flock knows where it wants to go. The shepherd's job is to see that the flock keeps moving and that strays do not get too far away, as one abbot phrased it. He is not really a spiritual father to all the community, though he may be a spiritual director to a few. Instead, he sets the spiritual tone of the monastery.

For a few years before the election of the present abbot, Fr. (or Dom) Daniel, the abbatial government in Palisades had been unsteady. One abbot resigned, the next resigned shortly after being elected, and a somewhat firm-willed superior was appointed by the mother house. Thus, it is significant that Fr. Daniel is rather young, very liberal in that he places much more emphasis on inner conviction than on tradition (though he still considers tradition important), spiritually oriented, open and friendly, energetic, democratically inclined, and nondirective in his counselling.

The reaction is mixed. Some of the old guard, the older and more tradition-minded monks, are suspicious. Many of the neoconservatives feel that he should rule with a firmer hand. The more liberal and radical monks, in contrast, want the abbot to be even more open, more collegial, less tradition-bound than he is. Because of this diversity, he is considered by many the best man for the times—not necessarily ideal, but the only one who could guide Palisades through its stormy situation following Vatican II.

The story is told of one monk who was going to visit his sister and asked if the abbot would care if he smoked while on the visit. The abbot's reply was characteristic: "I wish you would not, but you may if you wish." (Smoking is not permitted in the monastery, yet a few monks smoke.)

When Fr. Daniel was elected, he agreed to serve for five years. At the end of the term, when he told the monks that he would continue as abbot, there was virtually universal applause. The monks, then, may each have his own individual objection to Fr. Daniel as abbot. But with few exceptions, he is liked, respected, and given much of the support his office demands. Still, he resigned after his second term.

ATTITUDES TOWARD GOVERNMENT

The *Rule* of St. Benedict stipulates that monks are to live under a rule and an abbot (Appendix F). To a large extent, this is the way they want to live.[6] For almost half, the office of superior is holy. No matter how they may discern the personality of the abbot as distinct from his office, he is God's servant *to them*. However, almost one-third did not feel this way at the time of the study, and this proportion is higher in Palisades than among other Trappists in the sample.

Even those who felt that the office is holy were not committed to blind obedience. Approximately two-thirds felt that much traditional monastic government should be permitted to die out.[7] And though the will of God is expressed through the abbot, the vow of obedience is further complicated. Slightly more than a third were opposed to the idea that the vow means listening to the community "as it speaks through many voices."[8] In particular, the abbot and the *Rule* were not enough.[9] The community itself should have some voice, they felt, though the monks were not clear just how much. Most felt that the superior should seek approval for commands,[10] though only about a third would equate this with the vow of obedience.[11]

Regardless, the monks were relatively satisfied with the governing system at the time of the survey. Almost all questions from 338 to 644 (in Appendix F) show that approximately three-fifths of the monks approved of the practice of obedience as it was worked out with superiors: initiative was not stifled, there was little sense of red tape, the monks felt that obedience (as practiced) helped them to be responsible and cooperative, and they felt they were receiving enough direction and guidance. Yet the sense of democracy was strong: the monks wanted regulations determined by vote of all in the house rather than by elected representatives.[12]

Though most were satisfied with the governing system, there were still criticisms. There was concern that those in authority were too hesitant about correcting deviations,[13] and most felt that "they do not understand the individual's problems."[14] However, never did many monks express a "high degree" of agreement with these criticisms. Finally, the monks felt that those in authority did keep confidences, did not feel threatened, and did not exact personal services.[15]

The Chapter of Faults, referred to in Appendix F,[16] was an institution where the monks accused one another of various indiscretions. No one was allowed to defend himself or anyone else. The chapter was a thing of the past when the survey was completed. That over half expressed desire for change in the chapter is more an expression of disfavor over the chapter than of dissatisfaction over the conditions then at work. However, the monks have not substituted any system of conflict regulation. They are and have been operating largely through latent functions (such as discussion groups, personal conversations, avoidance). Most know who disagrees with them and why. But there is not much of an effort to reconcile differences, which may prove dangerous in the future.

Palisades monks were much more satisfied with their superiors than the total Trappists in the sample.[17] I suspect that this condition is due to the nondirective approach of the abbot at Palisades. He apparently has been more successful than anyone realizes in helping his brothers find their own way, and hence they are largely satisfied with him.[18]

A large amount of independence exists among the various monasteries. What happens in the order is watched with interest, and the decisions made at the regional and international levels are followed closely. But interpretations are left largely to the individual house. For example, some years ago, there was a general decision that all should wear the same habit. In particular, the brown habit that distinguished the lay brothers from the choir monks was eliminated. But still one monk at Palisades continues to wear the brown habit, and no one has expressed disapproval of this to me. Though relatively satisfied with the local house, however, the monks are not as satisfied with administrative conditions in the Church hierarchy outside the monastery.

The monks at Palisades Abbey tended to agree to a large extent with the other monks who took this survey. Most of the questions discussed in this chapter revealed no significant differences between Palisades and the other monasteries. Palisades tended to be somewhat more liberal, but even that difference is converging toward the larger population of monks.

LOVE, POWER, AND CONFLICT

This analysis should put to rest conceptions about a monastery as an authoritarian, prisonlike system, as Goffman's (1961) comparison with total institutions implies. The abbot of Palisades Abbey is in no sense an authoritarian (nor have been any of those who succeeded him). Obedience is very important, but so is the relation of the abbot to his monks. He is supposed to listen to them and be sensitive to their needs.

Monastic government is a mixture of power and love. The modern abbot probably does not have nearly as much power as abbots did when the *Rule* was written, nor even as much power as abbots in the Middle Ages, but the focus of the monastery is on him, and largely on him depends the fate of the abbey. Again and again, I have observed the way the role of the abbot is tempered and guided by love—correcting the misplaced energy of a young monk, patiently ministering to those not as well integrated into the monastery as others, sharing in monastic parties—the list could be extended. I have known three abbots during my study, and none have shown dictatorial tendencies. They have varied personally, but their concern has always been for the well-being of their brothers.

Palisades is not unusual in this matter. The longer I have known any abbot at other monasteries, the more apparent his love for the community has become. The question is not whether the abbot is liked, for the decisions he makes are often hard. Admittedly, the reason for the abbot's attitude of concern has to do with the selection process. He is the kind of person who would be concerned—the monks would hardly elect any other type of person to his position, given their orientation to agapé love.

Of course, all is not sweetness and light. Love does not preclude conflict. It even engenders conflict. Abbot James Fox of Gethsemani cared for Thomas Merton deeply. Yet there is no one in the monastery with whom Merton was in more conflict (Mott 1984). The source was largely personal. According to Mott (1984:279), "The two men would have found themselves on quite separate lines in any conceivable situation. One of the difficulties was Merton's own attitude to authority. This was ambiguous at the deepest level. He was rebellious by nature, a born critic and changer, yet he sought to appease."

Dom James Fox was a man of deep conviction, strongly conservative, notwithstanding that he was also a "brilliant pragmatist" (Mott 1984:282). He "was overprotective, not only of Merton, but especially of Merton" (Mott 1984:280). I discovered this in one of my own visits to Gethsemani— Merton was strictly off limits to the guests.

The main conflict "was over trust. . . . Dom James trusted Father Louis [Thomas Merton] within the monastery and he showed that trust. He did not trust Merton outside the enclosure walls" (Mott 1984:280). The two were by no means enemies. At the end of his life, Merton wrote to Fox: "Be sure that I have never changed in my respect for you as Abbot, and affection as Father. Our different views certainly did not affect our deep agreement on the real point of life and of our vocation" (Mott 1984:283).

Conflict is not merely interpersonal. In view of the "camps" mentioned earlier, one would be surprised if there was not political intrigue, and there was. Firsthand observation of such behavior is difficult, since I was not permitted to attend the Chapters (meetings) of the professed, where such conflict would be most likely to occur. But one monk, whom we shall call Father Angus, related the following incident as it developed soon after his solemn profession of vows. Before that time he was not permitted to attend the Chapter of the professed monks, where decisions were discussed and made. He had been oblivious of that part of monastic life. But once he began to see the politics going on, he did not like it. A certain monk was very influential with some others (all on the Abbot's Council). It was obvious that this man was out to be abbot and was trying to make the abbot look "stupid."

As part of the intrigue, ordination of Fr. Angus to the priesthood was delayed. He felt the delay was another part of a plan to get him on the side against the abbot. The abbot said he did not really want to make the postponement, but the council, under instigation of their leader, had complained that they were not consulted in the decision of Fr. Angus's ordination. They, using the word of their leader, said Fr. (then Brother) Angus was not mature enough.

What he was angry about (though he was not aware of the anger) was the way the ordination was prevented. Of course, all was resolved in a few years when the abbot resigned, but the villain did not become his successor— disappointed at not being chosen, he left the monastery. The new abbot had Fr. Angus ordained two weeks after his election.

How much can one generalize from such an incident? The "villain" has left, and the present abbot, Father Mark, assures me that the former camps have dissolved. Certainly the monastery was more peaceful in the late 1980s than when I first began my studies in 1969. Abbots vary in power, both in time and across monasteries. In one monastery, for example, the abbot's secretary took dictation on his knees (prior to Vatican II). In another monastery (more recently) it was reported that the abbot behaved consistently as if he were sensitive to the potential vote he could get in his next bid for election. Palisades does not seem to approach either extreme.

The problem with the association between love, conflict, and abbatial power is that conflicts seem more remembered than loving acts, at least in American society. As the years go by, the accumulated conflicts weigh ever more heavily on the abbot. This would seem to be one of the factors leading to the resignation of Fr. Daniel. We come to a point already noted: the need for methods of conflict resolution. Essentially, we are speaking of forgiveness, which is directly related to love.

LATER ABBOTS

Fr. Daniel served nine years (1967–76). He left the abbey after his resignation (a common practice for an abbot emeritus) and now is chaplain to a convent of nuns. He was abbot when most of the data for this study were gathered and during which most of the changes occurred. The church and other parts of the monastery building were remodeled. The decline in the population of monks was the steepest it had ever been. But much more important were the changes following Vatican II. During these years, a sharper emphasis was made on focusing one's monasticism toward the cloister rather than the guest house. Liturgy changed from Latin to English, the custom of silence was virtually dropped, and dormitories were abandoned for private rooms. Government also changed, particularly in shifting from lifetime elections of abbots to six-year terms.

Two other abbots followed Fr. Daniel. Fr. Donald (1976–84) had been a Brother and was appointed superior (by the Father Immediate of Palisades's parent abbey) two years prior to his election as abbot. He had been studying for the priesthood and was elected after he completed his studies and was ordained. He resigned after his first term and is still in the monastery. A brilliant intellect, he is deeply committed to monastic life. During his term, the community was consolidating after the upheaval of preceding years. It was quieting down and rediscovering traditional monastic values and practices. Fr. Donald on the whole encouraged this reorientation. He also was able to close the cattle department, which was a problem for a long time. Although somewhat more direct in his leadership than Fr. Daniel, he basically continued the nondirective style.

Fr. Mark (1984–) is probably the most outgoing and sociable of the three, though his spiritual roots are as firmly established in the monastery. He was, in fact, the community's liturgist. Easily reelected for a second term, he continues reorienting the monastery toward a more Cistercian milieu, though exhibiting a firmer sense of direction.

This succession of abbots has been accompanied by greater peace in the monastery. There are at least two reasons. All three of the abbots did what they could to increase peace. But much of this change was due to the exodus of monks, many of whom probably should not have been in the monastery at all. Some discovered that they either were not contemplative or could not put contemplation above other considerations. One monk that I considered extremely pious and well acquainted with contemplative prayer left because he felt called to be among the poorest of the poor. Another wanted more opportunity to be a counselor. Another wanted to be a priest. As the dissatisfied monks left, divisions in the monastery became less rancorous.

The following insightful summary is given by one of the monks:

It's very hard to separate the man from the epoch in which he lived as abbot. For instance, Daniel would undoubtedly appear much differently if he were abbot now rather than in the turbulent sixties. At that time the community was just coming out of an authoritarian system and sensing its new freedom; firm direction probably wouldn't have gone over too well (though many of us repeatedly asked Daniel for it). In the overall view, it would probably be truer to say that the community made the abbots rather than vice versa: the various styles of government were determined not so much by the particular abbot's personality as by the needs/demands of the community at the time. And often these needs and demands weren't clear, either to the abbot or the community. My personal feeling is that we've never been so well off as we are now.

CONCLUSIONS

Although the monk is not different from seculars in that he becomes involved in political affairs, he differs in degree of involvement. Indeed, he is probably less involved politically than economically. I know many monks who have been in the monastery a long time and are quite concerned over the abbey's economic situation. But all monks who were overtly concerned politically have left. Monks who are politically conscious at least do not attract attention. Not that there is no concern, particularly among the abbots. One of the abbots of Palisades, for example, became somewhat uneasy over certain passages in this chapter. Monastic politics is a delicate matter. It cannot be avoided, but if it becomes overbearing, it could destroy the monastery.

There is some conflict between love and authority, just as there is conflict between love and economics (see Chapter 7). "Love does not insist on its own way" (I Cor. 13:5), as authority must sooner or later if it is to remain authority.

But from another perspective, the apparent difference in love and authority does tell us something. Such things as political battle and the tensions with the abbot mark off limits of agapé, for they do not bear all things, believe all things, hope all things, endure all things (see I Cor. 13). There is little information to be gained about love from the data on the monastery's politics. For example, the questionnaires indicate that the monks have a strong sense of democracy and are generally satisfied with their superiors. These are important items of information to have about a government. But what does this tell us of love?

And yet, when the activities and efforts of the abbot are examined closely, love becomes a dominant theme, revealing itself even through different styles of abbots. Fr. Daniel was mainly nondirective. Though he was not alone in using this technique, others were more forceful. Abbots also range in ability, from being efficient administrators to being blessed with a patient and supportive staff. Yet administrative ability is an accidental quality, almost irrelevant to the office (almost, because efficiency and leadership are important). The essential quality needed for an abbot is a love for his community that enables him to sacrifice much of the very reason he came to the monastery—for prayer and contemplation. He has markedly less of these when he occupies the office. Thus, many abbots serve just a few terms and are happy to return to the status of being "only a simple monk," as one former superior put it. To the extent that such resignation shows a disinclination to sacrifice, there is less agapé. But one can hardly blame the abbots, from a human perspective.

Political development in the monastery is largely rudimentary. The monks are primarily concerned with prayer in community, and this concern short-circuits normal political activity. Were the monks to give up their concern with prayer, political activity would probably increase markedly.

Yet the monks do not (or should not) seek "community." Whenever a monk became concerned with community (which usually means concern with self-fulfillment), his monastic vocation was in jeopardy. Most of those concerned primarily with prayer are still in the monastery. The feelings of community in the monastery are a consequence of prayer, not a conscious objective.

NOTES

1. Note that the term "religious" is used in the Roman Catholic church to refer either to a religious attitude (he is religious) or to one who has made a religious vow (she is a religious).

2. App. E, Q. 125.

3. App. E, Qs. 125, 240.

4. App. E, Q. 596—referring specifically to those who do not complain about decision making.

5. See App. E, last two sections.

6. App. F, Q. 85.

7. App. F, Q. 86.

8. App. F, Q. 90.

9. App. F, Qs. 87, 88.

10. App. F, Q. 89.

11. App. F, Q. 90.

12. App. F, Q. 314, Q. 315.

13. App. F, Q. 321.

14. App. F, Q. 325.

15. App. F, Qs. 322–324.

16. App. F, Q. 463.

17. App. G, especially Qs. 428, 439, 625.

18. App. G, Qs. 443, 616.

Chapter 9

Stratification

with L. Richard Della Fave

Let [the Abbot] not advance one of noble birth ahead of one who was formerly a slave, unless there be some other reasonable ground for it.
—*Rule for Monasteries*, Chapter 2

Several questions are important to this chapter. First, given the heavy emphasis on the equal value of each individual in the monastic ideology, does status inequality exist? Second, if it does, on what criteria is the ranking based? Finally, does a system of stratification exist? That is, does status inequality correlate with institutional rankings within the community, such as whether a monk is a priest or a brother, the type of job a monk holds within the economic structure of the monastery, and whether he is an officer in the community? Also we wish to know whether the socioeconomic status of the monk's family of orientation has any influence on his position within whatever status ranking may exist.

It is important to distinguish *inequality* and *stratification*. Inequality refers to a rank ordering of individuals along one or more dimensions, whereas stratification refers to the ranking of positions that is institutionalized within a society, that is, a ranking system that persists beyond the lifetime of any set of role incumbents. Thus, while inequality among individuals can exist in the absence of stratification, stratification necessarily implies inequality.

A specific set of questions was used for this chapter: "What two or three persons in the monastery do you respect the most?" and its corollary: "What do you mean by 'respect'?" (Interviews were given in March 1976.) A

Chapter is adapted from L. Richard Della Fave and George A. Hillery, Jr., "Status Inequality in a Religious Community," *Social Forces* 59, September 1980, 62–84.

monk's status is measured by the number of times he is named as being among those most respected.

SOCIOECONOMIC CONDITIONS

A basic value position of the monastery is that it permits no economic distinctions among its members. For example, the abbot sleeps in the same kind of bed in the same kind of room and eats the same food as the novice. No monk owns property, not even his clothes.

Some inequality of power exists as a matter of canon law; in particular, the abbot is the main authority. The authority of the abbot, while great, is not absolute. There are instances specified in the constitutions where the abbot is bound, under pain of invalidity, to take the vote of the community, and at times he may not act against a negative vote (although he is not bound to follow a positive vote). Also, the local bishop has some supervision in liturgical matters within the monasteries.

Two of the promises made by these monks underline this authority: they promise to be obedient and to be stable. In fact, however, there are limits to the authority. The *Rule* of St. Benedict admonishes the abbot, "Do everything with counsel, and you will not repent when you have done it" (Doyle 1948, Chapter 3:14). Further, entrance into this community is entirely voluntary. Regardless of the power his vows are supposed to have, if a monk questions whether his God is still calling him to live this form of life, he is apt to feel that the vows are no longer binding, and he leaves—as many have done. Finally, the abbot in office during most of this study believes that a monk should live his life according to firm inner convictions. If anything, he has resisted pressure from the community to exercise more direct authority.

Personal power does exist. For example, one brother repeatedly sits on sensitive committees and is sought out for advice by many, but such power is idiosyncratic, nontransferrable, and thus unique. We should see that, if anything, there is *less* inequality of power than one might expect because of ideology, just the opposite of what is usually found in such comparisons. The existence of status inequality and stratification is much more problematic, however.

Findings

The status structure. Among the most interesting findings was the difficulty experienced by many monks in singling out those whom they respected the most. One monk objected to the question as "intimate" and simply named the superiors, avoiding invidious comparisons. Another, while giving the names of two monks, lamented, "In a sense, all of this is repugnant."

Others insisted that they could not really single out only a few. For

Table 9.1
Number of Times Chosen as Most Respected

No. of Priests	No. of Times Chosen	No. of Brothers	No. of Times Chosen
1	17	1	17
1	12	1	7
1	7	1	6
2	4	2	5
1	3	3	4
7	2	2	3
4	1	2	2
7	0	2	1
--	--	12	0
—	—	—	—
24	65	26	64

Source: Della Fave and Hillery 1980: 69.

example, a brother explained, "I have respect for persons for different things. Everyone has a particular grace, and you respect him for that." The abbot replied, "In almost everyone you can find something to respect. I hesitate to draw any lines—I respect them all." Still others had to grope for a criterion: "Never give it much thought. I have respect for all the monks. Now if it's fervor you mean—which monks are the most fervent—that's a different thing. All the monks are serving God, but from the exterior—some are more fervent."

Despite such problems, all but two of the monks gave the name of others whom, for one reason or another, they respected most. The results are shown in Table 9.1. The data reveal a marked degree of status inequality. Out of a total of 50 men—24 priests and 26 brothers—32 were named at least once as most respected. A total of 129 choices distributed among these 50 men gave an average of 2.6 choices per man. However, some far exceeded this average. The incumbent abbot, one priest, and one brother each were chosen 12 or more times. Only eight monks received five or more choices—only three received ten or more. Thus, though many insist that they respect all equally, and we believe that in one sense most if not all of them do, the research question on respect elicits the names of some with striking consistency while the others seldom or never appear.

The task now is to understand the criteria on which the status inequality is based. Here, one is struck by the consistency with which the monks apply the yardstick of their monastic ideals. A few examples will make the point clearer.

I respect Brother Henry, perhaps for his practicality, the others too. They are more realist than idealist. In a certain sense I find Christ that way. He had ideals but he was aware of the real.

Father Luke for his integrity—he's rather human, cheerful. He's a man of deep prayer, capable of loving very deeply. Brother Clovis, very prayerful person. He cares about and is interested in other people. He's cheerful and patient. Brother Ambrose, a man who has had to learn to be flexible. A person who can be very kind and considerate—very understanding and caring. The kind of person I'd like to be like....He is a very holy person. Brother Brian—striving to live the life and be true to his values. He's outspoken yet he has a real love and concern—desires what is good for all.

The qualities I most admire are personal integrity, fidelity—...personal, communal, and religious and spiritual fidelity—it is not a matter of being dedicated to himself.

To demonstrate quantitatively the criteria used by the monks, a content analysis was performed on their replies. From this analysis, a questionnaire was constructed, and the instrument was administered to three undergraduate sociology classes at a state university and to four other monasteries in this order. Students were used because they were a readily accessible population with essentially nonmonastic values. The replies are given in Table 9.2. (Since the classes of students did not differ significantly on any of the variables, they are treated as one population. The monks differed significantly on five variables and thus are listed separately.)

The rank orders for the broader categories of respect are similar for all populations (all correlations at the end of Table 9.3 are significantly different from zero, $p > .05$). The greatest differences between students and monks are in "basic monastic values" (humility, simplicity, obedience), spirituality, and sacrifice. Monks always use these values more frequently for assigning respect than do students. Instrumental values, integrity, and self-control present a mixed picture. Although monks rank instrumental values lower than students, only one monastery consistently shows significant differences (see Table 9.2). Love and friendliness as reasons for respect are not significantly different for either students or monks.

Both monks and students give similar weight to many of the same values when giving respect to someone. In these cases, both monks and students are drawing from a common pool. The greatest differences are in those values by which other values are realized. In what way does one become loving and friendly? How in practice does one achieve integrity and self control? The monks say it is through humility, simplicity, obedience, sac-

Table 9.2
Criteria for Respecting Persons, as Given by Students and Monks

Criteria for Respect	Percent of Students Using Criterion	Abbeys				
		Total	Second	Third	Fourth	Fifth
Love and Friendliness	74.0	79.5	73	71	98	78
Ability to love	73.8	70.5	46	77	100	56
Caring for others	79.9	88.6	91	77	100	89
Kindness	76.5	75.0	73	64	100	78
Generosity	72.5	81.8	64	77	100	89
Cheerfulness	67.1	81.8	91	69	91	78
Basic Monastic Values	22.6	66.7	70	59	85	52
Humility	26.8	70.5#	73**	61*	100#	44(a)
Simplicity	26.2	68.2#	64*	69**	82#	56
Obedience to Others	14.8	61.4#	73#	46*	73#	57**
Spirituality	22.8	80.7	77	92	86	61
Holiness	23.5	77.3#	64*	100#	82#	56
Love of Prayer	22.1	84.1#	91#	85**	91#	67**
Integrity	62.8	77.3	59	81	91	78
Integrity	60.4	77.3	55	85	91	78
Faithfulness	61.1	79.5*	55	92	91	78
Courage of conviction	41.6	70.5**	55	69	82**	78
Honesty	87.9	81.8	73	80	100	78
Sacrifice	47.7	77.3*	67	77	100**	67
Self-Control	38.3	62.5	45	60	75	72
Persistence	40.3	65.9*	45	77*	77	67
Strength	49.7	54.5	18	69	73	56
Ability to control anger	45.0	61.4	45	39	91**	79
Minds own business	18.1	68.2#	73#	54**	64**	89#
Instrumental Values	59.7	56.1	24	69	67	63
Intellectual ability	62.4	59.1	27*	77	64	67
Practicality	46.3	47.7	9*(a)	61	64	56
Common sense	70.5	61.4	36*	69	73	67
Number	149	44	11	13	11	9

*Difference from students, p < .05.
**Difference from students, p < .01.
#Difference from students, p < .001.
(a)Monks different, p. < .05.

Source: Della Fave and Hillery 1980: 73.

Table 9.3
Rank Order of Criteria for Respecting Persons, Students and Monks

Criteria for Respect	Students Using Criterion	Prime Study Site #	Ranks Second	Ranks Third	Ranks Fourth	Ranks Fifth
Love and friendliness	1	1	2	4	2	1.5
Basic monastic values	7	2.5	3	7	4	6
Spirituality	6	2.5	1	1	5	5
Integrity	2	4	5	2	3	1.5
Sacrifice	4	5	4	3	1	3
Self-control	5	6	6	6	7	4
Instrumental values	3	7	7	5	6	2
Spearman rank-order correlation with students	1.000	.838	.798	.881	.899	.984

(Columns "Second, Third, Fourth, Fifth" under "Other Abbeys")

Source: Della Fave and Hillery 1980: 74.

rifice, and spirituality. Students do not attach such importance to these values.

It is somewhat surprising that such things as instrumental values, which presumably are helpful to the interest of the community, generally occupy a low place in monastic values. Extrinsic attributes such as wealth, family social standing, education, and power are never even mentioned. Thus, the data show that at least in this community, with its highly selective recruitment, voluntary commitment, strongly religious ideology, and extensive isolation, status is reckoned very much by compliance with the normative ideals of the community.

Priests and brothers. Granted the existence of status inequality, the question remains whether this inequality is part of a system of status stratification. The first topic to be investigated is whether being priest or lay brother is related to the likelihood of the monk's being chosen among those who are more respected. The data in Table 9.1 do not lend much support to this hypothesis. The 24 priests were named as most respected a total of 65 times, an average of 2.7 times per man, whereas the 26 brothers were named 64 times, an average of 2.5 times per man.

Superiors. However, the data did reveal that the superiors of the community, the abbot, prior, and subprior, were highly respected. These three men were chosen 35 times, an average of 11.7, in sharp contrast to the community average of 2.6. This does not mean that superiors are invariably chosen most often. In fact, one could put together a combination of three other monks, none of whom are superiors, who were named as often as 31 times.

An important question arises here: Is the degree to which superiors are respected the result of their being superiors, or have they obtained their posts by virtue of their high esteem, or both? As was stressed earlier, the cross-sectional nature of the questionnaire data does not make causal inference possible. However, since the questionnaire was administered, a new abbot has been elected, and this has provided us with field observations that bear on the issue (see later discussion).

Economic positions. If anything, an inverse relationship was found between respect and the status of jobs held by the monks in the monastic economy. The three positions conferring the most economic authority are the procurator and the heads of the beef department and the farm. These were named a total of five times, an average of 1.7. In contrast, the abbot, named 17 times, drives a dump truck, and the brother most often mentioned is quite old and has not been able to work for many years.

It should not be concluded that there is necessarily an inverse relation between economic authority and respect. The data are not complete enough for that. More important, the monastery is set up as an economic organization in part for what the monks consider an incidental reason—they must make a living. They make a living, in turn, so that they can live the monastic life. The conclusion is that an ordinary means of assigning status in the secular world—that is, economic authority—is not considered important and is at times even negatively valued.

Family of orientation. How important is the relationship between the socioeconomic status of the monks' families of orientation and the extent to which they are respected by their fellows? In this order, the ideology strongly encourages detachment from family and forbids discussion of it. Therefore, the question is raised whether there is a relationship between the respect a monk receives and the status of his father's occupation. Occupations of the fathers were obtained for 34 of the 50 monks involved in the respect ratings. Chi-square analysis showed no significant differences between the respect rankings and the occupational ratings according to the Hollingshead occupational rating scale (chi-square is 0.129, with 1 d.f., $80 > p > .70$).

Summary and discussion. The egalitarian ideology of a Trappist monastery has been compared with the reality of its social structure. In doing so, three questions were posed: (1) To what extent does inequality of status exist? (2) On what criteria is it based? (3) Does a system of stratification exist, and how can its presence be explained?

There is evidence of rather clear-cut status inequality, a more highly skewed distribution than anticipated. Those who were most respected were also seen as best exemplifying monastic ideals, as expected. Although there is no significant overall correlation between respect and seniority (rank-order coefficient of correlation .357, N of ranks is 7), the most respected monks still tend to come disproportionately from the long-term members. This may be because it simply takes time for a person to learn to live the monastic life successfully or because it takes time before the members of the community can observe the extent a monk has been able to exemplify monastic values.

Since the perquisites of the abbot, the most "privileged" member of the community, are virtually nonexistent and his responsibilities many, to posit a relationship between status and privilege makes little sense. To see power, or in the abbot's case what might better be termed authority, as a source of status is more plausible. But even if such a relationship existed it would be highly circumscribed in that it would apply only to the abbot and perhaps secondarily to the prior and subprior, certainly not even to those who head the monastery's businesses. For the bulk of the monastery's population, status seems to be based on personal qualities that exemplify monastic ideals.

Stratification means here the extent to which inequality is institutionalized. In its least institutionalized form, inequality is based entirely on the personal attributes of individuals. It is not anchored in any preexisting structure of roles. An extreme form of institutionalization is present when incumbency in such roles is hereditary, quite impossible here. The next question is whether status inequality as observed in the monastery is part of a system of stratification. The indicators of stratification would be positive correlations of status (respect) with: (1) being a superior, (2) being a priest rather than a brother, (3) holding a leadership position within one of the monastery's business enterprises, and (4) coming from a family of high socioeconomic status. The findings clearly indicate that only the first of these variables shows a positive relationship.

Finally, the strong positive correlation must be considered between authority and status. Does the high correlation between being a superior and being highly respected mean that the office confers status on the man, or are these officers among the more highly respected individuals in the community to begin with and therefore elected at least partly for that reason? In the first instance, stratification would be said to exist, whereas in the second it would not. Without longitudinal data, it is impossible to choose rigorously between these alternatives.

For several reasons, the noninstitutional explanation is favored. First, the abbot at that time, Fr. Daniel, is known to have been a highly respected man well before being elected. Second, observation in other Trappist monasteries has shown that most abbots were chosen for their apparent spirituality. Several had, in fact, been hermits at the time they were asked to be superior. A man normally moves to a hermitage to devote himself more intensely to prayer. Administrative acumen, however, varies markedly among abbots. In extreme cases, the prior or subprior has been known to take over. Thus, spiritual qualities that are most closely associated with high status are the very ones that appear crucial in calling a man to be abbot, suggesting that status accrues before election.

Third, survey research conducted by Sister Marie Augusta Neal (Research Committee of CMSW 1969) reveals that a large majority of monks of this order reject outright the notion of blind obedience to superiors and feel the superior should seek community approval for his decisions (see Chapter 8). Such attitudes show that the monks do not look on the offices of superiors as such with great awe, although, as has been shown, they tend to hold the men raised to these offices in high regard anyway.

Shortly after the data for this study were collected, the abbot resigned and a temporary superior was appointed. This was a brother and also one of the men receiving the highest number of choices in the respect ranking. (Although this fact was unknown to the official who made the appointment, he did know that the brother was highly respected.) Since only a priest can be abbot in the order, the brother had to wait until he could be ordained before he could assume office (he had already been studying for the priesthood). Although he had been subprior, and thus could conceivably have gained some respect by virtue of that office, field observation suggests that he was appointed subprior because of the respect by the community. Almost a year and a half after ordination (and after he had assumed the role of superior), this former brother was elected abbot by the community. However, several monks observed during this time how he was "growing to the office." Thus, though the former brother had significant status before he assumed office, the office itself also granted him additional status.

Apparently, therefore, the office confers some status. At least two competing explanations appear plausible. The first was suggested at the beginning of this chapter, that is, that the abbot's authority derives from the laws of the Church. Therefore, the influence of this hierarchical formal organization on the egalitarian community, the monastery, is responsible for the limited form of stratification that exists. While plausible, this explanation leaves unanswered the question of why priests do not systematically enjoy higher status than brothers. The second possible explanation is a variant on the well-known halo effect. That is, the monks have invested something of their judgment in selecting one of their own to fill this important office. Once the selection is made, they feel the need to validate their judgment. It would appear that the second explanation has at least some weight.

Thus, despite the egalitarian ideology of the monastery, status inequality is clearly present. This community has failed to transcend completely the virtually ubiquitous tendency of making status distinctions. This chapter has also shown that at least this monastery has not been so heavily influenced or coopted by the formal organization of the Church as writers such as Kanter (1972) and Bennett (1975) have implied, at least not in its status structure.

The only system of stratification observed in the monastery is associated with authority, and even that singles out only one person at a time, for all other authority positions ultimately depend on the abbot. There are status inequalities associated with compliance to monastic values, but the respect achieved in that way is not associated with any other monastic position and is always contingent on the interpretations made by the individual. A monk is never recruited for what he can give to the monastery in skills—personal, social, or technical. Apart from considerations of age and medical and psychological health, the only criteria for his admission are his willingness to lead a life of prayer in conformity to the Cistercian lifestyle in this particular monastery.

IMPLICATIONS

In brief, then, the monastery has been discussed as a community that places little emphasis on stratification, but one where inequality of status among the members does prevail. Both conditions derive from the community's ideology. The monks believe in a basic equality of all before God, and thus there should be essentially no status differences. Yet, the common lot of mankind requires (so the monks believe) differences in authority. Thus, the monks have a leader, the abbot, and almost alone, he is the authority figure. Still, given their equalitarian ideals, the abbot is quite sensitive to the views of his brothers, and authoritarian tendencies are effectively dampened.

There are certain values that the monks prize highly, such as love, friendliness, simplicity, humility, spirituality, and integrity. Monks who consistently display these virtues, particularly for a long time, are accorded more respect by the others.

What is the function of status inequality for the monastery? There are extremely significant consequences. The monks are devoted to the worship of God through a life of prayer. Thus, whatever will reinforce such a purpose would understandably be prized. Consequently, an old and dying brother who is faithful in prayer and in attending the liturgical offices despite illness, who is judged to be simple and unaffected, who is always known to be kind and cheerful though in much pain—such a brother is accorded highest respect. That he is not a priest is incidental. It is not the office of priest that matters. Rather, what is sought is a living model, a person who can be regarded as evidence that the system works. Further, not everyone who may be eligible need be the model. According to the monks, there are probably more who should or could receive respect than do. What apparently is important is that someone be a model, although even this statement is a speculation. One may suspect (though of course we have no proof) that if this old brother had not been a model, someone else might have been, or if not one person, then perhaps a composite. The fact is that someone was such a model at the time status was studied in this monastery, and he was a model apart from the canonical office, from the sacerdotal functions, from the power structure, or from anything else that one would normally associate with status attainment.

The monks find themselves in a dilemma. They prize equality but recognize a need for authority. This dilemma results in a system of minimal stratification. Still, the monks have certain ideals about what a good monk should be, and thus the monks individually are given different statuses. But these statuses are constantly changing as monks come, leave, or die, and so the statuses never become stratified.

CONCLUSIONS

The most significant feature of the monastic status system is the importance love has in the status rankings. In fact, in most of the abbeys studied, and specifically in Palisades, "love and friendliness" was the most important criterion used in awarding respect. Moreover, even in monasteries where love and friendliness are not most important for respecting people, spirituality and sacrifice are, and these are important components of agapé.

Of course, people are respected for reasons other than love. Furthermore, there is a great range of respect among individual monks. If one makes respect a necessary (though not sufficient) criterion of love, then there is also a great range in the love monks have for one another.

Chapter 10

Monastic Prayer

> Let us therefore consider how we ought to conduct ourselves in the sight of the Godhead and of His Angels, and let us take part in the psalmody in such a way that our mind may be in harmony with our voice.
>
> —*Rule for Monasteries*, Chapter 19

Prayer is the heart of monastic life. The monk's day is marked off into "hours" when psalms (as a form of prayer) are sung and prayers are offered corporately. At other times, the monk is supposed to be in prayerful reading and meditation. Even in his work, his labor, he ideally should be making his living as an act of reverence. Thus there are different forms of prayer. Prayer is defined as any form of communication with God, including not only petitions and requests but also simply desiring to be in God's presence.

I have classified some forms of prayer in Chart 10.1. It shows two overlapping dimensions: focused and nonfocused (or diffused) on the one hand and conscious and nonconscious on the other. In focused prayer, one centers consciousness on some phenomenon, such as praise, requests (petitions), songs, or psalms, or limits one's behavior to one type of activity (such as speaking in tongues). In contrast, diffused prayer lacks focus. One is simply in a condition determined by one's belief in what God would want one to do.

Focused and diffused prayer have both conscious and nonconscious forms. In the conscious form, one is aware of what is happening. But one can also pray and not be aware of it, as will be explained. The overlap between the focused and conscious dimensions is not complete. Thus, petitional prayer cannot be nonconscious, and the distinction between consciousness and nonconsciousness is not applicable to contemplative prayer.

Chart 10.1
Selected Types of Prayer

	Examples	
Types of prayer	Conscious	Nonconscious
Focused:		
Exclamatory	Praise, thanksgiving, grace at meals	Glossolalia (speaking in tongues)
Petitional	Intercessory prayer, confession	--
Liturgical	Divine Office, Sunday worship, Communion	Certain times during chanting of the psalms
Diffused:		
Expressive	Choice of work	Prayer in work, prayer in behavior
Meditative	Thoughts on a passage of scripture; the stations of the cross	--
Contemplative	--	--

The emphasis in this chapter is on forms of prayer that are especially important in understanding monastic life. First, liturgy is considered, then expressive prayer, meditation, and contemplative prayer. In the last part of the chapter, the monks' opinions concerning prayer are analyzed.

FOCUSED PRAYER, WITH EMPHASIS ON LITURGY

Much if not all focused prayer in the monastery is highly structured, especially exclamatory prayer and petitions. Grace is said before and after each meal; the abbot leads such prayers at noon, the most important meal of the day for the monks. Petitions, especially, are incorporated into the Mass (see later discussion). The extent to which exclamatory prayer is used in other situations or spontaneously is not known. A monk may exclaim,

"Praise God!" or something similar from time to time, but this is rare. Similarly, I have heard monks speak in tongues (glossolalia), but not often.

By far the most important type of focused prayer is liturgical. There are two main forms: the Divine Office (otherwise known as simply the office, or more rarely, the hours), and the Mass. Their names, the hours they are held, and the times they occupy are given below:

Office Name	Starting Time	Elapsed Time
Vigils (Matins, Night Office)	3:30 A.M.	30 minutes
Lauds	6:30 A.M.	30 minutes
Mass	7:00 A.M.	40 minutes
Terce	9:00 A.M.	15 minutes
Sext	11:45 A.M.	15 minutes
None	2:00 P.M.	15 minutes
Vespers	5:30 P.M.	30 minutes
Compline	7:30 P.M.	30 minutes

These times are traditional and vary at other monasteries, depending mainly on the kind of work the monks have. The time for Mass is even more variable. On Sundays, Mass at Palisades begins at 10:00 A.M.

The ritual at the offices consists of singing psalms, with accompanying antiphons and hymns. This part of the liturgy was especially important to St. Benedict. Eleven of the 73 Chapters in the *Rule*, or almost one-sixth, are devoted to the conduct of the offices. The singing of the psalms is antiphonal: The choir is divided into two parts, facing each other on opposite sides of the church. One side sings a verse, then the other side responds, followed by the first side, until the psalm has been completed. After each psalm, the monks bow from the waist while singing, "Praise the Father, the Son, and the Holy Spirit, both now and forever, The God who is, who was, and is to come at the end of the ages. Amen." The melody is usually a form of plainsong (see Gelineau 1963:253ff). Since Vatican II, practically all liturgy at Palisades is in English. For some years this change generally precluded the use of traditional Gregorian chant (a loss keenly felt by some). During the office, a minute or more of silence is provided for meditation.

The psalms are so distributed through the hours that all 150 are sung in two weeks. More time is spent singing the psalms during the major hours (Vigils, Lauds, and Vespers) than during the minor or "little" hours (Terce, Sext, and None). The wording of some of the psalms caused problems when they were first sung in English, specifically those traditionally known as the "cursing psalms." For example, from Psalm 34 (Septuagint numbering; 35 in the Hebrew), verse 6: "Let their path be slippery and dark; let God's angel pursue them" (Gelineau 1963). Experimentally, this and similar verses were omitted for a time. However, efforts to delete them have been abandoned. As one monk put it, he conceives of the psalms as being sung by an old Jew, advanced in years of prayer, honestly bringing to God all of his problems and praise. Part of the devotion in the office is coming to understand how this old Jew felt.

The Mass is the most important part of the liturgy. It may be regarded as the dramaturgical reenactment of the passion of Christ. The analogy of the drama is even more appropriate with the concelebrated Mass, where monks who are priests gather around the altar and say the Mass with the chief celebrant (or president, who may or may not be the abbot). The concelebrants, the other monks, and the congregation act as the chorus in the ancient form of Greek drama.

The Mass has two major parts: the liturgy of the word and the liturgy of the eucharist. After the songs and prayers of the entrance ritual, there is reading from the Old Testament, the writings of the Apostles, and the Gospel, followed by a brief homily or sermon.

The liturgy of the eucharist begins with the bringing of the "gifts" (the unconsecrated bread and wine) to the altar. As the priest (or priests) offers prayers over the gifts, they are believed to become the substance of the body and blood of Christ. These prayers, as with virtually all of the Mass except the homily, are read from a large, bound, printed manual. After the prayers but before the bread is broken is a ritual of peace where priests and congregation shake hands or (which is more usual for the monks) give the "kiss of peace," a simple embrace. (For some, the embrace is more stylized and formal.) It produces a strong, positive effect. The bread is then broken and distributed to the monks (guests receive Communion wafers). The wine is served to both monks and guests in a common cup. The concluding ritual consists of prayer, a blessing, and a dismissal. There may be a closing song or procession. Music is variously accompanied by the organ, the guitar, or is sung a cappella.

All forms of focused, conscious prayer are incorporated into the Mass. Diffused prayer occurs in the interval after the sharing of the bread and wine. The Mass may thus be considered the ultimate conscious prayer of the Roman Catholic Church.

Built into the liturgical cycle of the monk's daily life and the two-week psalm cycle of the offices is the cycle of the liturgical year. This cycle revolves around the two major feast days of the Christian religion: Christmas and Easter. Christmas is anticipated early in December with Advent and lasts until Epiphany (January 6, or "Little Christmas"). Easter is preceded by the forty days of Lent (beginning with Ash Wednesday), culminates with Holy Week, including Good Friday, and ends with Pentecost (see Chapter 11). Interspersed throughout the year, even during the Christmas and Easter seasons, are other feast days. Some are important to the entire Church, such as the Solemnity of Mary the Mother of God on January 1. Others, such as the Feast of Saints Robert, Alberic, and Stephen (the Cistercian founders), are specific to Cistercian monasteries; July 16 is the anniversary of the founding of the abbey, celebrated as any major feast. On feast days, there are special prayers, psalms, and readings, so the Mass and the major hours last somewhat longer.

In nonconscious prayer, one is not *unconscious* but is simply not conscious of the prayer at the moment, even though the person is saying it. This type of prayer occurs in the liturgy, but its extent is unknown. An example was provided by one of the monks. Consider that the entire Psalter is recited every two weeks. When one has been a monk for decades, these 150 psalms can be learned by heart; and then without being aware of it, one can go into other forms of prayer such as meditation and contemplation while chanting the psalms.

The liturgy serves several purposes. First, it focuses attention on the monk's life as a life of prayer. Second, it brings the monks together physically and thus fosters cohesion. Third, it brings them together at specified times, thereby regulating the life and enhancing obedience.

DIFFUSED PRAYER

One may describe the expressive form of diffused prayer by the folk saying "Actions speak louder than words." That is, what one does on a day-to-day or even on an hour-by-hour basis is as important as any form of worship (Lawrence 1954). Expressive prayer can thus become important in any occupation. Indeed, some religious groups, such as the Hutterites, prohibit entirely certain forms of labor, such as tavern keeping, and extol others such as agriculture. The Trappist-Cistercians have a comparable tradition that agricultural occupations are desirable.

By his very presence in the monastery, the monk is involved in expressive prayer each moment of his life in everything he does. He has chosen to become a monk, which means following a way of life. He has further chosen this way of life in this particular monastery. Therefore, being where he is, doing what he does, it an act of communicating with God.

Expressive prayer differs in comparison to most of the others considered so far in that one does not necessarily or even usually think of God when driving a tractor or pulling beets or herding cattle. At best, God will rise to one's attention and then sink from consciousness as more immediate problems are confronted. The question then is, how can work be expressive prayer, especially when one is not conscious of God? A basic psychological assumption is that one cannot think two thoughts at the same time. If this is true, then the significance of nonconscious prayer becomes more apparent. When during one's occupation, attention is necessarily directed to the immediate problem at hand, then it can matter very much that the problem has been chosen because of one's initial commitment.

The next forms of prayer, meditation and contemplation, are incorporated into the life of the monks by a tradition known as *lectio divina* (divine or spiritual reading). The prayer begins with reading sacred or spiritually oriented texts. As the monk reads, a phrase or word may catch his attention: "For all have sinned" (Romans 3:23). "For the wages of sin is death" (Romans 6:23), or "Jesus wept" (John 11:35), or even "God," or "love," (the shorter the better). He ruminates on this phrase or word, considering what it means for his life, the relation with his fellow monks, and so on. This exercise is meditation. (It is diffused only in being unplanned.)

This form of meditation differs from spiritual exercises (or "mental discourse" in the ascetic literature), where one proceeds through a series of steps in order to reach some conclusion. The monk's meditation is not intended to achieve anything specific. According to Pennington (1982: 31),

In the early monastic tradition, meditation involved primarily a repetition of the word of revelation, or the word of life one received from his spiritual father or from some other source. The word...may be a whole phrase or sentence...quietly repeated over and over again, even with the lips.... In time, the repetition would tend to interiorize and simplify the word, as its meaning was assimilated. For during the repetition the mind...received the word more and more, entered into it more and more, assimilated it and appropriated it, until it was formed by the word and its whole being was a response to the word.

Finally, the monk may pass from such thinking to being simply in prayer, in a state of communion with God. In its advanced form, words are not needed, just as old friends can enjoy each other's company without speaking. This is contemplative prayer (also called centering, mental, or quiet prayer). It is not "thinking of nothing." The monk is instead in a state of loving surrender to his God; he is in agapé love (Johnston 1973, Peers 1960).

The difference between meditation and contemplation lies in the thought process. In meditation, one is thinking of something, usually quite actively. In contemplation, one strives to ignore thought, to go beyond thinking, and insofar as possible, achieve a state of total surrender.

CONTEMPLATIVE PRAYER

The monk does not divide his prayer into certain types. He looks on prayer as a unity. Thomas Merton (1969:29) uses the "formula" *psalmodia*, *lectio*, *oratio* and *contemplatio*: psalmody, reading, speaking, and contemplation. In this approach the monk uses the psalms and the office to begin prayer. Then he reads (*lectio*) reverently, letting his thoughts (meditations) dwell on whatever moves him (as discussed previously). From here he goes into contemplative prayer.

Pennington, also a Trappist monk, has a slightly different "formula": *lectio*, *meditatio*, *oratio*, *contemplatio* (1982:30). *Lectio* may involve reading. It may simply evolve when one is sitting in the woods or looking at the stars. Then one passes from meditation to vocal prayer to contemplation. But one need not follow such steps. One may pass directly from chanting the psalms in the office to contemplative prayer, or go from contemplation to spiritual reading.

Pennington (1982:34–35) does suggest some steps to contemplative prayer, based on the writings of the anonymous 14th-century author of *The Cloud of Unknowing* (Anon. 1973):

Simply sit relaxed and quiet (Chapter 44) [:130].

Center all your attention and desire on him and let this be the sole concern of your mind and heart (Chapter 3) [:48].

Gather all your desire into one single word that the mind can easily retain, choose a short word rather than a long one.... But choose one that is meaningful to you. Then fix it in your mind so that it will remain there come what may. (Chapter 7) [:56].

Let this little word represent to you God, in all his fullness and nothing less than the fullness of God. Let nothing except God hold sway in your mind and heart (Chapter 40) [:100].

Such is as close to a method for contemplative prayer as I have found (see also Keating 1986). One other comment, however, is needed. Contemplative prayer is highly individualistic. What works for one may not work for another. For example, some may object that one should not even think of God, for any thought of God is inadequate.

Obviously, contemplative prayer is not normally a group activity (Philippe 1990:24), and thus one can hardly provide a sociological analysis. However, contemplation is one of the basic reasons for the existence of Trappist monasteries, it is supported by the monastery, and it is taught by the monks (to the extent that it can be taught).

Although I first learned how to pray contemplatively at Palisades, I have few useful accounts of this prayer from the monks. They would volunteer comments, but when I asked directly, they would tend to be very hesitant. However, I have interviewed monks at another Trappist-Cistercian monastery who were highly articulate in discussing contemplation. Thus, though the following discussions are not with monks at Palisades, this is how they pray.

The main problem in discussing contemplative prayer is that, as is true with love, it cannot be done adequately. But as with love, one can say something, and though the expression may be exasperatingly incomplete, one who has had the experience will understand. In other words, contemplative prayer is experiential.

My first discussion of contemplative prayer was with Br. Bernard in the bookstore. He just started talking about contemplation. I asked him, "What does contemplation mean to you?" That opened a floodgate. Basic to his thought is that contemplation is an unfolding. His first word was: "Presence." Then, the next: "Listen." He cites the opening words of Benedict's *Rule*. "Listen, my son, to your master's precepts, and incline the ear of your heart" (*Rule*, Doyle 1948, Prologue:1). He said that it does no good to talk about it, because too much of ourselves gets into what we say.

I asked specifically, "How do you go about praying contemplatively?" He said that you have to learn to listen, again. Wherever you are, in prison, in a house of prostitution, wherever, you have to stop and realize that you are in the cone of God's love, and then you have to let it (God's love) unfold. All of us are mystics. He prefers the scriptural word "prophecy," the act of letting God speak.

One day I had a talk with Br. Erhard, the guest master. I asked him, "What does prayer mean to you?"

A: Communicating with God—speaking and listening. It also means adoration and worship. The first thing I do when I pray is adore God in all three persons: Father, Son, and Holy Spirit. I place myself in their presence and listen. I don't hear anything, but I listen. You might not hear anything then, but you are liable to hear something later on in the day. And it's because you listened.

It's also loving—between all three persons—Father, Son, and Holy Spirit. It's seldom asking, though I do use the prayer of petition. What I ask is the grace to do God's will and the grace to accept what God has for me this day.

Q: What does contemplative prayer mean to you?

A: Sitting in God's presence. Mostly listening and loving without words—though you use words occasionally. Because that communication of love seems to be the height of our prayer. It's a point at which almost all action stops. We're anxious to do God's will, but contemplative prayer is where we stop acting. It's God's union and love. It can happen anyplace. You can be walking in the woods and sit on a rock. It's union with God's love.

Q: You have talked of union with God. What is the meaning of that?

A: It's a quietness, a stillness, one in which you give yourself in union and joy. Your whole happiness is in this—it's complete union in friendship. It's the most important thing. Nothing else matters at that moment. You experience real happiness. You realize that real happiness is nothing other than this union with your most perfect friend.

These moments don't last too long, but out of that grows your relations with other people, because these relations grow out of your relation with God.

Q: Have these experiences increased since you have been a monk?

A: It would increase because of the environment. The atmosphere here contributes to a life of prayer. Saturday during your talk, Reverend Father [the Abbot] said that he made a distinction between contemplatives and the contemplative life [canonically]. There are contemplatives outside of the monastery as well as within it. I feel I have to answer a call from God—so I'm much better for being here. It's hard for me to think what it would have been like if I hadn't answered that call. I can't conceive of it, really. In a sense, I'm not here because I want to be here [he said this with a big, beautiful smile]. It's like being in the guest house [this is his fourth full year as guest master]. I do it because my superior told me to, and I find that there are graces for doing it because of that.

Fr. Ailred, the abbot, came by after None (the afternoon office) and we had a talk of about two hours. I mentioned the difficulties I had in getting responses on contemplative prayer at Palisades. He said that it was because they had been taught not to speak of such things, presumably by the Church. For him, contemplative prayer was any type of prayer that went beyond meditation. He said at one point, "If you've got to think about your doing it, you are not doing it." It takes many different forms. A very common form is an awareness of the presence, as discussed in the writings of Teresa of Avila. St. John of the Cross talks of the night of the senses, and experience of the absence of God. At times, when one is beginning to pray contemplatively, he will be conscious of such an absence. Trials that the Lord sends are sometimes not appreciated for what they are, as cleansings, simplifications, and so people try escapes—looking at television all the time or something like that. One purpose of the monastery is eliminating the escapes. Awareness of one's own sinfulness is part of the same thing. The good thing about the monastery, he said, "is that you can get to the point where you have nothing else to do and so you have to face yourself and your relation with God."

These accounts are not meant to be statistically representative. In the first place, only one monastery is included, and monasteries differ in this respect. Second, I quoted only those who wished to speak. Many will say, as some of the monks said, that it is impossible to discuss contemplative prayer—and they won't.

THE VOICE OF GOD

Prayer is defined as communicating with God. It follows that prayer is a two-way process. How then does the monk hear God speaking? Most of the time, there is no sensory contact. Ideally, the monk prays about something and trusts that God hears. Some wait for a feeling of peace following their decision. Others are sensitive to circumstances. One monk was just entering the monastery and narrowly missed being in an automobile accident. This circumstance prompted him to conclude that God intended him to be in the monastery. He eventually became abbot. Such sensitivity is part of a more general attitude, which one monk described as "the gift of the present." Every moment that God gives to us is a special gift, and it is up to us to appreciate it for what it is. Most often the circumstance is simply a gift: the freshness of a morning, a good meal, the peace of a given moment. At other times, God is trying to tell us something in the situation.

Others have more apparent communication, such as visions. One monk, a simple and unaffected person, had a vision in which God showed him the whole world at once. I asked him what it was like. He said that he was surprised that God could get so much into such a little head. He had had other visions about the nature of God and about various monks.

The most tangible manifestation I have heard concerns a man who later became an oblate. He had purchased a grove of redwood trees, and was walking in it in the moonlight. It was so beautiful that he wept. Then he heard a voice telling him that the grove was God's gift to him, but that God would want it back some day. Shortly after, a group of Trappistine nuns came to him looking for some land on which to build a convent. He gave them the grove.

Such open answers to prayer are not normally sought by the monks. They are usually content to offer their lives to God, with confidence that God will do what is best.

DEVOTION TO MARY

The founders of the Cistercian Order decided that all houses would be dedicated to the Virgin Mary. St. Bernard (see Chapter 1) had a strong Marian spirituality and had a decided influence on all succeeding generations of Cistercians. The names of Trappist monasteries begin with "Our Lady of," though popularly these words are seldom used. Thus, Our Lady of Gethsemani is known simply as Gethsemani.

Until the mid-1950s, the Little Office of the Blessed Virgin (a complete set of liturgical hours) was sung before each canonical hour of the office. This has been replaced by a simple commemoration of Mary at each hour. Palisades has a sung antiphon at the end of each office except Vigils; at Compline the hymn to Mary, "Salve Regina," is the last song of the day. Palisades has at least six icons of Mary within the enclosure. Formerly, each monk began his religious name with Mary and then signed his name, Br. M. Paul, Fr. M. Thomas, for example. This practice has largely stopped.

Although devotions to Mary have declined, she is still honored. One monk estimated that two-thirds of the monks say the rosary regularly.

Such remarks fail to show the emotional side, the devotion to Mary. One monk expressed himself thus:

One aspect of my personal relationship with her is consecration: I have (like Pope John Paul) turned my whole life over to her to do with as she pleases, and I interiorly renew this act many times each day when "talking" with her. I trust her absolutely to bring me to God, to Jesus, in this life and the next: this is the role I believe God has given her in the plan of salvation, to "mother" us (in the order of grace) just as she did Jesus in the natural order....

All this, of course, presupposes the absolute subordination of Mary (who is, after all, only a creature) to Jesus in our Christian life. Jesus is everything—without Him, Mary is just another Jewish girl who lived and died 2,000 years ago. But in fact, we *do* have Jesus—and hence Mary's unique role in God's scheme of salvation, and in our (my) personal salvation. God's mother is my mother.

This intensity is not evident in all. At the other end of the spectrum is the more intellectual approach: Mary is a role model, one particularly appropriate for monks since she too stood alone before God. One monk said he would not pray to Mary in words, but noted that his prayer is becoming increasingly nonverbal (contemplative) anyway. He admitted that he had been criticized for not giving enough attention to Mary in his homilies, but he thought he had!

ATTITUDES CONCERNING PRAYER

Statistics are available from the contemplative survey (Research Committee of CMSW 1969) on how the monks feel about contemplative prayer, liturgy, and conditions for prayer, particularly silence and place. (The questions are found in Appendices H to J and are numbered according to the sequence used by the survey). The tables show that Palisades is very close to the other Trappist houses in matters of prayer.

Almost all of the monks—over 80 percent and at times over 90 percent—had very positive attitudes about prayer. For practically all, prayer was to some extent "a contemplative way of participating in the salvation of the world by petitioning God for the world's needs, thanking him for his kindness, praising him for his creation, and making retribution for the sins of man."[1] For almost as many, prayer was a conversation with God.[2]

The monks usually did not think of prayer as a means of self-realization ("to go down into myself"). Some of them thought it was some of the time,[3] but often they did not, and many objected (approximately one-fourth). Nor was prayer in contrast to an active life.[4] Many monks would make this contrast, but over a third did not.

Though impossible to describe completely, and certainly not described statistically, some aspects of mental (contemplative) prayer can be enumerated and are mentioned in Appendix H.[5] Many monks (both at Palisades and among the other Trappists) rejected the statement that prayer is "a stillness which God fills," though most accepted it to some extent.[6] Even more did they reject the idea that prayer is "the occasion to go down into myself and to be really present to myself."[7] The contemplative objects to the purposiveness in both questions. God may or may not fill the stillness, but the prayer is still there. The monk does go down into himself and is therefore really present to himself, but he sees this as one of the ultimate distractions, something he must go *beyond*. In a deeper sense it is something that happens because of and even after mental prayer—but it is not its purpose. Very few monks surveyed thought of prayers simply as spiritual exercises.[8]

Whatever mental prayer is, as one abbot told me, "that's what the life here is all about." Most of the surveyed monks enjoyed mental prayer or value it deeply.[9] Almost three-fourths felt that their prayer was always or sometimes contemplative (mental), and practically all felt that they practice mental prayer at least occasionally.[10] Similarly, almost all felt at least somewhat informed concerning methods of mental prayer, with about half feeling "very well informed."[11] Thus, though the monks may not have been able to tell the uninitiated what mental prayer is all about, they were extensively involved in it.

The Trappists were formerly known as monks who did not speak. Though this is an exaggeration, strictures upholding silence were a part of the formal structure until 1968, when the rule of silence was heavily modified. None of the monks wanted the near-total silence of former days (and most experienced it). Still, most did not know quite how to change. The option adopted at many monasteries, including Palisades Abbey, is one of specified periods and places for silence.

Silence is an aid to contemplation as well as a monastic discipline.[12] But silence is not enough. During the days of more extensive silence, sign language was used as a means of communication, and this had the unintended effect of often disrupting one's solitude. Mental prayer is, at least at first, a very demanding discipline and can be disturbed rather easily. Monks communicating by signs can be almost as distracting as whispered conversation. Thus, preserving certain places of silence means there are more likely to be places where one can have solitude (since persons who wish to communicate are more likely to go where they can communicate).

Most monks were satisfied regarding change toward having less silence,[13] but a significant minority felt that "we should not have this," or "we have gone too far on this." Palisades monks felt more this way than did the monks at the other monasteries. It is my impression that Palisades did in fact have more talking than the other monasteries. Certainly there was little indication that the monks wanted less silence.[14]

Closer to the meaning of solitude is enclosure and separation from the world. In the study, enclosure was seen as "somewhat" of "a physical separation for the sake of a spiritual involvement with the world."[15] The idea here is to be physically separated from the distractions of the world so that one may pray for it—that is, become spiritually involved. Enclosure, however, did "not at all" mean that no one saw you.[16] On this subject Palisades departed rather sharply from the other Trappist monasteries. Most monks at Palisades rejected the notion that they should not seek to know outsiders well, whereas most of the other Trappists who were sampled would have agreed that such contact is at least "somewhat" of an infringement on the spirit of enclosure.[17] Only a minority of Palisades Trappists felt that "withdrawal or hiddenness from the world" is essential to being a contemplative.[18]

Having a place of retreat was important to many Trappists, but not most.[19] About one-third wanted more time for prayer, but most felt that the current conditions (1968) were "just about right."[20] Trappist life was more than prayer and retreat, however; penance was essential according to almost two-thirds.[21] Though penance is more than deprivation, the association of suffering and denial with transcendental communion is a condition experienced in many cultures.

Being a contemplative, therefore, means prayer, both liturgical and mental, it means silence and more especially solitude, and it means deprivation or sacrifice. However, the meanings of being a contemplative are not always clear, especially as one leaves the topic of prayer. Being a contemplative does not mean being "of service,"[22] and the monks feel that there should be some changes made in the focus of renewal and the rules of their order, but they are not entirely clear about the nature of the changes.[23] Most want change through renewal, and most feel that the renewal should be in the interior life, but there is significant opposition and uncertainty.[24]

In summary, most of the monks surveyed had very positive attitudes toward prayer, contemplative prayer in particular. But it is not meaningful to describe prayer as a means to an end. Respondents felt that liturgy is essential, particularly praying the Divine Office together (at least some canonical hours). They did not regard the changes made in the liturgy as radical (no matter how extensive they were in actuality), and they valued the new liturgy. Most supported a limited form of silence (at certain times and places, or speaking only when there was a good reason), and most felt that the monastery should not move toward a condition of less silence. The monks at Palisades differed most sharply from other Trappists in that most at Palisades did not feel separation is essential to being a contemplative; most other Trappists feel it is. But Palisades did move substantially toward more separation from the world in the decades that followed this questionnaire.) Having a place of retreat was important to many but not most. Penance, however, was considered essential. Finally, though the monks were not always certain about the changes they would like, they felt that the central focus of renewal should be on the interior life and that major revision should be made in the rules.

SOME DIFFERENCES

Palisades monks are very much Cistercian in their attitudes toward prayer. No more than 5 of the 25 questions examined (not all of which are presented here) showed Palisades monks differing significantly from the others (that is, more greatly than would be expected by chance).

The largest difference concerns withdrawal or hiddeness from the world.[25] Monks at Palisades generally did not feel that seeking to know outsiders well, "even though you remain within the cloister," was an infringement on the spirit of enclosure, whereas other Trappists tended to feel that it was.[26] Also, Palisades monks were more willing to change rules.[27] However, more Palisades monks felt "we have gone too far" in trying to have less silence,[28] and more Palisades monks believed in the "meditative search for the meaning of life" through scripture and other writings.[29]

On one side, since separation from the world is a Cistercian ideal, then Palisades monks are less Cistercian. On the other side, having less silence runs counter to traditional Cistercian custom, and of course the meditative search for the meaning of life is more Cistercian, and Palisades monks showed themselves to be more Cistercian on both issues.

Thus, according to these data, Palisades monks are if anything more Cistercian than the other Trappists. For most of the questions, however, the differences were no more than would be expected by chance.

CONCLUSION

Prayer itself is an act of love, and in all its variations it is one of the chief forms of agapé. Prayer is the essential reason for the monk's presence in the monastery. We tend to become desensitized when prayer is accompanied with such terms as "adoration," "worship," "surrender," and even "obedience," but each of these terms have been used because they express various facets of love.

Of all the forms of prayer, the liturgy is the most formal, and this formality masks the expression of love it contains. But the liturgy exists to remind the monk of the love relation to his God and to remind him of the love he must bear toward his fellow monks. This love can be sometimes almost unnoticeable. One monk told me that he was much comforted and greatly strengthened when he came down to the church at 3:30 in the morning to find some of his other brothers already there. These monks were probably unaware that they were having such an influence. Liturgy contributes to cohesion, and cohesion is a form of love.

But cohesion is a love of group members, a love of people. Though the monk expresses his love for God in the liturgy, many feel that the deepest expression of that love is in contemplative prayer, the wordless, loving surrender of one's entire heart, mind, soul, and strength to the presence of God.

Love, as used here, is always transcendent—one transcends out to others or out to God. Concern for self is probably the single greatest threat to monastic life. Whenever a monk told me that he was not finding self-fulfillment in the monastery, I knew he was soon to leave. In contrast, whenever a monk was most concerned about prayer, no matter how he might complain about the difficulty, that monk would stay.

Whether in contemplative prayer, liturgy, or merely in one's work, love requires a going out from self, a transcendence. Prayer is a major means of achieving such a state.

NOTES

1. App. H, Q. 234. Percentages were obtained by combining the first two responses for each answer.
2. App. H, Q. 237.
3. App. H, Q. 240.
4. App. H, Q. 238.
5. App. H, especially Qs. 239 and 240.
6. App. H, Q. 239.
7. App. H, Q. 240.
8. App. H, Q. 10.
9. App. H, Q. 365.
10. App. H, Q. 386.
11. App. H, Q. 588.
12. App. I, Q. 476.
13. App. I, Q. 611.
14. See also App. I, Q. 609.
15. App. J, Q. 303.
16. App. J, Q. 304.
17. App. J, Q. 305.
18. App. J, Q. 306.
19. App. J, Q. 370.
20. App. J, Q. 630.
21. App. J, Q. 308.
22. App. J, Q. 458.
23. App. J, Qs. 459, 460.
24. Ibid.
25. App. J, Q. 306.
26. App. J, Q. 305. Responses "high degree" and "somewhat" are combined.
27. App. J, Q. 460.
28. App. I, Q. 611.
29. App. H, Q. 241.

Chapter 11

Asceticism and Recreation

[On whether monks ought to have anything of their own] This vice especially is to be cut out of the monastery by the roots. Let no one presume to give or receive anything without the Abbot's leave, or to have anything as his own ... since they are not permitted to have even their bodies or wills at their own disposal.

—*Rule for Monasteries*, Chapter 33

Normally, one would consider asceticism the opposite of recreation, and in a sense, this is true. But the schedule of life in monasteries combines the two so that recreation alternates and combines with asceticism extensively. Asceticism is the ground, the general tenor of monastic life. Recreation is present within a context of asceticism. The two activities are distinct; yet, as the present chapter will show, they are often inseparable in practice. ("Recreation" is used in its broadest sense, meaning "to restore or refresh" and not only "fun and games.")

Asceticism in the monastery is accomplished mainly by living the religious vow of obedience and through poverty and chastity. The discussion begins with obedience. Poverty is included with abstinence. Normally, chastity would be considered here, but it has already been treated in Chapter 6. Another form of asceticism, though not a vow, is certainly part of the monastic life: solitude. (For a discussion of Benedictine vows, see Van Zeller 1959:48.)

According to Thomas Merton (1949:377), asceticism is "the doctrine and practice of self-discipline and control of ... the natural faculties in order to arrive at moral, intellectual and spiritual perfection." Of course, monks do not expect extensive perfection in this mortal life. But Merton continues: "In the highest sense, asceticism means the effort of man's soul, aided by God's grace, to deliver himself from every attachment ... that falls short of

God himself." In other words, asceticism is simplification, "the active practice of virtues, with the help of God's grace, preparing [the monk] for or
accompanied by mystical contemplation, in which the chief work is performed passively in the soul by God himself" (Merton 1949:378). Asceticism, then, is simplification that will aid the monk in walking closer with
God.

OBEDIENCE

Obedience is ascetical in that it simplifies the monk's life and it requires
mortification of self-will. It was intended "to minimize internal dissension
and liberate the monk for his primary spiritual concerns" (Renna 1980:3).
The life of the monk is not slavish obedience to an abbot. More properly
speaking, the monk works with his abbot and the abbot works with him.
Though a dictatorial rule may well have been possible in former years, I
know of no abbot who acts in such a way today. As it is lived, obedience
is found in conforming to the "usages" of a particular house. The usages
are "a set of monastic customs, determining ceremonies and conduct in all
aspects of communal monastic life" (Merton 1949:388). These rules govern
the times when the monk will rise, when he will join in liturgical prayers,
when he will eat, work, go to bed, and so forth. Usages vary from house
to house, but there is a remarkable similarity. Their main purpose is to
enable community members to live in close association. But the usages also
aid in simplification, since the monk need not concern himself about details
of living: when he will sleep, eat, work. He is freed to be concerned with
only one thing: how he is relating to God and to his fellow man, which for
him will be mainly monks.

The one area in his life in which the monk can spend time freely is his
spiritual development: What will he read? How much? How will he pray?
How long? Such questions should be the ultimate concern of his life, and
obedience to the usages permit this.

POVERTY AND ABSTINENCE

Poverty is discussed in Chapter 7. The focus here is on poverty as asceticism, wherein one turns from acquisitive desires and attempts to lead a
simpler life. The monk owns nothing. In a sense, however, this statement
must be qualified, for he has his own place in the refectory, his room, his
place at liturgy, his clothes, and so on. But these statements say no more
than that the monk has his personal space, for he is not free to do what he
wants with these "things," such as give them to guests, for example.

The vow of poverty may be traced to the Acts of the Apostles (2:44–45):
"And all who believed were together and had all things in common; and
they sold their possessions and goods and distributed them to all, as they

had need" (see also Acts 4:34–35). The *Rule* (Doyle 1948, Ch. 33:51) is even more stringent: "for all their necessities let them look to the Father of the monastery.... Let all things be common to all, as it is written, and let no one say or assume that anything is his own."

The spirit of poverty concerns not necessarily the amount or quality of what the monk has but his very having of things at all. Somewhat related is the practice of abstinence, which means surrendering even "legitimate" pleasures, such as tobacco, sex, certain kinds of food (the monks are generally vegetarian), and alcohol (save for communion and occasional celebrations). Though two or three monks have been or are alcoholics and a few smoke, such acts are performed surreptitiously, though most of the monks are aware of what is happening.

Fasting is institutionalized. The monks eat no meat of animals or fowl (although St. Benedict only prohibited the flesh of four-footed animals). There are seasons of fasting, such as from September 15 to Advent and from Ash Wednesday to Easter. (Advent formerly was also a season of fasting but is no longer so for these monks.) During such times, only one meal is ordinarily taken each day (at noon). The entire community always eats this meal together. Since breakfast and supper are served cafeteria-style and one can eat at any time within approximately an hour, one may skip breakfast and supper without anyone's knowledge. In other words, one may fast in secret.

Silence is the rule at all meals, but at the noon meal, one monk is appointed each week to read aloud to the community. The reading may be a biography, history, theology, novel, or even sociology (this book was read in an earlier draft). There is no discussion of the reading during the mealtime.

Normally, the monk has seven hours of sleep (8:15 P.M. to 3:15 A.M.). Some do with less, either staying up later or rising earlier (as for prayer). One monk told me that he considered sleep a luxury.

SOLITUDE

The life of the Trappist-Cistercian monastery is structured to maximize opportunity for solitude, so that one may more effectively commune with God. Solitude may be absolute or relative. Absolute solitude occurs in the monk's cell, during solitary walks, in retreats, during the Great Silence (8 P.M. to 8 A.M.), and in other places such as the cloister walk, at church, and in the library, where speaking is not permitted. Relative solitude occurs at meals, in liturgy, and at work.

Solitude is a state of mind rather than a form of silence. The monks invented a sign language to communicate without unduly disturbing the solitude of others. Before Vatican II, the monks did not have private rooms (cells) and had to find solitude elsewhere. However, the monastic cell has an ancient place both in the cenobitic (communal) and the eremitic (hermit) life. The following quotation is from the "Sayings of the Fathers" (in Merton 1960:30) attributed to the hermits and monks of Egypt, Palestine, Arabia, and Persia in the fourth century: "A certain brother went to Abbot Moses in Scete, and asked him for a good word. And the elder said to him: Go, sit in your cell, and your cell will teach you everything."

RECREATION

Recreation is a universal human phenomenon, found even in places where severely curtailed, as in prisons and mental asylums (Hillery 1968). It exists in both institutionalized and uninstitutionalized forms. When institutionalized, it may be defined as patterned and pleasure-giving behavior performed in groups. Activities that make up recreation in the narrow sense are feasts, games, music, songs, dances, and stories.

These activities occur in monasteries, but primarily within the context of religious celebration. What is most impressive is the way ascetical practices alternate and integrate with recreation. The interplay is exhibited nowhere more clearly than in the liturgy of the hours and in the celebration of the Mass. Though these ceremonies are in themselves asceticism, they are also recreation. Ascetically, the monk must stop what he is doing seven times a day and perform these rituals, always in common. But singing is pleasurable and is a universal form of recreation. Thus, in the asceticism of the liturgy, the monks find refreshment in song. Also, one should not overlook the effort of the monks to beautify the church where this liturgy is conducted.

Therefore, recreation restores or refreshes the monk in his ascetical practices. Not only is recreation contained in asceticism, but asceticism is found in recreation. The celebration of Christmas and Easter, for example, require preparation, extra time in liturgy, and loss of sleep. Hard work itself can be recreation, as in sports, jogging, and so forth.

Feasts and festivals are the most universal forms of recreation. Two major festivals in the monastery are given special attention, Christmas and Easter. Of particular interest is the way recreation persists and is even cultivated (as in these feasts), in spite of the prohibition of St. Benedict on laughter: "But as for coarse jests and idle words or words that move to laughter, these we condemn everywhere with a perpetual ban, and for such conversation we do not permit a disciple to open his mouth" (Doyle 1948, Ch. 6:21; see also Chs. 4 and 7). Laughter occurs in the monastery probably as often as anywhere else, and the monks displayed no guilt over this. And though "coarse jests" are in principle excluded, festivals are not. It is to these that we now turn. Other recreational forms are considered at the end of the chapter.

CHRISTMAS

What follows are excerpts from my field notes of 1971.

December 21: Yesterday, I saw Fr. Peter. He had some lights and pine branches as Christmas decorations in his shop—"for a bit of the Spirit," he said. This and the decorations in the refectory are all that I saw. In the refectory, there is an advent wreath and a tinsel-and-peppermint colored wreath. That's it.

Fr. Simon brought me a large candle for Christmas in a holder made from a gallon wine jug.

Notes from the bulletin board: "It was suggested that the Advent (Gregorian) Kyrie be sung at Mass a few times this season.... It has also been suggested that the Gregorian 'Puer Natus est' be sung at Mass this Christmas. Responding to these and to other requests for occasional pieces of Gregorian Chant, we have decided to incorporate some of the more beautiful chants in our repertoire and sing them now and then." (From the Liturgy Committee).

Christmas Eve: More decorations appear as Christmas nears. There are lights on one of the trees in front of the monastery. Today wreaths abound: on the Abbot's door, one in the Church, and one on each of the three front doors. The Advent banner in the church, HE COMES, has been changed to, GREAT JOY TO ALL MEN. There is a big tree in the refectory, put up after the noon meal today. At noon we have ravioli made by Brs. Giovanni and Umberto from an old family recipe of Br. Giovanni. Tables are freshly painted in the refectory. We'll have new table cloths, too.

The novices put up a big poster in the entrance to the sanctuary with all the first names of the men in the community. The names were arranged in the shape of a huge dove.

The season seems to be one for visits. Various kinds of people have appeared, including a priest who used to be a monk here. The spirit in the house is good. I miss the expectance of Advent at home, with presents under the tree and children and family excitement, but there is an atmosphere here all its own. Fr. Job told me that he decorated his room with a tree and tinsel. "I guess I'm just a little child at heart when it comes to Christmas," and he had a big smile. He gave me the shove to do what I had been considering, and I went out and got some pine branches for my room. I bought some candles and a 25 cent creche from the Gift Shop. Br. James gave me a box of Christmas tree ornaments. My room smells now of beeswax and pine and glows red and tinsel. I miss my family but have peace. It is very quiet. I'll go to bed (7:45 P.M.) so I can get up for Midnight Mass.

Christmas Day: The bells are joyful (there's no other word). Mass went on until 1:15 A.M. Fr. Winnie complained that it should have been longer. Fr. Roger said, "The time just flew," and he beamed. There was a "collation" in the kitchen after Mass, which was really a cocktail party with Tom and Jerries for refreshment. Fr. John smiled at me over his and said, "Happy New Year!"

"How many have you had?" I asked.

"Where I'm from, this is a New Year's drink."

This was the "light repast" after the Mass that had been "advertised" on the bulletin board. How do you describe joy? Poetry helps: "The bright noise of this morning glittered back and forth among the Abbey walls." Smiles were everywhere, everyone talking to everyone else, even if in little knots of people. No loners, here. After some time, I left, but could still hear the gentle din from the floors below. Not loud, but unusual. I am accustomed to walking these halls in silence.

Then, the quiet of my room in the early Christmas morning, the rest between celebrations. The last I remember, the clock read 2:50 A.M.

The Christmas bells woke me at 6:30 A.M. I thought they were for Lauds, but they were for Mass. The colored lights from the Night Mass were lit, again. Green, red, and blue spotlights on one side, red, blue, and green on the other. Carols were the only hymns.

After Mass, Br. Bill came by. I asked him which was the more important, Christmas or Easter. "Easter, of course." Then I asked which had more excitement. He thought for a second, then, "Christmas, I suppose."

"Funny," I said, "I would have said Easter."

"It depends on what you mean by 'excitement.' "

I said that I really meant joy, "but that's a loaded term."

"Not at all," he said. "I would say Easter has more joy. But you have to remember, we've gone through extended fasting." He smiled, and then said, "So there's more to joy than spiritual things."

Community Mass was in the refectory. The tables (with new flowered table cloths) were arranged in a circle. I was late going down, and Fr. Job came to get me. The Mass was quite beautiful, and the acoustics were a wonderful relief after the old chapel, which had a tendency to smother sound. I did not commune, as usual, but the hugs (kiss of peace) from Br. Ted and Fr. Job were warm and sincere. Then supper, a feast, really, with wine, ice cream, soup, nuts, Waldorf salad, something like turkey dressing. The works. I swapped puns with Fr. Edgar and Br. Ted. Jokingly, I reminded them of the *Rule* and levity. Fr. Edgar: "But St. Benedict would understand that this is a special occasion."

December 26: I talked with Fr. Roger and Br. Keith about Mass last night, noting that the acoustics were much better. Fr. Roger: "We need all the praise we can get, like Peanuts needing all the friends he could get." Then I asked which season has more excitement, Christmas or Easter. Fr. Roger responded immediately, "Easter." Br. Keith did not know. They were too different to compare. Fr. Roger said, "Now if you had asked, which is more important, that would have been easier." I told him that I knew what he would say, but I wanted to hear him say it for himself. "Easter," he said.

"It's like the difference between childhood and adulthood," said Br. Keith. "You can't say which is better." Fr. Roger and I both thought adulthood was better. Then I asked, "Which is which?" Br. Keith: "Easter is adulthood. It represents maturity. Christmas is childhood."

EASTER

Easter symbolizes most of what is central to Christian and thus monastic faith. This is what the monks believe: Holy Communion, which the monk normally "celebrates" (with bread and wine) at least once a day each day of his life, was instituted by Jesus on the night he was betrayed and the night before he was crucified (1 Cor. 11:23–29). His death on the cross is a fulfillment of ancient prophecies (Psalms 22 and 69, especially verse 21) by which he became the sacrificial lamb (John 1:29), bearing on his body and through his death the sins of the world (Isaiah 53:1–11). His prayer of forgiveness on the cross (Luke 23:34) is realized in the resurrection, an event to which each of the gospels gives particular attention (Matt. 28, Mark 16, Luke 24, John 20–21). By rising from the dead and appearing on Easter morning, Jesus revealed himself as the Son of God. All of this is necessary to Easter.

The period before Easter is accentuated in several ways. According to the *Rule*, fasting begins on September 15 and lasts until Lent, which begins a more stringent fast broken by Easter (Doyle 1948, Ch. 41:60). Lent itself is a period wherein the monk is to be particularly solicitous of his spiritual welfare (Doyle 1948:Ch. 49). Finally, the last week in Lent, Holy Week, is marked by two special services: Maundy Thursday, on which Jesus celebrated the last supper with his disciples, and Good Friday, the day of his crucifixion and burial. Thus, Easter has a long preparation with increasing intensification of penance and is both a physical and a spiritual fulfillment. This development is described in the extracts from my field notes:

I arrived at the monastery to observe Holy Week on Wednesday, April 7, 1971. Fr. Pascal pointed out that "you were really lucky to get a room. We have been turning away people for months." The guest master had had a note appended to the retreat schedule: "Should there be any change in your plans, please call us collect immediately, as others are waiting should there be any cancellations." The number of cars in the parking lot gradually increased as the day went on. There seemed to be about 30 or 40 people for supper. The guest master expected 50 or 60 eventually.

Maundy Thursday: The fasts during Holy Week have not affected the quality of cooking in the monastic kitchen. The meals are as tasty as ever. And fasting and penance does not stop the monk's sense of humor. The following notice appeared on the bulletin board today:

The Voice of the Turtle Is Heard in Our Land

The natural changing of the season and monastic tradition dictate that at stated periods the monk shall go through his sordid possessions, ruthlessly casting aside, for the poor or for the dung heap, all that is superfluous and vain.

Let not him who is content with less be envious of him who needs more [from the *Rule*, Ch. 34:52], but let him who needs more not let his possessions stretch across the floor from door to door.

Each Son of Benedict, even though he only hang his hat within these walls, will be expected to clean his place or places, within the bootroom, from top to bottom within the next couple of days.

The angel of destruction will pass by and any place that does not bear a living name overhead shall feel the living weight of his sword.

The same shall apply to your place or box in the washroom. If your box or boxes are not marked, all within shall perish in the purge.

This edict has been posted following a suggestion of Fr. Abbot.

Prior

The next day, the following notice appeared, posted above the "edict":

I guess I didn't make myself clear. We are expected to dust and clean our places in the bootroom and in the washroom as well as getting rid of our accumulated junk and clothing.

Prior

And another note:

Washing of the Feet

As in the last years, the ceremony takes place during the Eucharist, after the Gospel. The abbot washes the feet of those in the front rows, only a gentle reminder to those priests and brothers to pre-wash their feet.

Saturday: Fr. Carl was complaining about the barley soup we had during Lent. He thought it was too much, that we should have just had bread and water. Eating the barley soup was for me a greater penance than just having bread and water. Even the cook's good graces could not improve it.

Easter Sunday morning began at midnight with the Pascal vigil and the lighting of the fires in the garth (courtyard). The community went in procession to the church. Candles were lit, then Mass was said. After, cake and cookies in the refectory and in the guest house. It was noisier in the guest house than in the cloister, but everywhere there was an air of celebration. I can say it best in poetry:

Paschal Meditation

> White robes, black night.
> Golden flecks of candle light.
> Deep soul words intoning God's history.
> Slowly, slowly, the expected blooms.
> The Lenten debt, the sorrow wait,
> Is over.
> A laughter ripples soft beneath the surface
> And shines forth in their eyes.
> The buried bells break out
> And sing their wonder.
> God has gone the end of grief.
> The world is Genesis again.

(Hillery 1991)

OTHER RECREATION

Numerous feasts are celebrated throughout the year, and though not as central to Christian theology as Christmas and Easter, they are still important. With special foods and at times a glass of wine, all these feasts include as part of their celebration music, songs, and stories (for example, the pertinent biblical accounts and other relevant traditional literature are read at each feast). Excluding Sundays (when work is never performed), there are 21 days on which no labor is done. For three of these days, work is optional. Four are secular holidays: Memorial Day, Independence Day, Labor Day, and Thanksgiving. The only things omitted that are normally found in communal recreation are games and dances. Some argue that even the dance is not ignored, as when the monks bow after singing each Psalm. Processions may also be considered a form of liturgical dance.

On reading this material, one monk observed that recreation in the monastery was made up of many little things: a sunset, variations in the seasons and in nature, and visits from one's family. One attains a heightened sense of perception. Recreation re-creates a sense of life, almost as if one stepped out of the pattern, but recreation is basically a part of the subdued rhythm of the liturgical year. Thus, it is understandable that the monks do not show much interest in additional recreational pursuits. Other recreation seems sporadic and idiosyncratic, such as an occasional volleyball game at the Fourth of July picnic. This lack of pattern is shown in conversations with several monks.

Br. Philip began thinking about recreation when speaking with the novice master, who remarked how serious the present cohort of novices were— perhaps too serious. This made him wonder why the order did not favor recreation as such. He thought that the monks needed some stimulus from outside themselves, that it was good to have a spirit of competition where one could get his emotions out. The smorgasbords (on the major feast days) were not really enjoyable for him.

I asked Br. Philip if he had any form of recreation, himself. He said he does some light reading occasionally, but that was about all. I asked: "Do you go on walks or anything like that?" He said, "I walk to work over at the barns, but that is not recreation. I remember once that someone was walking the guests around, and one of the guests asked if there was any recreation, and the monk said, 'Oh, no. Our manual labor takes care of that.' "

He thinks that there is a need for recreation, since this is a serious house. He would not have it every day and is against the "forced" recreation found in other orders. He talked with Br. Ben about his ideas but could not convince him. When he was at another monastery they made a visit to some nuns who were schoolteachers. They played a French game, something like monopoly. He was way ahead of the others, and then got "caught" by a series of bad cards, which kept him in "jail." He became quite frustrated and was able to express his frustration. It was the best experience of the six months, but it did not seem to help when he came back from the visit.

Br. Philip said his time after work is too important to give up for recreation. An hour now given to work could be used for it. He said that they used to play football a few years ago, but it just tired people out. It only lasted for a couple of Sundays. He felt he was in pretty good shape, because of his work around the barn, forking silage.

I asked Br. Henry what type of recreation he did. None, other than spiritual reading. Were there any other types? After dinner he glances at the newspaper. Occasionally he looks at other kinds of books in the library, but these are more distractions than recreation.

I pointed out the terrariums that Fr. Simon made. Br. Henry said, "I've made pottery. I could have the time for it now, but I would have to give up my spiritual reading." I asked if he made the pot that was used for ashes this morning (Ash Wednesday). "That was Brendan. He keeps at it. I have trouble kicking the fly wheel. If we had a mechanical wheel, I might be more attracted. What I like to do is sculpture."

Br. Ronald and Br. Victor carve wood. Br. Giovanni does craft work, as does Tom—he's also involved in remodeling the garth. Some finish chairs. Br. Alphonse works on rocks. Phineaus bakes. "We don't allow him to go over the deep end about it," said Br. Henry. "Some like to watch things grow, but they can overdo it—we have to give tomatoes away, and things like that. Fr. Tim and his apple orchard is an example." I commented that there is apparently no system of recreation, as such. A lot is combined with other things into something useful. I asked if anyone played chess, checkers, or cards. He said, "No. Once when I was a novice I saw someone playing cards. There are some jigsaw puzzles up in the infirmary that some people play with when they are sick."

"Are there any crossword puzzles?"

"Yes. I noticed one in the paper the other day that had been worked. Never noticed it before. More a mental thing probably." Some would take up mathematics as a change of pace, or some language. Calligraphy, that is, chancery script, is used as a form of meditation. Some listen to tapes and records. "I don't do very much of it. It's too much trouble to find the records. When renewal came, we tried movies and TV, but that tapered off." I asked him when the last time was that he read a novel that was not spiritual. He said it was *The Gang Who Couldn't Shoot Straight*—about six years ago. "It wasn't spiritual, but you could get a lot of spiritual insights from it." He also read a novel about a destroyer. "Went on a Gandhi kick some years ago, trying to find out what they had that we didn't. Most of the things like that have been since the renewal. You couldn't have read those things before, nor would you have wanted to."

I asked Br. Fred about his playing the guitar. "I used to," he said, "but not so much now."

I glanced at a wood carving he was making. "What about carving?"

"I wouldn't classify carving as recreation, though I do that."

"Why not?" I asked.

"It's a diversion at times, but not recreation."

ASCETICISM, RECREATION, AND ART

Though art and recreation overlap heavily, there would seem to be little connection between art and asceticism. Yet one of the fundamental principles of the ascetic is also vital to some art forms—simplification. This principle is most evident in the abbey's church. Stark walls and floors of stone, high beamed ceilings, plain wooden choir stalls, and a large block of black granite for the altar combine to produce an awesome experience. The simple white and black robes (only white in winter) and the plainsong and chants of the monks only add to the total aesthetic experience. But the primary purpose of this simplicity is not to create beauty but to worship God. The beauty is a by-product of that love, a love expressed in an ascetic response.

Not that the monks are insensitive to beauty. The church was intended to be beautiful; so is the singing. But the simplicity of the style reveals the purpose. The style is indeed purposeful. In the last century, there had been a tendency, not only at Palisades but in other Trappist monasteries as well, toward architectural embellishment, even rococo. But the call for renewal from the Second Vatican Council has stimulated the monks to return to the Cistercian simplicity that motivated the beginning of their order.

CONCLUSION

Monastic asceticism and recreation are part of the same process. To a significant degree, the asceticism of the monks is relieved by designated celebrations, which include feasts, music, songs, and stories—in other words, recreation. These practices are clearly embedded within a religious context. Asceticism is never completely withdrawn. The monks must always be celibate, for example. There are no monastic bacchanalia. But recreation has been part of monastic life since before St. Benedict's *Rule*. One should thus not argue that the alternation of asceticism and recreation is intentional. St. Benedict merely adapted monastery life to the Church calendar, and he probably did not think of the feast days as recreation, nor do the monks. But the behavior in feasts can be labeled as recreation in virtually any communal organization in the world.

Of the two processes, only asceticism can be directly related to love, specifically a love for God (agapé). Merton's (1948) definition of asceticism quoted earlier is relevant: delivering oneself "from every attachment...that falls short of God himself." Liturgy thus is a formal act of love for God, and this applies especially to the Mass.

It is more difficult to associate recreation with love, since recreation is pleasure seeking for its own sake and accordingly has an inherent self-orientation rather than being concerned with others. Its integration with asceticism therefore becomes that much more interesting. Whereas asceticism is sacrifice for love, recreation from this perspective becomes cessation from that sacrifice, a relief from it, though only a temporary one (as in the alternation of asceticism and recreation in the liturgy).

Chapter 12

Invalids and Death

For these sick brethren let there be assigned a special room and an
attendant who is God-fearing, diligent and solicitous.
—*Rule for Monasteries*, Chapter 36

THE INFIRMARY

When one first sees the infirmary at Palisades, it appears much as any
ordinary hospital, with patients' rooms lining the corridor, an office for the
infirmarian, a supply room, and something resembling a day room where
Mass may be said. But the infirmary is in fact quite different from a hospital
precisely in that it is in the monastery. There is no dichotomy between the
hospital and the outside, between patient and monk. One might view the
infirmary as simply another dormitory wing of the monastery, with the
distinction that the monks are in varying degrees not well and so have
conveniences that other dormitory wings do not have, particularly a private
bathroom for each room.

There were ten monks in the infirmary when the data for this part of the
study were gathered (1975). (The large number is because of the aging
population.) The infirmarian was there, of course, but he was also a patient
in that he had multiple sclerosis, with prospects of becoming more infirm
as the years went by. One brother helped him, since he could do no heavy
lifting. Those who stay in the infirmary are older monks, and some spend
more time there than others. Five slept in the infirmary because they had
heart conditions or arthritis and needed a toilet or hospital bed in their
room. Four monks were full-time patients: one dying of multiple myeloma,
one paralyzed by a stroke, one psychotic, and one with an undisclosed
illness. Thus, five of the monks participated fully in the life of the community
and the others only partially.

Mass is said in the infirmary three times a day (though one of the monks thought it was only twice). Several priests celebrate these rituals as a service to their brothers. Some of the patients attend all the Masses held there and also the community Mass in the morning, as one monk said, "because it is part of their piety."

According to the former infirmarian (for 33 years), himself now five years retired and a semipatient, four to six persons were usually in the infirmary, except during an epidemic of influenza—then every bed possible was used. He commented that the *Rule* gives care of the sick first place. ("Before all things and above all things, care must be taken of the sick, so that they will be served as if they were Christ in person; for He Himself said, 'I was sick, and you visited Me,' and, 'What you did for one of these least ones, you did for Me' "—Doyle 1948, Ch. 36:54.) He remarked that the infirmary is an important place in every religious house. Work is usually provided for the patients. "Our brothers can't work, but there is a bindery up there for some of them." None use it now. They do make rosaries. Some help clean the infirmary. "There's always some little thing they can do, like putting on stamps."

One is never too old or too ill to be a monk. An old monk volunteered to be part of a new monastery the abbey was founding. They asked him, "Father John, why do you want to go?" His reply: "Maybe I can start the graveyard." He became senile, and the abbot of Palisades offered to take him back, since Palisades had an infirmary. The reply was, "No. Father John belongs to us."

Being in the infirmary suggests a greater awareness of the monastic calling, since one is closer to death. As one monk who slept in the infirmary put it, "The old men there really know what it is to be a monk. They have reached the end of the line for them and are aware of it." He continued, "We are not so much concerned with dying or death as with life hereafter. But St. Benedict says that we should always keep death before our eyes. This is what gave rise to the old legend that Trappist monks dig one inch of their graves each day of their lives, so that the idea of death is always before them." He also said, though I am not certain whether this was legend or fact, that the monks were once supposed to keep a skull at their place in the refectory, so that they would know that the food was just to satisfy their bodily needs and so that they should not be gluttons. (There are no skulls on the refectory tables today.)

This monk felt that the experience he and the community have had with people in the infirmary is an intensification of the monastic life. A man is in the infirmary what he was before. Another key word he felt one could use was "simplification." Coming into the monastery is only the first step. It seems to be the most radical step, but it really is not. The infirmary is a continuation of a process of simplification that should characterize all the monk's life.

Another monk, who at one time helped in the infirmary, observed that the way the men respond to death is strongly conditioned by what they've been taught. The infirmary room of one of the invalid brothers, for example, "is crammed with junk that is part of his Celtic background. He has books on saints, he has shrines, statues. These things are probably relating him a lot to his own past." His point was that the monk's expression of death is not different from the rest of his life. One's anticipation of death is related to the way one has lived. Working in the infirmary changed this monk's ideas of death. His parents are waiting to die, and his sister is dying. These experiences have deepened his ideas of mortality, but they have not altered them. (He was in his thirties at the time of the discussion.)

I wondered, however, whether there was not a quantum jump when one had to face one's own death. I said to the brother that I suspected that the old priest, Father Clement, had had a quantum change in his attitude in the last few days, since he had just been diagnosed as having cancer. Without denying that, the brother wondered how much of a change it was. The monk does not change his life-style. I countered that the monk who died of leukemia a few years ago, Br. Alfred, certainly changed his life-style, as did the brother who is now paralyzed by a stroke. One day he was walking around the monastery; the next day he was out of commission for the rest of his life. The brother agreed, but said that he was thinking more of Father Clement.

The brother noted that we were also dealing with a special case. Many of the older men are Irish, and the typical Trappist-Irish view is one of persevering until death. Living within the structure and dying here is all you have to do, or almost. Such behavior is supposed to justify everything that has gone before. The Irish have a veneration for the dead; the world of the dead is a very real one for the older monks here. There is a certain harshness in the Irish attitude toward death: "You're going to be caught where you are, so you had better be ready."

According to the infirmarian, a day doesn't go by that a monk doesn't think of death. It is a part of being a monk. I asked him about the initial reaction to a diagnosis of terminal illness. "Naturally," he said, "I would be thinking in Christian terms when something like that comes along. It often crushes a person at first, but he responds. Like Father Clement. When I first told him, he blanched. But then he responded. The nurse [in the hospital] walked out of the room. She wasn't going to tell him, but of course, knowing Father Clement, I told him right away. Such a thing all fits in with being a monk. It is no obstacle.

"Elisabeth Kubler-Ross [1969] discusses five stages of dying: denial, anger, bargaining, depression, and acceptance. At none of these points would the monk have the usual reaction, largely because he is a monk. He certainly wouldn't deny it, or if he did, it would be momentary. And why should one be angry with God? We are here [in the monastery] to prepare for death. As to bargaining, it doesn't make sense when you view life as a pilgrimage. There should be no depression." And, as far as can be discerned, very little depression occurs.

I asked whether it was conceivable that he would withhold the information of an impending death from a monk. He said, "Generally no, but there are exceptions, such as one monk who really shouldn't be here. He would be much happier out. He is rather neurotic and has not really been able to face life, much less death."

I interviewed Brother Ambrose, who had had a heart attack. I told him I was interested in his reactions to his illness, particularly in any change in his attitudes. He said that he didn't feel that he was particularly close to death. "Thought I first had gas, and since it did not go away, I went to the infirmarian. It might be something more. He agreed, especially since I had a pain in my left arm, and so I went to the doctor. There was no fear. Nothing struck me at the time, because maybe it wasn't my heart. I was in the hospital two days, and the diagnosis of a heart attack was confirmed. By that time, I was adjusted to it. Nothing fearful came up. There was a willingness to go if God's love required it. In fact, I kind of enjoyed it. I told the nurse, 'I wish everyone could go through this experience.' She said that not everybody felt that way."

I told him, "You were close to death, you know."

"But part of the heart was still beating," he said.

I replied, "But it could have killed you."

He thought for a second. "Yes, I suppose so."

I then asked if there was any change in his spiritual life because of what happened. He felt there was. He notices more the unimportance of material things. His attitude toward death has changed somewhat. He is also more aware of chest pains and checks his pulse regularly. "Just before I go to sleep, I say that little prayer that kids say, you know: 'Now I lay me down to sleep,' And I tell the Lord that if he wants me, to take me. I don't know if I'll feel this way when I'm really facing death. But you do change your whole way of life." This monk shows a mixture of attitudes: trying to take things as they come, trying to minimize the importance of death, a heightened sensitivity to his physical condition, and even some apprehension.

The behavior of the monks toward one particular brother is instructive. This was the infirmarian with multiple sclerosis, mentioned earlier. As the disease progressed, the monks continued to provide for the demands of his increasing paralysis. They equipped him with an electrical wheelchair, an extra large room (he called it "my suite") that could accommodate not only the wheelchair but a special bed and a computer system that could be operated with one finger. Such functions as opening doors and switching on lights could be controlled through an electrical system operated from his wheelchair. His room was spotlessly clean, and his every need was cared for. He observed that if he were not in the monastery he would have to be in a nursing home, a thought he did not enjoy. As things were, he was still a monk.

His response was not only gratitude but a deepening spirituality. He kept a journal in which he collected meditations on the meaning of sickness and suffering, such as "For this slight momentary affliction is preparing for us an eternal weight of glory beyond all comparison" (2 Cor. 4:17). Death seemed to hold no fear for him. Indeed, he appeared to look to it with the same gratitude that he felt toward his fellow monks.

If there is any reason that life in the infirmary is an intensification of the monastic way, it is that the monk is reminded that he is closer to death. Of course, he could die in any other place, so the infirmary does not mean he is closer to death ipso facto. It only reminds him.

A MONASTIC FUNERAL

Each monastery has its own graveyard, and though it is not a focal point of activity as is the church, it certainly represents a destination, or more properly a gateway to a life that the monk is promised in scripture.

The line separating life and death is not sharp in the monastery. Once I was listening to a conversation between two monks about a certain brother. I did not know who he was, though the tone of their remarks suggested strongly that he was a member of the community. I knew all of the others, so I asked who it was that they were discussing. "Oh, that was Br. Joachim," was the reply. "He died a number of years ago."

The funeral described here is an event that I witnessed in January 1973. The monk in question, Br. Alfred, was 84 years old when he died, and had been in the monastery 44 years. He came from a large Catholic family (13 children) and worked for the railroad before joining Palisades Abbey at 40 years of age. He was the guest house cook for 30 years, renowned for his cooking and his sanctity. One of the guests had written to his sister (herself a nun) many years before his death:

Everyone praises the delicious meals he serves. One half of the praise he receives for his excellence in the culinary arts would turn the head of any housewife were it bestowed on her. But to me, the outstanding and fascinating trait in the good monk is his deep spirituality. And with true humility does the good man carry that inestimable treasure. Frankly (and I'm not writing in a mood of hyperbole), when I've stood in the kitchen at the monastery chatting with Bro. Alfred, I've had the feeling that in that brown-clad monk, I'm in the presence of true greatness.

There was evidently a love that shone through Br. Alfred, a love that was not lost on the community, as will be evident.

I had discussed with the abbot the significance of being able to witness a monastic funeral, since it was one of the more important rituals of the life. Thus I was somewhat prepared for the telephone call. "Our old Br. Alfred seems to be going on us. In fact, he told Br. Bernard [the infirmarian] that he was dying. He keeps his eyes closed all of the time and he can hardly talk." The abbot continued, "He could go any time. If you can't come until Friday and he should go before then, we'll hold the funeral for you." I was on my way the following day.

Br. Donald met me at the airport. I asked about Br. Alfred. "He's still here. I guess it's just that old Irish stubbornness." He had been given the last rites a few days earlier, before the abbot's call. Br. Donald remarked on how beautiful it all was, how Br. Alfred had been constantly in his prayers, how everyone in the house seemed to have a "good attitude." Everyone was in fact very cheerful when they met me.

One of the older brothers, himself in the infirmary, had remarked earlier in the day that Br. Alfred was "not going to die yet," and of course he had not. I mentioned to another brother what I perceived to be a general relaxed attitude. He remarked, "Not that there's not some sadness, though," and as I noticed later, there certainly was. Perhaps the relaxed attitude was related to Br. Alfred's age and the fact that, as Father Kevin remarked, "He's fooled us several times before." But when I mentioned the possibility of this being a false alarm, Father Kevin assured me it was not. "Two or three days, at the most," he said.

At 7:20 P.M., the church bells rang. They were not being tolled—the single strokes, slowly and regularly repeated, that signify death. I was talking with Br. Roger at the time. "What's that," I asked, "Compline?"

"All it could be at this time is Alfred. Do you want to come?" And we hurried to the infirmary. Ten monks were already there. They were saying a litany, the monks responding to the abbot's prayers, "Lord have mercy. . . . Lord have mercy." In a few minutes it seemed like most of the community was standing in the hall. Few tears were noticeable, and those that were came mainly from novices. Father Simon, after it was over, and with a big smile, said, "Well, he had a good send-off!"

Roger noted that the monks would stay up all night, taking turns praying over the body through reading psalms.

Very little attention was given to Br. Alfred's death at Vigils the next morning. The office was sung as usual, except that the abbot read from John 17 and after the Angelus, the bell was tolled. On the bulletin board was a notice: "After 7:30 A.M., the community will gather in the infirmary to bring Alfred's body to the chapel." A schedule was posted that the monks could sign for praying by the body, vocally or silently, until burial the following afternoon. The schedule called for half-hour sessions during the day, hour sessions at night. By 6:00 A.M. all the night sessions were filled; only a few of the day sessions had been taken. Br. Alfred's passport and naturalization certificates were also on the board (he was from Canada).

At 7:30 A.M., as scheduled, the community met in the infirmary. I did not go, thinking it might have been a private ceremony. I know now I could have gone, but as it was, I got a very good seat in the church from which to view the procession when the body was carried in.

According to Father Matthew Kelty (1971:224), a monk writing about the Abbey of Gethsemani, by this time the body had been washed and clothed in a fresh habit. There is no embalming. A cloth is wrapped around the head and under the chin to keep the mouth closed. At least at Gethsemani, the eyes have been sent to an eye bank. The face is not painted or "made up" in any way.

When all was ready, the solemn procession went from the infirmary to the church. One monk entered, bearing the Paschal candle (a large, thick four-foot candle used during the Easter season). The four pallbearers with Br. Alfred followed. They carried him in a bier, a plain, shallow white pine box or pallet. He was robed in white, his hood on his head. The bearers brought him to the center of the church, between the choir stalls, followed by the other monks. The abbot said a brief prayer, and the community was dismissed.

Later Br. Donald came to my room. I asked about going to the funeral tomorrow. No problem. I told him that I hadn't been sure about going to the service in the infirmary. He said that it was quite beautiful. He had noticed that I wasn't there and felt somewhat bad about it. He had meant to come and get me. Then I asked whether I could view Br. Alfred in his bier. We went. Br. Fred and Father Joshua were reading psalms. It was very quiet and impressive. Br. Alfred had thin, finely chiseled features, somewhat emaciated by age and loss of weight. I saw his arms yesterday, no bigger than thick broomsticks. Now he was completely robed in his white cowl, his arms folded on his chest. Only his face showed—still, white, with a look of dignity that I have not seen in anyone, anywhere.

Br. Donald and I stood through two or three psalms. I commented later on the relaxed attitude that prevailed and wondered whether this was because Br. Alfred was so old. Br. Donald wasn't sure whether "relaxed" was the right word. He mentioned the word "sobriety." I asked him to compare what was going on to Christmas and Easter. He felt that this was more of a celebration. "This was the expected and hoped-for consummation of what we've been working for all our lives." I remarked that what was happening was completely honest, with no show, and that's where I got the term "relaxed." It was unlike any wake I have ever attended. For one thing, no wailing or crying was evident. Simon and Winnie both had beautiful smiles. For another, there was no stench of flowers. It is admittedly somewhat intense, yet it is a very peaceful celebration.

Br. Donald mentioned that he felt ambivalent when he looked at Br. Alfred. He said that there was "identification with a dead person. I can't help but realize that he's dead when I look at him. There is a sense of fear of the unknown, and one of judgment." He said that a few days ago Br.

Keith had told Br. Alfred, "Soon you'll be in heaven." Br. Alfred's answer was—and he could just barely get the words out—"I hope so."

I asked, "How long has he been dying? When were you fairly certain about it?"

"When he stopped eating."

"When was that?" Br. Donald thought for a moment. "Probably last Sunday."

"You mean he's had nothing to eat since then?" (He died Thursday night.)

"Br. Bernard [the infirmarian] said he took no more than a bite of bread, just a bite. And a sip of Sanka."

I noted that the bier seemed to be just the right size. "Was it made especially for him?"

"No. We have different sizes. We'll probably lift him out by straps and place him in the ground." Two members were buried in caskets. One died in the hospital. Both were embalmed, though embalming is exceptional.

The funeral Mass was dedicated not only to Saints Robert, Stephen, and Alberic, the founders of the Cistercians, but also to Br. Alfred. He died on the feast of the conversion of St. Paul, was waked on the feast of Saints Robert, Stephen, and Alberic, and is to be buried on the feast of the Memorial of the Blessed Virgin. I pointed this out to Br. Bernard, the infirmarian, and he smiled cheerfully. "He sure timed it right, didn't he?" he said.

Vespers was held earlier because of the Bible-reading service at 7:00 P.M. Before the service, I was talking to Br. Fred. He told me that he had worked as a novice for Br. Alfred. "Some of the things he did aggravated me, but still he impressed me very much. He came here at 43 [sic] years of age. He had worked as a teletype operator. One day the secular cook for the retreatants was out drunk, and Dom Eugene asked if Br. Alfred could cook. Br. Alfred said he'd try, but the only cooking he'd done had been baching for himself. That's the only job he ever had at the monastery. Some people here looked down on him because he wasn't a community man, but that was because he couldn't come to the offices. He was really more of a community man than most. He told me once that in all the time he had been here, he had never once been tempted to leave."

The service was very simple: hymns or psalms followed by a Bible reading followed by other hymns or psalms, and so forth. Then prayers for Br. Alfred.

I saw Father Zachary in the kitchen after noon dinner. He told me that at the moment of Br. Alfred's death (he was mistaken—see later), he was walking across the fields and heard a wailing, as if by a dog. "It was the strangest thing I ever heard. It wasn't like any animal cry. The only thing that comes to me is that it was some demon who got deprived of something he wanted to get. You know those jungle birds that you hear in the movies?

Well, it was something like that, only it wasn't like that. And it kept getting more persistent as I got closer to the monastery."

"Louder?"

"No, not louder. Just more persistent."

"How long did it go on?"

"Oh, for about 5 minutes. I'll tell you, I was scared! And the first thing I said when I saw Br. Keith was, "How's Br. Alfred?" He did not know Br. Alfred was dead at the time.

"What time did you hear it?"

"About 10:00 o'clock [P.M.]." Br. Alfred had been dead for about three hours.

I asked the abbot whether it wasn't true that the novices seem more oriented to sorrow at death than the older monks, and he agreed. He speculated (he used that word) that they are more used to thinking of death as sorrowful and they are not used to the positive thrust in the monastery. For another thing, some of them have actually been cooking for the monks in the infirmary and have had more contact with people like Br. Alfred than they ordinarily would. This contact has been planned. The abbot thinks it is a contact that they should have.

On the bulletin board, carefully printed in artistic script on beautiful paper was the following:

It happened shortly after Vespers of our solemn celebration of the Cistercian founders.

As Alfred, he was my brother for a very short while.

Today, now that he has died, all that we have left of him remains in a wooden box, in the chapel. There we will watch, awake—today and through the night.

Tomorrow, after noon, we will place the body in a hole dug in the earth and then fill in the hole again, covering the body. There will be no procession from the grave site.

Dying is coming to be able to face oneself.

Saturday came. It was cold, with a light drizzle. The community prepared to bury their brother. The Mass was longer than usual. The abbot gave the homily. The theme was about a simple man, serving many, unknown to many. "I was hungry, and you fed me," he said.

The body had been moved from between the choir stalls to a place where the guests could see it, near the altar. There were numerous guests—not as many as at Christmas or Easter, but I have seen many Masses with fewer guests. Laymen viewed the body all day long. Because he had been the guest house cook, Br. Alfred had met more people in the outside world than would be true of most monks.

After Mass, the community gathered around the body for more prayers and hymns; then they filed out, followed by the pallbearers with the body, the guests last. A monk with the Paschal candle led the way, next came a novice with holy water, Father Theodore with the thurible, Father Simon with the burial cross (which will be the grave marker), and the rest of the community. All solemn faces. All in white robes. Down the stairs to the guest wing, out to the sidewalk behind the monastery and to the cemetery. Br. Alfred is to be buried beside his natural brother who died as a guest (layman) here almost 25 years ago to the day. All gathered around the open grave, including the guests, even the women (who ordinarily are not allowed in this part of the abbey grounds, within the enclosure).

More prayers, the grave was incensed, we recited the Lord's Prayer and sang a hymn: four monks singing the verses, with the community singing the chorus. Rigor mortis had left: the head lolled, the jaw sagged. The body was lifted from the bier and lowered into the coffin, a plain four-sided wooden box with handles. The coffin was lowered into the grave. (The use of a coffin is an innovation. The monk customarily is buried without one.) Each pallbearer used a shovel to begin filling the hole. They stopped, finally, when the outline of the coffin could just be seen. (Later they would get a back hoe to complete the task.) As the body was being moved to the grave, hymns were sung.

Faces solemn, but no tears from any monk—only from two old ladies. About half the guests came to the cemetery. I was impressed for the first time by the number of crosses there. There were more than the number of monks who had lived in the community. (This cemetery had 129 markers; the one a hundred yards away had 31.) Br. Donald says not all are monks. Some are lay people who lived around here. (Later, I counted nine non-monastic graves).

Some random thoughts about the funeral: After it was over, I was struck by the emptiness of the church—for the first time since Friday morning when they moved the body in, 31 hours ago. Father Peter kept saying, "Poor old Alfred, poor old Alfred." The hole made by the grave seemed so very dark. The circle of white robed monks around the grave. Singing that was more natural than speaking. It seemed as right for Br. Alfred to be sung to his grave as for the sparrows to be singing in the monastery garden. The white face in the white cowl. How much dignity the human face can have!

Father Winnie told me of a visit he had with Br. Alfred during his last year. As he left, he said, "Well, good-bye, Brother. I'll keep you in my prayers." At this, Br. Alfred (with no teeth), perked up, raised one broom-stick arm, trembling, and answered, "Yes, Father, I know. He's right here, now. And he will take me with him...if I'm ready." This last in lowered voice.

Father Winnie was impressed with this most because he felt that Br. Alfred was a very holy man, one who had truly succeeded in "hiding himself in Christ." For Br. Alfred to add, "if I'm ready," was a sincere and striking evidence of humility.

I asked how much it had cost to bury Br. Alfred. The abbot's immediate response: "Oh, no more than the cost of turning off the light switch." Br. Fred felt that it was certainly less than $50.00. There was the cloth for his habit and the cost of the screws and handles for the coffin. The lumber came from the abbey's mill. (There was no cost for a hospital or embalming, of course.) The abbot said that the greatest expense was phone calls to other monks and to Br. Alfred's relatives. I asked about the plaque for his cross (grave marker). The abbot said that it was donated. The man who made it is an old friend of the monks.

I talked about the funeral, first with a novice, Br. Ted, and then with an old monk, Br. Melvin. Ted seemed a bit solemn, but his general impression was that "this was what he had been expecting—and for so long!" Br. Mel (who could be the next, himself) was as cheerful as Ted was solemn. I asked what he thought was the biggest difference in the way monks used to be buried. "It's more natural, now. There is much less tension. Before you had to kneel down every so often on the way to the cemetery, to say prayers, and everyone had to go two by two. Everything was formal and had to go by rule. There is much less tension this way."

The next day was a session on reminiscences of Br. Alfred. The abbot first read written accounts. One said that during the winter he would say extra prayers whenever he had the time, so that he could store up graces for the summer when there was too much work to do to pray. Br. Tony gave by far the longest account. He said that Alfred took time as he found it. In particular, he spoke of his "understanding heart, how he could perceive other people's troubles." Throughout Tony's talk, and during all of the talks, there was an air of careful attention, dotted with little spaces of laughter. Again, no sadness (cf. Mott 1984:461), not even in Father Peter's account (which this time contained no mention of "poor old Alfred"): Alfred had a bumptious sense of humor, he said. He had told Father Peter a tale of a "lady" who had been arrested. The judge asked her how she got in court. She told him that she had slid in on a moonbeam. The judge then told her he'd give her three months in jail to get the splinters out of her rear. And Br. Alfred was apparently very shrewd. Once, when he was a railroad ticket agent, a man got away without paying. Brother announced to all in the waiting room that there was something wrong with ticket number so-and-so, "and you can't get on the train unless it's fixed." The man said, "I have ticket number so-and-so." Br. Alfred took him into his office, took the ticket from him, and then told him he had not paid.

Br. Alfred was lavish with praise, making it a point to tell you when he liked something you had made. He would take advice readily. He did have some irritating habits. He was always trying to save things. A bumper crop of anything, especially fruit or vegetables, would mean that he would work overtime peeling and preparing. He would casually ask you to help, much to your regret when you saw the work he would bring. But you couldn't complain, because you knew how much he had already done. He and Br. Tony never had a real falling out. Br. Alfred would walk away rather than argue.

Br. Alfred became more patient as time passed. Each sickness seemed to change him, always for the better. He would tell people, "You better pray for me, or I'll come back and haunt you, that's what I'll do." Br. Ambrose noted that he'd never seen Br. Alfred impatient. He also had wisdom. When someone was applying to become a member of the community the (former) abbot would always ask Br. Alfred's opinion.

The abbot then asked, "Should I add anything?" (Laughter.) He said that he never knew him to start a conversation. He was beyond complaining. He wasn't too careful about his own appearance but was especially careful about the way the food was prepared for the guests. He simply forgot about himself. What impressed the abbot was his devotion to the rosary and the Way of the Cross. He was always saddened at infidelities, especially when anyone would leave the monastery. When he was in the infirmary, he was dying every day. He would say, "It's just as if the Lord is waiting for me, but He isn't ready for me yet." There was no doubt in the abbot's mind that Br. Alfred was in heaven. He knew personally four persons in the house who had experienced a frustrated devil. Br. Alfred was lost to the devil and he (the devil) was taking it out on someone else.

With this, we adjourned. As we were leaving (I think that almost all of the community had turned out), Father Kevin came up to me. "Just a few extra things I wanted you to write down." (I had sat in the back so I could take notes.) "Br. Alfred used to make little visits to the Blessed Sacrament (in the church). He used to remark on how peaceful it was there and how fortunate we are to live in a monastery. And something else: he used to say how glad he was to be at the end of his life, hearing about all these crimes and how even the priests were not obeying the Pope."

Br. Alfred's death, from his last breath in the infirmary to this final meeting, had been a rite of intensification. It provided a continuity to the tradition of the monastery for the novices, a sharing of experience for all, and a reaffirmation of basic things, one of which was the love they felt for a gentle little man. The Cistercian values of liturgy and labor, poverty and chastity, and the vows of obedience, stability, and conversion of manners were very much there.

CONCLUSION

The attitudes of the monks toward their brothers is nowhere shown more clearly than in their behavior toward the invalid, the dying, and the dead. No one complains because an invalid monk is not working or is a burden to the community. A monk did comment on the fact that one of the men in the infirmary complained about his own condition. The monk concluded that he was a sissy. But this was the only exception. If anything, the old and dying monk who does not complain becomes more of a source of pride.

As noted, one of the monks said that life in the infirmary is a continuation of the monk's earlier life. If he was striving for agapé before his illness, he will continue to do so. Of course, being in the infirmary is in itself not an act of love. One is in there because he must be. The important question is, how does he act when he gets there, and how do the others act toward him? This question is intensified when the monk dies, for then he cannot act. It is only others who act toward him. Though everyone in the monastery does not pay attention to the invalid (in that they know he is being cared for), most if not all pay attention to the newly deceased. Their brother has left them physically, and they have one more chance to say good-bye. They do not wait for death to do this. The leave-taking begins when it is evident that the monk is dying and continues until the community meeting after his burial. In their behavior, there is foremost a concern for that particular monk. The reaction is positive. Because they love their brother, there is expression of joy at his departure, especially if he is an old monk, full of years and piety. They are not entirely happy. After all, they are losing a brother. But the reaction is not negative. It is an affirmation.

Chapter 13

The Relativity of Deviance

If a brother who has been frequently corrected for some fault, and even excommunicated, does not amend, let a harsher correction be applied.

—*Rule for Monasteries,* Chapter 28

Durkheim (1938:68–69) claimed that even in a society of saints there will be sinners. So it is in the monastery. The deviant monk is defined both by monastery rules and by those of the outside society. Through understanding the deviant, we will better understand the rules of the monastery, especially those rules considered important to the operation of the system.

"Deviant" is used in a neutral sense to mean anyone who deviates in practice from ordinary behavior. There are both positive and negative deviants, that is, those who deviate from normal practice that are approved, and those who deviate that are not approved.

Positive deviants are qualitatively different from the negative kind, which is the sort most think of when they use the term "deviance." Positive deviants may be treated as harshly as the negative. They tend to arouse jealousy and threat reactions (Jesus was crucified, Gandhi was assassinated). Nevertheless, they are used as ideals toward which people orient themselves. Negative deviants, in contrast, mark off the boundaries of things society will not permit. Both positive and negative deviants clarify social values, but each in a different direction. Our interest in deviance, therefore, is not in showing what is wrong in the monastery but is in describing more accurately the structure of rules—what is encouraged and what is disapproved.

POSITIVE DEVIANTS

Some express the norms of the society by doing more than is expected of them. These tend to be few. In the tradition of Durkheim (1938:68–69), even in a company of the extremely pious, a small number will stand out as more pious. Two examples can be noted. Both men were very old and lived in the infirmary for some time before they died. For Br. Alfred there is only anecdotal and retrospective evidence (Chapter 12). He was honored by the community, there could be no doubt of that. But whether he was more honored than most is not known. Br. Clovis, however, shortly before his death was the most respected member of the community (Chapter 9).

Several things contribute to the estimate of piety for these men. First, they persevered. Each remained true to his monastic commitment for more than 25 years. Second, they maintained this commitment despite major obstacles, including long and debilitating illnesses. Third, their piety was unobtrusive. They were known to be pious mainly by their persistence, by maintaining the ways of a monk over many years and in adversity. These men served as role models. It was of no importance whether they accomplished anything outstanding. What was important is the simple faith that could endure.

Positive deviance is displayed in various ways. Most abbots I have known have been very capable. One in particular, before his selection as an abbot, had been a brother, not a priest. He was very respected for his intelligence and for his deep faith, both of which were held in a quiet and unassuming manner. (Still, I recall asking him, after he became abbot, whether he had ever thought he would become abbot when he first entered, and he candidly said, "Yes.") When the reigning abbot resigned, this brother was appointed temporary superior, ordained a priest, and elected abbot by the community.

The prior, as second in command, also tends to be of superior intelligence. A former prior, Br. Henry, apparently has no intention of becoming a priest and thus will probably never be abbot. But he is widely respected and serves on most if not all important committees.

Still, persons of unusual talent generally have difficulty remaining in the monastery. The temptations of Thomas Merton to leave Gethsemani are well documented (Mott 1984). At Palisades, in various places in the abbey, there are beautiful sculptures by a former monk. Several novice masters, highly intelligent and dedicated, are no longer in the abbey. The same may be said for some priors who have left the monastery because they could not or would not subordinate their talent to the demands of being a monk. Many who remain could make outstanding contributions in the secular world, for example, artists of unusual ability, a highly qualified lawyer, engineer, chemist, and so on. However, they have been able to shelve their talent to follow a quiet life of prayer. The ability to simplify life to a single focus on God is the only aptitude that eventually counts in the continuing development of a monk. Men with few or less-developed talents may thus find it easier to persevere. The exceptionally gifted have more to surrender.

Another positive deviant is the hermit at Palisades. But he was once a negative deviant in that he wanted to be a hermit, which was then at variance with monastic life. Many disapproved of what he felt to be a calling. As he persevered in his hermitage, however, he was increasingly respected, particularly for his spiritual counseling. Thus, the *monk* had not changed. Rather he had changed from a negative to a positive deviant because the attitudes of the *community* toward him had changed. Nor should one assume that being a hermit necessarily means that one is only a positive deviant. The hermit at Palisades eventually left and became married. Merton himself was involved in an erotic love affair while he was a hermit (Mott 1984:435–54), and he generally had the respect of his community.

Positive deviants help to show that which is valued in the monastery. But the same is true of other deviants.

NEGATIVE DEVIANTS

These appear more numerous, although they are still a minority. Out of 50 monks, I estimate that approximately seven were positive deviants and 17 to 20 were negative (excluding those who left). Usually, negative deviance is limited to a single trait. Otherwise, the deviants make good monks. Some would never be thought deviant in the world. For example, the chief value of the monastery for some is the security it offers; others are attracted to the guest house. Both could be admirable traits outside but are deviants monastically. Others would be deviants in the world as well as in the monastery: the mentally ill, alcoholics, and homosexuals. For a time, Father Sean was a deviant only in the monastic sense. He had developed what some called an apostleship for nuns. They came to the guest house for his counseling, and it occupied much of his life. Pressure gradually arose from the community, part of which was community gossip. His monastic calling meant more to him than his apostleship, and the visits eventually ceased. There was no hint of anything sexually irregular. But two things seemed inappropriate: the sexual selectivity of those being counseled (though he also counseled men), and the counseling itself. A monk is not supposed to be a counselor to outsiders.

Father Sean was not alone, however. Several monks felt it their duty to spend time with the guests discussing spiritual matters, and many guests came for such discussions. One monk, Br. Jacob (see later discussion), spent practically no time in the cloister besides sleeping there. He took his meals with the guests and generally kept their hours. For some, he became a guru. This monk was an extreme case. Nothing could dissuade him, and he maintained this pattern until he died.

The abbot's position in this matter of "apostleships" was one of attempting to remind the men where their "center of gravity" was, in the guest house or the cloister. For some the pressure of community opinion and abbatial counsel was sufficient and they changed. Some, however, though they lived and worked in the cloister, felt another calling. The point is, Trappist-Cistercian life is separated from the world to pray for the world. Extensive interaction with the guests detracts from the separation. The *Rule* (Ch. 53) is explicit on this point: "On no account shall anyone who is not so ordered associate or converse with guests" (Doyle 1948:74).

Several monks wanted to become priests, but the abbot would not grant them permission. Two left the monastery and went to seminaries, though one eventually returned and died as a brother. A priest is hardly a negative deviant outside, but a Trappist-Cistercian monastery is not an order of priests, and this desire ran counter to that orientation. In each case, because of the abbot's disapproval, their aspiration was contrary to the spirit of obedience. Their only recourse was thus either to desist or leave.

This pattern of negative monastic and positive worldly deviance is even more pervasive. Some monks are especially work oriented and would work much more than they do if the abbot would let them. But a monk is supposed to divide his time between labor, liturgy, and prayer. Those who emphasize work upset this balance.

Leaving the monastery is also deviant. One monastic vow is stability, and part of this vow is a decision to remain a monk all of one's life. To leave the monastery permanently is therefore an act of infidelity (unless one goes to another monastery on the orders of the abbot). From this view, most who were at Palisades have been deviant over the last twenty years. During that period, the population of the monastery has gone from approximately 150 monks to 35. (Only a few of these died.) According to the *Rule*, a monk may leave the monastery no more than three times before reentry is permanently denied (Doyle 1948, Ch. 29:48).

Though the monastery keeps no systematic record of those who leave, one monk was able to describe the status of 21 priests and three brothers who left since 1970. Most are still priests. Seven of the priests have married, four are serving as diocesan priests elsewhere, five are "exclaustrated" (out of the monastery but still affiliated with it), two are on extended sick leave, and the rest (one each) are semiretired, still single, and deceased. Of the three brothers, two are married and one is a hermit.

Another form of deviance is found among those who leave the monastery temporarily without permission. For example, a few monks have been known to visit the local bars at night. Some were even able to tell me precisely where I could purchase a very good, locally brewed beer.

Sexual deviation does not seem to be common. A few have confessed to me their problems at one time with masturbation. A few others have mentioned temptations to having various sexual experiences, ranging from homosexuality to bestiality, but these were recognized by them as deviant acts and were never consummated. Several have been tempted to marry. Some have succumbed.

I know only four monks who were homosexual at Palisades, and only one remains. Two left at the same time, and some of the monks believe they became active homosexuals. One was diagnosed as latent homosexual and also left. As far as is known, there is no practicing homosexual in the monastery today. The latent homosexual is an instructive case. He realized that something was wrong when he became overattached to one of the monks. He left the monastery in order to attain a better perspective. On obtaining psychiatric counseling, he learned of his latent homosexuality. He will not return to the monastery, but he is convinced of the validity of his call to the priesthood and celibacy. Thus, though homosexual, he is sociologically not deviant. I doubt very much whether he ever will be. Leaving the monastery was not easy. When I spoke with him a few months after his departure, he was still in some confusion, yet he felt that he had peace. Apparently, he was coming to terms with who he was and what he had to do.

Several monks have been alcoholics. One was from time to time found inebriated to the point of unconsciousness in various places in the monastery. Another was openly confronted with his condition and underwent treatment, which appears to have been successful, but he has left. One remains an active alcoholic. I personally never have seen any of these monks in an inebriated condition, and thus their alcoholism was well hidden from the public.

Mental deviants are equally rare. Only five at the most were known to me, and of these, two were more neurotic than psychotic. Two were in the infirmary. One was senile, the other lived in his own world. He would not eat food from the monastery kitchen, because he was afraid it was poisoned. He claimed that the Virgin Mary was the fourth person of the Trinity. The other three were able to perform their duties in the community effectively. One talked out loud to himself. One was usually in a state of depression. The third was suffering from combat stress. The casual observer would never recognize these last two as mental deviants.

Reaction from the monks is almost always tolerant for all deviants. Only twice did I observe negative interaction, in both cases directed to the monk who talked to himself. In each case, there was no more than a slight reprimand.

Violence, such as striking someone or threatening to strike someone, is most rare. I know of only one such incident at Palisades. The monk was sent to another house where he is adjusting well. I know of only three such incidences among all twelve of the monasteries for men that I visited. Though the frequency is undoubtedly higher, it is rare enough to constitute a scandal each time it happens.

Despite these acts of deviance, the monks are not very deviant as the world considers deviance. Consider the main types of crime one finds in any major city in this country during a year: murder, rape, robbery, assault, burglary, larceny, auto theft, forgery, fraud, embezzlement, vandalism, prostitution, drug abuse, and vagrancy. To be fair, of course, neither do we find Olympic champions, Nobel prize winners, millionaires, senators, and presidents in monasteries. The monk avoids most positive deviances also.

THE MONKS AS DEVIANT

I have been speaking of deviance relative to two populations: deviance in the monastery relative to monastic norms and deviance in the world relative to norms of the world. The monk, as a monk, is also deviant relative to the world. In particular, the monk is celibate and is more religious than people outside. These differences are especially important in terms of their consequences.

Celibacy

Monastic chastity is discussed in Chapter 6. Celibacy is treated here as a deviant form of behavior. Most people in the world marry. All monks should be celibate, and I found no exception in any of the monasteries. If a monk had difficulty even in controlling his thoughts about sexual matters, it was a problem for him. If he could not control himself, he left the monastery. Of course, I have no way of knowing if any monk was actively but secretly disobeying his vow of celibacy.

Outsiders have asked me more questions about celibacy than about anything else in monastic life. People seem especially fascinated by the way in which the monks control their sexual appetites. Repeated questioning has revealed no special techniques. Generally, the monks expect a man to have attained control over his sex behavior before he enters the monastery. One abbot maintained that a candidate should have no voluntary orgasm for six months before entering.

Religiosity

The monk, of course, has explicitly renounced everything so that he could follow a religious way of life. The world may think him odd for doing this, but it nevertheless respects him. For this reason, people go on retreats at monasteries and go to monks for spiritual advice. In this sense, the monks are positive deviants.

There are many other ways in which monks deviate from the norms of the world, but the world is not usually aware of these, or is indifferent to them, so there is little or no criticism (or praise). For example, the monk owns nothing, he is a vegetarian, he wears a habit identical to those of his brothers, and so forth. Technically, in all these ways he deviates from the norms of the world, but not of the monastery.

AN EXAMPLE OF DEVIANCE IN CONTEXT

In summary, the monks appreciate piety, simplicity, perseverance, and commitment. Ability is honored also, for example, intelligence, learning, and craftmanship, but ability should fit within the values of piety, simplicity, perseverance, and commitment, not to mention obedience and the other monastic promises. The monk's life should be devoted to prayer, separate from the world and even separate from many of its "good works," such as counseling outsiders. Not that the monk is to refuse requests for help from guests, but he should avoid going out of the cloister to help others. The monk forgoes ambitions even in the area of religion, such as becoming a priest. His task is to remain in his cloister, ideally in his cell, devoted to a life of prayer, in chastity, obedience, poverty, and stability, seeking always to convert his own life closer to Christ.

But monks stumble occasionally, some more than others. When they do, they know that there is the forgiveness both of the community and their God. One example will suffice. It concerns Br. Jacob, mentioned earlier in this chapter. He seldom came to choir and seldom attended community meals. Though he did more or less regularly attend community Mass, he spent most of his time with the guests and usually was not concerned with rules. He died in 1984 after 44 years in the monastery. I quote from the abbot's eulogy:

Br. Jacob died peacefully in his sleep last Friday afternoon. He...was napping in his chair when the Lord called him to himself. Above his head on the wall of his room...was a small banner on which was written: "There are no rules about leaping into the new because no one has even been there before...."

I think he would like the part, "there are no rules." He was not a rule man. It was difficult for him to stay within the limits of rules—not, I believe, out of contrariness but because he saw a greater need—a need for love. And if there is anything you could say about Br. Jacob it is that he loved people, all kinds of people. He loved them deeply—and maybe to a fault—but he loved them.

In a sense, Br. Jacob was to Palisades what the Statue of Liberty is to America. The Statue is called the "Mother of Exiles" and inscribed at its base are the famous words "Give me your tired, your poor,/Your huddled masses/...Send these, the homeless, the tempest-tost, to me."

We have the spiritually homeless and the tempest-tost, the spiritually tired and poor coming to our door and Br. Jacob was always there with open arms to receive them and make them welcome. He loved everyone who came and never refused anyone. Young people flocked to him because he was good to be around, always encouraging, always saying the affirming word, giving the kind smile. This means a lot to people who are frightened or struggling with life. I remember how fearful I was that August day in 1958 when I entered the community. I was eating in the monastery refectory for the first time, afraid to lift my eyes off the plate much less look around, but I did look up once and there across from me was a giant of a man in a brown habit with his hood up—right out of a Robin Hood movie—beaming a giant smile my way. It went a long way to silence my fearful heart. How many thousands of times in his life time has Br. Jacob reassured a frightened soul with a kind smile or affirming word? Love for people is Br. Jacob's hallmark. It is a gift he had from his earliest youth. . . .

Br. Jacob did not think in terms of structure or categories, or class distinctions. He had one great charism in life and that was to respond to people's need to be affirmed and loved. . . .

Philosophers and theologians can speculate about what is needed for our modern world but I think that Br. Jacob's simple message cannot be surpassed: to spread God's love. People need to know God loves them. There is no greater hunger in the world, no greater famine than the famine of love.

Today's Gospel was chosen especially because it is a story of the last judgment. A story about how people who helped others during their life will enter eternal life. "I was a stranger and you made me welcome, thirsty and you gave me drink, hungry and you gave me food." How many people were strangers in love, were hungry and thirsty for some small island of peace in their life and found it through the kindness of Br. Jacob? These will be the ones who open the gates of heaven for him because Christ dwells in them, and to touch them is to touch Christ.

The last book Br. Jacob was reading was entitled, *A Gift for God, Meditations of Mother Teresa of Calcutta*. She says: "To show great love for God and our neighbor we need not do great things. It is how much love we put in the doing that makes our offering something beautiful for God." Br. Jacob is something beautiful for God. We are all beautiful to the God who made us. Br. Jacob had the gift to see this. He was able to see beauty where others saw blemishes, he was able to like the unlikable. To love everyone was his impossible dream (a song he liked especially well) and in his case the dream became a reality. To love everyone—the stranger, the weak, the unlikable. A true work of art.

Of most significance is the abbot's statement that Br. Jacob "was not a rule man"; what made him deviant was that he lived in a communal organization very tightly structured by rules, both general and specific. The reaction of the monks varied from those who clearly rejected him to the tolerance and understanding shown by the abbot at the funeral.

CORRECTION

In earlier years, before Vatican II, an institution of correction operated in Trappist-Cistercian monasteries known as the Chapter of Faults. At this meeting, a monk was expected to stand and accuse himself, that is, openly confess before the abbot and his brothers some transgression of the community norms. Alternatively, he could be "proclaimed" by someone else, but he would be expected not to defend himself. The institution was abandoned after Vatican II, mainly because it was felt that it was not in keeping with modern customs. Some felt that at times the Chapter of Faults was used as a means of revenge—monks proclaiming others in order to "get back at them." I have no evidence that this ever happened, but the fact that it was considered by some to be a possibility is itself significant.

Today, there are four major means of correction: selection, training, peer pressure, and the abbot. Men in need of constant correction are not selected to be monks, as discussed in Chapter 4. During the years in the novitiate, the novice master becomes an important source of discipline. Once the monk has made solemn profession, the major mechanisms of correction left are peer pressure and the abbot.

Peer pressure can be powerful, as in the case of Father Sean and his guests. In my conversations with him, his concern for the opinions of his fellow monks was quite pervasive, and his change in behavior was due in part to this perceived pressure. He is not alone in this sensitivity, though his was the strongest case that came to my attention. Not all monks are this sensitive, and some appear not to react at all. Br. Jacob did not change, and others who appear similarly impervious are known.

The abbot is the only institutionalized source of correction in the monastery. Though the bishop may object to liturgical practices, he must work through the abbot. Most of the time, the abbot corrects by suggestion, advice, and example. He also has the power to invoke a canonical warning, but the power is used rarely. If a monk receives three such warnings, he is expelled. Though monks have been warned, I never knew one who was expelled during my study. As one monk said, "If you give them one canonical warning, they are as good as gold after that." The abbot has the authority to send the monk to another monastery, and this step has been taken, particularly in the case of monks who cannot get along with each other.

The abbot can himself muster peer pressure. This happened to an alcoholic. He was called to a conference with the abbot, some of the monks, and others who were involved, and was openly confronted with his condition. He eventually allowed himself to be committed to an institution for treatment.

The role of the Father Immediate should also be mentioned. The abbot of the mother house from which the monastery was formed periodically visits his daughter houses and interviews the monks. He then makes recommendations, but these must ultimately be enforced by the abbot of the daughter house.

There is not much occasion for the use of correction mechanisms, but the mechanisms exist and are used. I learned of the existence of peer pressure on my first visits to Palisades, and it was still functioning on my most recent visits, especially through gossip. The need for corrective mechanisms may be less in the monastery than in other types of communal organizations, but it is still there.

In closing, we may cite in detail the reference made to Durkheim at the beginning of this chapter (1938:68–69): "Imagine a society of saints, a perfect cloister of exemplary individuals. Crimes, properly so called, will there be unknown; but faults which appear venial to the layman will create there the same scandal that the ordinary offense does in ordinary consciousness."

CONCLUSION

A consideration of deviance provides a clearer picture of what monastic life is like, especially its norms. We learn the extent of the monk's surrender to his God. Monks are serious when they proclaim a life of asceticism and when they attempt to lead a life of solitude and separation from the world. A society has the kind of deviance it needs, particularly to serve as boundary markers for its members, to show what is right and wrong.

Deviance is usually not an act of love, at least not to the people from whom one is deviating. Thus, one testimony to love in this chapter is to be found especially in the low level of deviance. But another testament is the way the deviant is treated. Father Sean was gently pressured, and because he loved his confreres, he conformed. Brother Jacob was also pressured, but he would not conform. Still, he was loved. Love, for the monks—agapé—is a matter of choice. One chooses to love, and one should be able to love the unlovely. Though he hate the sin, the monk must love the sinner.

Part III

Conclusions

Chapter 14

Community, Freedom, and Love

The treatment of the monastic community has been thus far entirely analytic, considered as if it were made of numerous discrete parts. But the abbey is also a whole, a unity, an entity with a purpose. In this concluding chapter, I attempt to bring that unity into its own. But this cannot be done using the traditional model of the community found in the vill. As the normal human community, the vill and the monastery are built around three main foci: the family, cooperation, and space. The monastery lacks the family, and thus it is not a vill. This is more than merely a matter of definition. Because it has no biosocial family, there are no children, no need for elementary schools and countless other things associated with childhood, and, not least important, the monastery has no competition for its loyalty. Thus, because there is no biosocial family, there are differences in the behavior of monks as compared to the citizens of vills.

The monastery is, however, highly institutionalized and does not give primacy to specific goals. Thus, the monastery is the same general class of things as a vill: both are communal organizations. A central hypothesis that has guided this research is that if a communal organization lacks one of the foci of the vill, it will compensate by emphasizing something else. The monastery compensates by emphasizing agapé love, a love that can only be obtained through disciplined freedom. Accordingly, this chapter shows the way in which community, freedom, and love are integrated. These three things form a basic unity, so that each attains its fullest realization only in union with the others (Hillery 1982:198).

COMMUNITY AND FREEDOM

Because of the diversity of meanings in the term "community," a more restricted concept is needed if we are to communicate effectively. The essential distinction, as discussed in Chapter 3, is between communal and formal organizations. The importance of freedom to communal organizations is most simply understood by contrasting them with formal organizations, which are defined, after Parsons (1960), as systems that give primacy of orientation to the attainment of specific goals. Communal organizations are systems that do not give specific goals primacy. (Both types, it will be recalled, are heavily institutionalized—see Figure 3.2.) Because they are thus less restricted, communal organizations are able to permit more freedom, so that they can give primacy to people rather than things. In my studies, members of communal organizations perceived less deprivation of freedom, and more disciplined, conditional, and ego freedom than did members of formal organizations (Hillery 1978:26, 1982:190). It is particularly significant that monasteries have higher scores on disciplined freedom than most other groups (see Appendix C).

Disciplined freedom is at the center of monastic life, providing the basis for its stability. In reality, egoistic freedom (to "do one's own thing") is most unrealistic and naive. It cannot last, because reality intrudes itself quickly, and freedom is at best conditional. However, when people commit themselves so that they learn and master the forces that surround them, then they become disciplined and thus free. Stated in this manner, our life is filled with disciplined freedom—handling of multitudinous tools from automobiles to computers, playing musical instruments, and on and on. The monk has learned that only through disciplined freedom and the required commitment can one be significantly free.

But more, the monk has learned that it makes a difference what he commits himself to. Commitment can provide the basis for either freedom or slavery. The two may become frighteningly close, as for example, those committed to Nazi ideology. That the monk continues to feel free, and is free, as so many have demonstrated by their leaving, attests to the wisdom of his choice.

In Chapter 2, I proposed a fourth type of freedom, unconditional. This type seeks to realize self through a transcendental identification with Jesus Christ. Its most significant reality is spiritual (see Figure 2.1). It arises from such a complete commitment that one is no longer concerned about rules. The person who lives according to unconditional freedom is the ultimate communal being, completely conscious of all rules and yet constrained by none. Admittedly, we are talking of an ideal type, as was pointed out in Chapter 2. Most of us will never attain unconditional freedom, but such freedom suggests the ultimate union between freedom and community.

There is, of course, a reciprocal relation between community and freedom. The monk learns of the need for disciplined freedom first in the novitiate and then throughout his life in the monastery. The novice must learn the customs of the particular house, the meaning of monastic spirituality, the liturgy, contemplative prayer, and so forth. In learning these things, he is learning disciplined freedom.

In return, disciplined freedom provides a structure to the community. The monks must be disciplined in their freedom not only by practicing a celibate love but by obeying the rules that free them from concerns with clothing, shelter, food, corporate prayer, and all the other norms of monastic life. Subjection to these norms provides, among other things, the free time for contemplative prayer, where the monk may direct his thoughts to God in whatever way he deems best—within the structure provided by the monastery.

FREEDOM AND LOVE

The relation between love and freedom is somewhat paradoxical. Erotic lovers can do nothing but love. There is no reason, no volition. In this sense, eros is unfree. But eros is free in that it cannot be forced, ordered, or commanded. No one fully understands why people "fall in love." But however it happens, eros cannot be coerced.

In contrast, agapé is completely a product of the will. One practices agapé love because one decides or wills that it is best to do so. Agapé is, for the monks, a duty, something required by Jesus: "A new commandment I give to you, that you love one another" (John 13:34). But this injunction is given in freedom, in two senses. First, one is completely free to love or reject the God of the New Testament, as the life of Jesus attests, and as any atheist can demonstrate. One can reject God and not be swallowed by the earth or struck by lightning. Thus, the decision of the monks to love God is free, in the sense of ego freedom. Once that decision is made, however, the monk must obey God if he is to love God. He can of course choose to hate his neighbor, but he will not please his Beloved. This is the meaning of the statement by Ladislaus Boros (1973:29), that the proper name of freedom "in its deepest sense is, after all, love." To love, we must be free. The second sense, then, in which we are free is through discipline. To be free, we must commit and sacrifice through love. We must obey the commandment.

To be unconditionally free, we must love unconditionally, which is the meaning of agapé in its fullest sense, and it is the ultimate lesson of the monks. But agapé is not something to be attained. It must be acted on. It is not a condition, it is a process. To quote Boros again (1973:29): "The absolute freedom of a finite being means that even when it has attained perfect fulfillment it is still advancing and is never definitely fixed."

Nevertheless, even in agapé, to love is to give up some amount of freedom. If I allow my beloved to respond in his or her own way, this means that I surrender any power I may have over the beloved. In the ultimate sense, the lover allows the beloved to do anything the beloved wants, even crucifixion. The lover may not approve of what the beloved is doing, but to coerce the beloved is to that extent to destroy the love.

As in its relation to community, disciplined freedom provides the structure in which agapé can operate. Particularly in that agapé is created by the monk's choice, he cannot love by means of agapé in any way he chooses. The love must be diffuse rather than focused, it must be capable of being given unilaterally. It must not be possessive; rather, it must be detached. Agapé must be inclusive, universalistic, and disciplined rather than exclusive, particularistic, and undisciplined (see Figure 3.1). In turn, agapé supports disciplined freedom in providing the value that disciplined freedom is good, something to be desired.

COMMUNITY AND LOVE

One of the problems in maximizing love is the practice of power, defined here as the ability to have others do as one wishes. Power ultimately is very ego centered in that the one who has power denies it to others. The more power I have, the less someone else has. Still, the basis of power is in the social structure. No one has power unless others permit it.

But where power is ego centered, love is ego transcendent. Love must involve someone else. It has less concern for self than for others. We have defined love as doing what is best for the beloved. As we have seen in the fullest development of love, the beloved is never coerced. Love and power are thus inversely related. The more I love, the less I insist that the beloved do what I wish. However, power is a characteristic of any human relationship. We seek to get things from others—food, shelter, service, and love. The lover courts and pursues the beloved, most often desiring to have the lover return that love. As natural as that may seem, it is still the beginning of an act of power. The relation can proceed to the aberrant form noted in the Inquisition, where people were burned at the stake "for their own good."

Power corrupts, and it corrupts love as well. Since we are human, and since we (to some degree) seek to exert power over our beloved, our love is accordingly corrupt. Thus, we must qualify our definition of love (no definition of love can be complete). In seeking to do the best for the beloved, in our human selfishness, we deny the freedom needed to love. Doing the best for the beloved may well require doing nothing at all, which is one meaning of contemplative prayer.

The monastic community teaches its monks the importance of agapé, just as it teaches the importance of disciplined freedom. This teaching starts in the novitiate and continues after, especially in the Mass but also in numerous customs that are part of monastic life, such as monks serving their brothers at mealtimes, preserving the Great Silence at night, and even working to support the community.

Agapé in relation to disciplined freedom, supports the communal organization with the value that one must love one's neighbor as one's self (Mark 12:30–31), and the closest neighbor is one's brother. More specifically, agapé love supports the community by increasing solidarity and cohesion. It does this chiefly through such things as liturgy (especially the Mass), through common labor, and in general through the mechanisms of commitment mentioned by Kanter (1972).

INTERRELATIONS

The preceding material can be summarized more systematically by noting that the community teaches, disciplined freedom provides structure, and agapé gives support. More completely, community teaches disciplined freedom, which structures agapé, which supports the monastery. And, proceeding in the opposite direction, disciplined freedom provides the monastic structure, which teaches agapé, which supports disciplined freedom (see Figure 14.1).

This summary is intended to show only the most systematic linkages between community, freedom, and love. Of course, in reality these connections are not as abstract and symmetrical as the discussion implies. Indeed, this book has suggested that the relations are subtle and various, extending to most of the monk's life.

THE MONASTERY AND OTHER ORGANIZATIONS

To say that communal organizations do not give primacy to specific goals is to speak negatively. Scientific evidence can hardly do more. We can infer that this condition means that one *may* thereby give primacy to people instead of things. But it is more complete to say that communal organizations attain their fullest potential when they maximize love.

The argument of this chapter, and indeed this book, is that the monastery is a communal organization, but that it is rare, if not unique, in that it is founded on agapé love. In fact, the monastery cannot be understood without understanding love. But love is also important in vills (see also Varenne 1977). Following Parsons (1966:12), we may say that kinship always orders eros.[1] That is, kinship always specifies the particular members of the kinship unit (and even nonmembers) with whom erotic love is permitted. Since the family, and thus kinship, is a focal component of vills, love at least in erotic form is therefore important in all vills.[2]

The monastery is simpler in that it emphasizes only one kind of love. It radically excludes eros and seeks to subordinate all other forms to agapé. Thus, the monastery is a radical experiment in community, not only in excluding the family but in substituting agapé for all other forms of love through its religious ideology. Accordingly, from the monastery we learn that it is not the family that is so important to communal organizations but

Figure 14.1
Relations between Selected Types of Community, Freedom, and Love

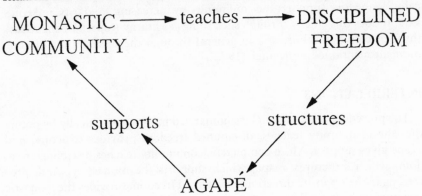

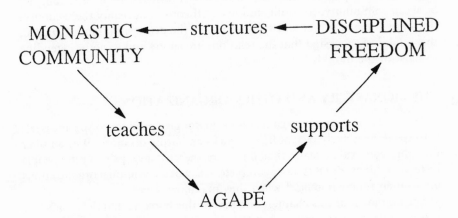

love. And it is not any form of love that is important, but it is agapé. The family can be strong and well, yet the community can fail (Banfield 1958). Only when the family is transcended through cooperation can a community grow in maturity. Only when the cooperation becomes motivated by agapé can the community reach its full potential.

Thus, the monastery is a valuable type of system in the study of communal organizations. It acts as a limiting case: as a communal organization that eliminates the family and thus erotic love, the monastery substitutes another form of love. This finding agrees with the compensatory hypothesis introduced in Chapter 3: a communal organization that does not emphasize the family or space will compensate by emphasizing something else.

Consequently, the theory of communal organizations shows the importance of the family in the normal village and city (that which I have called the vill) and the importance of love in the monastery. Agapé is as necessary to the monastery as the family is to the vill. That the monastery is the most long-lived effort to reorganize communal organizations is in itself significant. Other experiments in communal organizations, popularly known as communes, die out most often within a year, particularly if the family is modified too heavily or eliminated in "free love." The data for monks therefore strongly suggest that love in some form is important to any communal organization.

The community is a product of the human condition. From the broadest perspective, one may say that communal organizations are ultimately oriented to life.[3] In this orientation is the essence of the difference from formal organizations. Communal organizations must deal with all of life; formal organizations deal with only part of it (in giving primacy to specific goals). The monks suggest that there is a potential in community, a potential that is probably not reached very often, and that potential is agapé love. In the normal community, the vill, love is anchored in the family, both in affection and in eros. The monastery, because of the proscription against eros, must go beyond the normal arrangement. It must rely on something other than the encapsulated islands of love developed by the family. This used to be done through Gemeinschaft (Toennies 1957; see also Bulmer 1986) the kind of community based on kinship, mutual aid, and locality, but we move around in modern urban life too much for Gemeinschaft to be fully developed, and so something is lost. Perhaps the monks can point the way.

As a product of the human condition, the monastery is not to be understood merely by its external characteristics—for example, its size, age, and so forth. It is composed of people who have values and purposes. In this book, human groups are classified partly by their values, by the kinds of goals or ends for which they are constructed. Negatively, one may say that communal organizations do not give primacy to specific goals. We are able now to provide a positive criterion: To be fully developed, communal organizations should be primarily oriented to love.

This criterion does not maintain that communal organizations are primarily oriented to love, but that love is needed for communal organizations to develop their full potential. Communal organizations may exist for many reasons: because of the need to survive, as religious or political or educational centers, and so forth. But if the communal organization exists for no reasons other than these, one could argue that the task could be done more efficiently by formal organizations, and thus a case could be made for the eclipse of community (Stein 1964). Yet, to conclude that an eclipse has occurred is premature. Communal organizations continue. They continue also to confront the problem of love.

Both formal and communal organizations have sets of values that determine the primary direction in which the organization is oriented (whether it will be successful in proceeding in that direction is another matter). The values of formal organizations are oriented primarily toward efficiency. The values of communal organizations are oriented primarily toward love. Thus, to realize its condition as a fully developed system (expressive and informal groups are never fully developed), the members of the more institutionalized organizations must strive toward some kind of value. It is entirely possible for an organization to exist for some time in a partially developed condition: Many (perhaps even most) formal organizations are not very efficient, and many (even most) communal organizations are not very loving. But neither condition negates the importance of the value. Formal organizations that are inefficient are regarded, often by their own members, as not doing what they should do, as, for example, a business that does not maximize profits, a hospital that does not cure many patients, a university that does a poor job of training students, and so forth. Such groups can continue in their inefficiency perhaps forever, that is, they can exist and still be recognized for what they are: inadequate.

When one says that a group is primarily oriented toward a certain value, one is saying essentially that the group (that is, the members) *should* be striving for that value. Thus, formal organizations *should* be efficient. Communal organizations *should* attempt to maximize love. Though no form of love is sharply separated from the others, there is a different emphasis within communal organizations: the married couple should be erotic, the family members should be affectionate, neighbors should be friendly. It is in the communal organization as a whole that agapé should be emphasized. Probably most social problems of the modern city can be traced directly to the lack of love, whether this is brought on by population size (it is difficult to love millions of people) or rapid mobility (it is difficult to love people when little or nothing is known about them).

The efforts of monks to develop communal organizations (monasteries) based on agapé serves to emphasize a condition that should be true for all communal organizations. Love can be developed on a diffused, unilateral, detached, inclusive, universalistic, disciplined, and spiritual basis (and then it is, agapé). Of course, monasteries are simpler communities in that they lack the biosocial family, and possibly this is a key to their achievement. In lacking the biosocial family, they had to develop agapé if they were to continue to exist.

If love is so important to communal organizations, what can the monks do to help us? Primarily, they demonstrate that it is possible to choose to love because one wills it. Each of the other loves has something external that helps it in some way. Eros, of course, has its physical component, as does affection. And both eros and friendship have that unknown quality that draws people to each other. But agapé is the type of love that has nothing natural to prompt it. Agapé develops because one chooses to develop such a thing.

What I am saying is that it is not enough to build a community on the basis of eros or affection or friendship. The family may as well divide a community as integrate it (Banfield 1958; Romanucci-Ross 1973). Friendship and affection are limited in the number of people to whom these loves can be directed—friendship by its nature (we cannot be close friends with everyone) and affection because we can only be in physical contact with a limited number of people. But agapé can be directed to everyone, even one's enemies.

In view of the importance I have attributed to love in communal organizations, why do so few communities realize it? Perhaps the problem in communal organizations is analogous to that in individuals. It has been known for thousands of years that love is important to the welfare of people. In the Book of Proverbs (15:17), we read: "Better a meal of vegetables where there is love than a fattened calf with hatred" (New International Version). And again, in the Book of Leviticus (19:18): "Love your neighbor as yourself." Nevertheless, Jesus still had to emphasize the importance of love to his apostles (John 15:12). Apparently, the poor development of love is pervasive.

Similarly, efficiency has always been desirable for organizations designed to attain specific goals (that is, formal organizations). But not until the industrial revolution was efficiency developed to an appreciable degree. I suggest that the importance of love to communal organizations is a matter of social evolution. We probably will not develop agapé until we are forced to, until crime, poverty, familial disintegration, and government fraud become so widespread that we become desperate and realize that without agapé, the communal organization, society, and thus humanity may cease to be.

The efficiency of formal organizations could be antithetical to communal organizations. Certainly, it should be clear that efficiency is not a primary value of community. For example, children can be produced much more efficiently through ways other than heterosexual erotic attachments. But children survive poorly if at all without affection. To strive primarily for efficiency in communal organizations may ultimately kill such groups. Yet, especially in cities, formal organizations have been raised to their most important position in history, such that we cannot do without them. But they compete strongly with the family and place friendship and affection in second or worse place. Until communal organizations gain control over formal organizations, communal organizations may be hopelessly crippled.

SOME FINAL REMARKS

Though the monastery is a fully human community, there are important differences from the normal communal organization, the vill. It is instructive to remind ourselves of these differences if we are to understand how agapé can be strengthened. First, we have considered agapé only in a religious community, and in only one kind of religion. To what extent can agapé be developed in other religions, and can it be developed outside of a religious context? Second, the monastery is a drastically simplified community. It has only one sex and no children. The innumerable problems that occur in the family do not impinge on monastic life. Also, the monks are shielded from the outside society more than is true of adults in the family. Finally, the monk deliberately simplifies his life through asceticism so that he may offer himself more completely to God. On the other side of the problem, the monk is able to interact more closely with more people in a face-to-face situation than is true in the family. There may well be a connection between simplification and the ability to relate intimately to more people.

Agapé is not the only form of love found in the monastery. We have observed close friendship there, and affection also. Different forms of love support each other: the data suggest that the more we love in one form of love the more we can love in other forms. In the normal communal organization, there are also multiple forms of love. Eros has never existed alone. Perhaps we can learn from the monks how to supplement eros not only with friendship and affection but with agapé as well.

The chief problem in maximizing love in the vill is that eros and familial affection are so powerful that they easily obscure both friendship and agapé. Development of agapé in the vill requires unceasing vigilance. This task in our society has been generally left to the Christian church. But the church tends to lose its commitment to agapé, especially as it develops institutionalized modes of adjustment to other organizations in the community, such as the Christian accommodation to power and wealth. For the development of love in the community involves a commitment to the ideal of love in all its dimensions (which inescapably always requires a personal relationship). It requires a disciplined freedom that must itself be built into the normative structure of the communal organization. The monks would say it requires grace.

The modern world, particularly in the West, can be compared to a condition witnessed in physics in the form of high turbulence. One of the characteristics of such a state (called "far-from-equilibrium") is chaos, in which laws that normally hold in calmer conditions no longer apply (Gleick 1987). The rapidity of social change in the modern world brings us close to if not into chaos. In such a condition, agapé is even more important to the urban world in which we live. In spite of our material success, and perhaps because of it, we are impoverished in love. We do not treat each other very well. The increase in homelessness, unemployment, divorce, and crime all document this basic fact. Our capitalistic society has little conscience and less heart. Max Weber traced this condition to the development of bureaucracies, the ultimate of formal organizations, which would imprison humanity in an iron cage. Somehow, we must learn how to develop agapé. For unless we do, humanity will have to live in an ever-more inhuman system.

Our record also shows that the other forms of love are not enough, for most of us are well acquainted with eros, affection, and friendship, yet this knowledge is insufficient to stem the tide of social disorganization (chaos) in which we live.

What is wrong with our world? (I am speaking, of course, of the industrial West.) Sorokin (1937–41) states what I think is the best diagnosis. Ours is a decaying society. The culture that developed over the past centuries was based on truth defined as verifiable knowledge perceived through the senses (the "sensate" society). This culture is breaking down. We no longer are sure of what is right and wrong, beautiful and ugly. The decline of the family and the increase in crime that Sorokin predicted more than 50 years ago are but symptoms of this decay. Sorokin concluded that there is only one way our culture can become integrated again. As the former system based on materialism breaks down, we must turn to a more spiritual system, in which truth is defined as based on faith and love (an "ideational" society). This love must go beyond the family or we will be no better than before.

The monks are a repository of the love we need. They show that strangers can come together and develop love that goes beyond physical attraction (eros and affect) and personal predilection (friendship). The problem is that the monks, too, may become victims of our collapsing society. Monasteries are not receiving enough novices. But where can they find them? Our decaying society does not value lifelong commitment, as is shown by the ever-rising divorce rate.

The monastic decline, however, is not universal. It is found only in the industrial West. Monasteries in the Third World are growing. We may have to turn to them to rediscover agapé. Even here, the danger is not past, because the Third World wants the materialism of the West. Perhaps the question is one of time. Can our society last long enough for it to turn again to the ideational values it so desperately needs?

NOTES

1. More literally, Parsons (1966:12) says: "Kinship always involves an ordering of the erotic relations of adults," though we should certainly include children.

2. In both the monastery and the vill, eros is to some degree treated negatively: the rules designate the persons with whom one should *not* have erotic relations.

3. I am indebted to Irving Louis Horowitz for this observation.

Ending: A Personal Summing Up

The main thrust in this book has been sociological. But community, freedom, and love each also has an individual dimension. In summing up, it is appropriate to show what these dimensions have meant to me as I have experienced them in the monastery. For although I began this study strictly as a sociological venture, my involvement with the monks has come to be more than sociology. It has been a personal and spiritual experience as well.

It is not possible to study a group and be uninfluenced by it, if only because in studying it we gain new knowledge. But the extent of the influence varies. Since I have been influenced by the monks in more than simply a cognitive sense, the reader deserves to know the extent of the impact.

Monasteries have been attractive for me in several ways. The sociological attraction came first. There was a problem to be solved. Monasteries were communities without the family. How did they operate? But attraction quickly moved beyond that. I recall vividly my first nights at Gethsemani and then at New Melleray, the first two abbeys I visited. For many reasons, I was so excited I could not sleep. I had been reading Thomas Merton's *The Seven Storey Mountain* (1948). I am a committed Christian. My visits were the realization of a long-standing sociological interest. And there was, of course, the beautiful monastic solitude. It was not just quiet. It was also very peaceful, and the gentle chanting in plainsong of the monks only emphasized that peace. As the years went by, the excitement, like first love, wore off. But the attraction never has. I suppose that as long as there are monasteries, I will be going to them for one reason or another. If I cannot find some sociological project, I will simply visit or go on retreat. Discovering monasteries has been discovering a gentle passion.

With all the attraction, why then am I not a monk? Part of the story has been told: I am married and am a Protestant. A few words are needed to show more clearly what is meant. First, I am more than married. My wife and I have formed our own community, and it has grown stronger over the years. I understand something of what Elizabeth Barrett Browning (1932:432) meant: "And if God choose, I shall but love thee better after death." Our love has created problems for this research, for I cannot participate in monastic life as fully when my wife is with me. There is, then, a very significant choice to be made each time I go to the monks. I *must* go. I miss the life too much after a while. The world begins to get to me. But it is never difficult to leave for home.

My Protestantism has proved almost as much of a problem. I have come to know Roman Catholicism, and it has a great appeal. But I remain Protestant. In fact, my work with monks has sharpened my Protestantism. I now feel that both Protestants and Roman Catholics need each other. Protestants need the Romans because the Romans have a center. We Protestants are too fragmented for our own good. But the Romans need Protestants, because the Protestants represent a critical voice that cannot be silenced.

More specific reasons are not relevant here. Of greater importance, the monks are my brothers in Christ. I know experientially that we worship the same God who became incarnate in the body of Jesus. I have prayed with them too long and too often not to know that they are sincere and that our goal is the same, though we walk by somewhat different paths. Above all, I now realize the importance of Jesus' statement, "Judge not, that you be not judged" (Matt. 7:1). For as convinced as I am of the truth of my Protestant position, I know that they are equally convinced of the truth of theirs. Further, neither of us will come to our God because of our sincerity. We will come to God on the mercy of Jesus Christ or not at all. This *we* believe.

Such common dedication has meant much to this research. It has given me insight as nothing else can. The monks have responded to me as a Christian brother, also. I love all the monks I have ever met. Not all are my friends. Many are, but by no means all. Friendship is not the same as agapé. And the monks have shown me that, too.

I have alluded to the peace and solitude as major attractions. No peace is as deep as one can find in the solitude of a Trappist monastery. This peace is especially evident when the world is asleep, whether in the late hours of the night when monks and guest alike have retired, or just before dawn when many monks are at their own silent prayers. It is a peace so great that it is almost palpable. One can understand one monk when he said that the silence one experiences in prayer *is* God. I have visited 19 Trappist and Trappistine monasteries in six countries, and in every case I have experienced this peace. I sometimes take students with me, and their experience apparently is much the same. I recall especially one student—a good sociologist and also an agnostic. He evidently experienced something, for after we had left he said to me, with a touch of awe, "You know, Dr. Hillery, that place was *spooky!*"

Freedom, of course, has been a major theme in these pages. The monks have taught me most of what I know. The best statement I have read on the absence of freedom is by Roger Rosenblatt (1986:98). He speaks of the chaos young Americans now find themselves in:

> Freedom gains meaning from restraint.... For thousands of years, various, and very different, definitions of freedom—Aristotelian, Cartesian, Augustinian, Kantian—have all related freedom to significant choice.... If freedom has no restraints and embraces everything, then it risks becoming tyranny, since logically it must include tyranny among the things it embraces....
>
> The fact is that no wide social community exists, no village of common thought, in which personal freedom may be judged, guided and made valuable....
>
> Odd that the basic balance of forces sustaining the country seems to have been abandoned by the American family, ... a naturally closer community and potentially a happier one.... Little murders are committed daily in homes where Mom and Dad sit planted in front of pieces of paper..., while the children lie still as dolls on their beds and gaze at ceiling fixtures, like stations in a dream. See how free everybody is. The only things missing are the essentials: authority, responsibility, attention and love.

True, the monks do not receive much attention, either from the world or in the monastery—though they do receive some attention there. But they definitely know authority, responsibility, and love.

Quite related is the concept of community, for the monk's perception of freedom is one in community and of community. I see community differently now, after having viewed it in the monastery. The normal community, based mainly on families cooperating in a local area, can be much more. I see a potential for community to move beyond the immediate involvements of eros, friendship, and affection. These are undeniably beautiful sentiments. I will never willingly surrender them. But they can also point to something larger. The monks have taught me that the community is not built on the effort of its members toward self-fulfillment. A community is built not on self-fulfillment but on commitment, sacrifice, and dedication. As likely as not, self-fulfillment can come through these as an unanticipated by-product, but one is not apt to attain commitment, sacrifice, and dedication when seeking only for oneself.

We have here the classic dilemma between the person and the group. Without the group, humans could not exist. But each human creature is inescapably separate from every other. In this separation is to be found a basis for freedom. Too much group control would stifle the freedom; too much individuality would erode the community.

The world appears to have been growing away from community for a long time. In this, Maurice Stein (1964) was correct. Though we still have many communities, we have less and less community, less and less love. Ego freedom has been growing at the expense of discipline (though this need not be). Rosenblatt (1986) feels, and I can only agree, that this path leads to chaos. Perhaps the monks again can help to preserve civilization, as they did in the Middle Ages. But instead of manuscripts, they will preserve something far more important: a way of life in which freedom is built in its more substantial sense to maintain a love that is transcendent.

Appendix A

Methods Used in the Study of Monasteries

Scholarship requires that one be sensitive to what others have done and that one be able to innovate when necessary. Were innovation not required, there would be no need to discuss methodology. The methods to be presented here are not statements of how research should be done but of how it was done. Any research ultimately is a compromise with the possible. For example, because I had very little funding, the research had to be done in bits and pieces and has taken a very long time: two decades, in fact. I would not argue that all research should be so expensive. But some ideas require nurturing and evolution. For example, I did not see the significance of love in monastic life for approximately fourteen years.

The research could be given several labels. It is mainly sociological in its study of community structure. It is heavily anthropological since data were gathered largely by living with the monks and attempting to understand their values, beliefs, and ideals. It is also theological in that I have been guided in this study by St. Benedict's *Rule*, the Bible, and other theological materials. It is mystical because I have participated with the monks in their prayers and have used this participation to understand them. And it is scientific in that objective data (that can be verified by others) have been used wherever possible.

THE RESEARCH METHODS

Five major research tools are used in this study. (1) Participant observation is a research technique where the researcher lives among the subjects, participating in their life. (2) The questionnaire is a list of printed questions that the research subject answers. (3) The interview differs from the questionnaire in that the researcher verbally questions the subject. (4) Documents are written observations about the subject, whether made by the members of the group or by others. (5) Triangulation

---

Only enough of the methods are discussed to enable the reader to understand the research done in Trappist monasteries. For additional comment see Hillery 1981b.

Table A.1
Types of Data Employed in the Study of Monasteries

Mona-stery[1]	Approx-Size of Mona-stery	Days Spent in Participant Observation or Visiting	Type of Questionnaire and Number of Monks Sampled				Inter-views	Docu-ments
			Freedom	Respect	Love I	II		
Palisades	50+	259	50		22	22	X	X
King	15+	46			6		X	X
Ascension	15+	10	15	11	11			
Bernard	30+	8	9	13	10			
Cana	50+	5	21	11				X
Elim	30+	19	16	9			X	
Fountain	50+	4					X	X
Genesis	30+	5						X
Horeb	<15	1						
Immanuel	50+	3			5			
Jericho	50+	15			25	10	X	
Mark	<15	3						
Solitude	20+	15			9		X	
Waters	<15	6			7	7	X	
Yoke	<15	--	10					
Zion	<15	5						X
Total	557[2]	404	121	44	60	74		

[1]Pseudonyms
[2]Data for male monasteries only as of 1986.

is a combination of these (Denzin 1970). It involves their interaction and is thus a phenomenon that is more than the sum of its parts.

All 12 Trappist-Cistercian abbeys in the United States have been visited, as well as one experimental monastery, two Trappistine monasteries, and another contemplative one for nuns (Waters, Yoke, and Zion—pseudonyms are used throughout unless otherwise noted). The extent to which these research tools have been used in the various houses is shown in Table A.1.

PARTICIPANT OBSERVATION

There are various types of participant observation. (1) The participant is simply a member of the group. The works of Thomas Merton fall in this category. (2) The participant-as-observer is a group member who is trained in observational techniques and uses his own group as a subject for study. Heilman's (1976) report on *Synagogue Life* is an example. (3) The observer-as-participant participates as much as possible without becoming a full-fledged member (that is, without "going native"). (4) The observer does as the title suggests: he or she observes but does not participate (Gold 1958; Pearsall 1965).

My role was observer-as-participant at Palisades Abbey, Bernard, Cana, and Elim. In the remaining monasteries I was more of an observer. I slept in the guest house at Palisades but ate and worked with the monks and was allowed largely free access to the cloister. I had an occasional job of helping the baker. I was obviously not a monk but was accepted by most as having a right to do research in the monastery. I lived with the monks as much as possible. There were only four limitations: I was asked to avoid the dormitory and bath areas, I did not sleep in the cloister, did not sing in choir, and did not attend Chapter meetings. The last two limitations were compensated for in other monasteries.

King Abbey also allowed freedom to move about the cloister, and to some degree this was true of Bernard and Cana. I sang in choir at Palisades when I was in the Monastic Center (see Chapter 3) and also at Cana, Elim, Solitude, and Bernard. In all, I have taken part in most aspects of the life of a monk, though not all at any single monastery.

Perhaps the most valuable participant observation at Palisades took place while eating in the refectory with the monks, generally not permitted for laymen. I requested this privilege at the start of the study and never regretted it. True, there is no speaking at meals, but I was able to see most of the men at one time (other than in choir), and the nonverbal communication is probably more valuable than I understand intellectually. This part of the research enabled me to know the monks better than any way short of direct interviewing. I ate in the refectory for six months (spread over an 11-year period).

My own changing perspective through time was also important. I recall one monk in particular: on first meeting, I was charmed by his behavior and impressed by his piety. Then, on seeing the reaction of other monks to him, I concluded that he was essentially shallow. But as I observed him through the years, it became apparent that he was deeply committed. He did not follow the rules as scrupulously as the others, and he was no intellectual, but the search for God was foremost in his life. Only observations over many years could have shown this.

An essential aspect of participant observation is obtaining the help of someone in the group with whom one can converse in depth. Technically, the anthropological term for such a person is "key informant." When first studying Palisades, I asked the abbot to appoint an informant for me (I called him a "guide"). He turned out to be excellent. As time went on, other monks also came to fill this role.

Several papers have been written by me and my colleagues on various aspects of monastic life. Each of these has been read by a committee of up to three monks at Palisades, not for censorship but for correction. Corrections have decreased as time passed, but in the beginning, especially, use of the committee prevented serious errors. I have also made several sets of recommendations to the monastery. Simply the effort to make them forced a crystallization of my thinking and was more instructive than the feedback—though both were important.

The entire manuscript was also, in an earlier draft, read to the community during the noon meal in the refectory (the one exception being Chapter 13, on deviance; the monks were requested to read it privately). Corrections were mainly typographical. Some monks were uncomfortable about the deviance chapter, but I and several others pointed out that its omission would raise serious questions about the integrity of the entire book. There was also discussion about using the real name of the abbey, and so I asked that a vote be taken. The result was overwhelmingly for a pseudonym.

There are limitations to participant observation. First, it is largely unsystematic. Thus, I have used questionnaires and systematic interviews as well. Second, the perspectives are limited to the person doing the observation. Participant observation has provided a picture of only one monastery. How do I know that Palisades is not an extreme case? The answer is to visit other monasteries. In addition to the American monasteries, I have now been to Trappist monasteries in six countries. More than a week has been spent in six abbeys besides Palisades, and comparable, questionnaire data have been collected in several (see Table A.1). These observations show that Palisades is not extreme.

What of the dangers of overidentification? Or, to use more technical terminology, how does one maintain proper role distance? If one gets too close, the perspective is lost. Role distance was achieved more by necessity than virtue. First, I cannot be a monk because I am married. In monastic parlance, for me to become a monk would be in essence to break my vow of stability. Second, I am a Presbyterian and thus cannot share in the Mass in all monasteries. I can do so only where the bishop permits, but that is not the situation at Palisades. Third, I now live many hundreds of miles from Palisades. I cannot go there whenever or as often as I wish, and this helps in maintaining role distance (both geographically and socially).

Some disadvantages can be advantages. Being married means that long periods of time cannot be freely spent away from my wife, my own community. And so the more than 250 days at Palisades were broken into shorter visits. This condition has required that observations be planned more carefully and has provided ultimately a longer time perspective in which the monks could get to know me. This practice of "observation, separation, consideration, and return" (OSCAR) may be regarded as a research technique in its own right. It is not meant for quick results but can provide a perspective as nothing else can.

A few additional words about the advantages and disadvantages of OSCAR: It permits one's work to evolve more fully. Instead of having research begin and end over the normal grant period of a year, one observes, writes a report, checks with the subjects, forms new perspectives, gathers new material, writes another report, and so on. OSCAR thus becomes an embodiment of the point-to-point approach of W. I. Thomas: "Progress in method is made from point to point by setting up objectives, using certain techniques, then resettling the problem with the introduction of still other objectives and the modification of techniques" (Blumer 1939:166). Finally, one may use this technique when it is not possible to be absent from other duties except for limited periods.

There are disadvantages. OSCAR is obviously time-consuming. There are also occasions when extended stays in themselves can be an advantage. For example, I have never fully learned the Trappist sign language and probably would have during longer spans. As another case in point, it takes several days to become acclimated to the slower pace of monastic life. Visits that are too short also put the researcher in the role of a visitor (observer) rather than a participant. My minimum preferred stay is ten days. (Note that in anthropological field research the investigator often leaves the site after a week if possible, if only to rest. OSCAR can thus be fitted into a rhythm of field research.) A final disadvantage is that one misses things when leaving for a period. It is an advantage to be a part of the community over the entire span of the research. "Catching up" after a period of separation can never be complete.

QUESTIONNAIRES

Because only limited financial resources were available, the questionnaire was especially valuable. Since the monks are literate, this instrument generally presented no problems. In fact, in some ways it is advantageous, since answers are more anonymous than in interviews. Four questionnaires have been used. The first, the "Freedom" questionnaire is a broad one requiring 30 to 45 minutes to complete. Questions range over such concepts as freedom, cohesion, conflict, religion, and alienation (Hillery, Dudley, and Morrow 1977; Hillery 1978; Hillery, Dudley, and Thompson 1979). The second questionnaire was more narrowly directed to the reasons for which people respect each other (Chapter 9). The last two instruments, the "Love" questionnaires, repeat many of the questions in the Freedom questionnaire and also focus on various kinds of love. The first Love questionnaire attempted to collect data on the number of love experiences had by the respondent, and it was not successful. The second, using data from the first one, developed Likert-type questions that ultimately produced two factor scales (see Chapter 3).

As far is known, the first two questionnaires have posed no problems except for questionnaire fatigue. Six monasteries have been "questionnaired" more than once. In four abbeys, fewer monks filled out the questionnaires the second time, though several years intervened in each case. They can hardly be blamed. These men are conscientious, and completing a questionnaire for some can take hours, even days. The usual college student completes one of these in about half an hour. Of course, the effort of the monks is appreciated, but questionnaire fatigue remains a problem. In fact, several monasteries have decided simply that it would be best not to participate at all in filling out these documents, though other forms of research were fully permitted.

Thus, I am more careful about asking monks to fill out questionnaires. The attitude I take is: Suppose I only had one questionnaire to administer to this monastery; would this be the one? Such a question is especially pertinent to the first Love questionnaire. Approximately half of it concerned questions on love. Evidence has shown that asking questions about love may be threatening. If the interpretation is correct, then it means that the data will perhaps pertain to those monks who are not threatened, and the data should be so interpreted. (The second Love questionnaire was further modified to remove the threat, especially by omitting questions on eros, which were not informative of monasteries, at any rate.)

There is another weakness of questionnaires: one cannot probe for additional answers or clarification. If someone offers no comment in a space provided for one, that is the end of the matter. Or if someone offers an unintelligible remark, it must remain unintelligible. Only interviews offer a remedy. Finally, what of falsification of answers? Though this has not been a problem with the monks, at times one suspects that they may give an ideal answer more than a real one.

What is the value of the questionnaire? First, it systematizes (assuming also adequate sampling). One may *feel* that the monks are free. It is decidedly superior information to know that monks have more disciplined freedom than any other group and less ego freedom than most (Chapter 2). Through questionnaires the meaning of freedom is elaborated quantitatively in a way that it cannot be through participant observation.

INTERVIEWS

This method also includes several types. At one extreme is the formal interview, where the interviewer asks questions from what would otherwise be a questionnaire (and the questionnaire then becomes technically an interview schedule). At the other extreme is the informal interview, which becomes in essence a part of participant observation. Thus, interviews share many of the failings and advantages of each of the other methods, though there are differences. In comparison with the questionnaire, the interview is more expensive and is not as anonymous. However, it is more flexible in permitting probing, elaboration, and various degrees of clarification. Compared with participant observation, interviews are more purposive. One usually has a specific objective in mind. For monks, interviews have been used mainly to understand status (Chapter 9), occupations (Chapter 7), and prayer (Chapter 10).

DOCUMENTS

Numerous kinds of documents were used. Some of the monasteries have had books written about them. To use real names, this is true of Gethsemani (e.g., Merton 1948, 1953) and Genessee (Nouwen 1976). An excellent article about Conyers by Colman McCarthy appeared in the *Washington Post* (March 23, 1980). Three of the monasteries have been subjects of a lengthy and detailed questionnaire Research Committee of CMSW 1969 administered in 1968 by Sister Marie Augusta Neal (1970—see also Chapter 1). Palisades, especially, provided an extensive assortment of self-study materials, diaries, reports by visiting abbots, newsletters, travel records, financial reports, and other materials.

IN CONCLUSION: SOME OBSERVATIONS
ON TRIANGULATION

One often hears criticisms about these methods—the unsystematic nature of participant observation, the superficial findings of interviews and questionnaires, the incomplete nature of documents. Each of these charges, and others, are true. In reply, though each is inadequate when used alone, they can tell us much when used together. I argue for the importance of triangulation, or using several approaches in the discovery of truth. In closing, comment is appropriate on some problems of triangulation itself.

Denzin (1989:237) speaks of four kinds of triangulation: data, method, investigator, and theory. Data triangulation was achieved in this investigation by combining participant observation, surveys, questionnaires, interviews, and documents. In addition, data was gathered over varying segments of time as well as cross sections of single time-periods. Methodological triangulation also involved participant observation and survey analysis, for these are analytical methods as well as data-collection techniques. Participant observation, for example, requires that the subjects teach the investigator what is needed to understand their society, rather than having the investigator test some hypothesis. The survey analyst does in fact test hypotheses. Mine were concerned with freedom, love, and community.

I have used different investigators in triangulation no more than partially. Though I have worked with others, such as Charles Dudley and Richard Della Fave (see Chapters 2 and 9), they were involved mainly in the analysis of data rather than its collection, and they worked only in limited segments of the study.

Three disciplines have been used: theology, anthropology, and sociology. Theologically, I have been able to share in the prayer life of the monks. This experience has led me to explore such topics as prayer and agapé and in the end to build my central hypothesis around love: Monasteries compensate for the absence of the family by emphasizing agapé. Anthropology has not only been responsible for my use of participant observation; it has prompted me to study the monastery as a whole, as a unit. Sociologically, I have employed both functional and conflict perspectives. My major concern has been to understand how the monastery works, how it is put together. I used the conflict perspective on such subjects as change, the novitiate, the economy, authority, and deviance. Nonetheless, my main approach has been functional. I have tried to understand how the monastery works, how it is put together. Conflict has not been a dominant focus.

Even with such a brief summary, one is impressed with the amount of energy required in triangulation. Nevertheless, a single person has largely done the triangulation in this study, and to this extent there is always the problem of bias. What is needed is an account that several observers can affirm as real. A plea is thus being made for others to become observers and surveyors, so that their reports may be checked against mine. The problem, of course, is not with triangulation per se, since other researchers with other theories would contribute to a solution. What is being called for is more triangulation, not less.

But there are still problems. First, some observations can never be checked, such as experience in contemplative prayer or in agapé love. Second, the monks should not be studied too closely, or they will suffer. Monasteries are not unique in this respect, but it is nonetheless true that they are not meant to be studied by social scientists. They are meant to be places where one can seek God. Further research must be done carefully, or the object to be studied will be endangered. The question here is, How far can triangulation be carried at one research site?

Still, the present research has tried to show that even when only limited triangulation is used, findings are possible that could be attained in no other way.

Appendix B

Factor Scale Scores on Freedom for Selected Groups

Group	Disci-plined	Condi-tional	Ego	Deprivation of Freedom	Number of Cases
Yoga Training School					
Staff	1.067	2.450	4.367	4.120	5
Trainees	1.727	2.273	3.924	3.691	11
Nuns					
Monastery 1	1.370	2.844	4.204	4.000	10
Monastery 2	1.524	2.659	3.788	4.367	7
Monks					
Monastery 3	1.481	2.222	3.685	3.885	9
Monastery 4	1.519	2.450	3.741	3.860	10
Monastery 5	1.711	2.464	3.844	4.014	15
Monastery 6	1.733	2.550	3.767	4.040	5
Palisades	1.818	2.511	3.818	3.727	22
Monastery 7	1.867	2.500	4.100	3.600	11
Monastery 8	1.883	2.375	3.738	3.920	20
Monastery 9	2.121	2.659	3.788	3.673	11
Monastic Center					
Clergy	1.667	2.511	3.543	3.852	23
Married	1.905	2.463	3.488	3.738	28
Single	1.907	2.645	3.591	3.620	56
Staff Groups					
Women's Prison	1.782	2.060	2.868	2.469	29
Men's Prison, Administrative	1.850	1.673	2.497	2.131	49
Men's Prison, Custodial	2.434	2.121	3.172	2.552	33
Delinquent's School	1.944	2.167	3.764	3.617	12
Boarding School	2.048	2.518	3.726	2.743	14
Regimented Groups					
Drug Rehabilitation School	1.800	2.085	4.200	2.640	15
Women Military Cadets	1.931	2.552	3.957	2.936	29
Men Military Cadets	2.321	2.644	4.121	2.709	215
Fraternities					
Fraternity 2	2.000	2.119	3.286	3.314	21
Sorority 1	2.034	1.828	2.908	3.517	29
Fraternity 3	2.069	1.860	2.909	3.606	34
Sorority 2	2.135	2.042	3.226	3.714	42
Sorority 3	2.185	2.222	3.444	3.244	9
Fraternity 1	2.273	1.909	3.152	3.721	33

Group	Disci-plined	Condi-tional	Ego	Deprivation of Freedom	Number of Cases
Communes					
Caphas Volunteers	2.000	1.944	3.056	4.222	9
Caphas Members	2.024	2.446	3.500	3.771	14
St. Samuel	2.061	2.000	3.561	2.709	11
Walden Two	2.394	2.083	3.010	3.636	33
Old Age Homes					
Dale	2.196	2.853	3.293	2.557	46
Tatt	2.357	2.464	3.310	2.879	28
Prisons and Students					
Women Prisoners	2.375	2.806	3.871	1.875	40
Boarding School	2.400	2.536	3.782	2.898	55
Delinquent School	2.741	2.917	3.398	2.111	18
Men Prisoners	2.837	3.322	4.048	1.511	45
Citizen Groups					
Parents of School Children	2.179	2.000	3.628	4.167	15
Police	2.444	2.417	3.167	2.900	6
Trailer Park	2.533	2.850	4.167	3.760	15
Suburban Community	3.000	2.222	2.800	3.943	17
Social Workers	3.205	3.038	4.013	3.262	13
Military Groups					
Medics	2.167	2.350	3.767	1.700	10
Women's Corps	2.567	2.450	3.150	2.180	10
Military Police	3.152	3.223	4.192	1.725	46
Student Groups					
Black Students	2.667	1.545	3.424	2.948	25
Scouting Fraternity	2.722	2.321	2.881	3.014	15
Women's Dorm 1	2.724	2.159	3.142	3.468	41
University Sample 1	2.794	2.250	2.571	3.543	21
Men's Dorm 1	2.811	2.500	3.261	2.897	37
Football Team	2.884	2.427	3.451	2.409	23
University Sample 2	2.944	2.817	3.828	2.600	30
Classroom	3.104	2.439	3.131	3.264	53
Women's Dorm 2	3.182	2.386	2.763	3.388	33
Men's Dorm 2	3.255	2.985	3.647	2.659	17
Cooperative Boarding Houses					
Anarch	2.852	2.278	2.481	3.289	9
Coop	2.939	2.545	2.621	3.982	11
Martin House	3.000	2.531	2.653	3.225	24
Housing Projects					
Candice	3.067	2.900	2.917	2.460	10
Carouthers	3.111	2.917	3.593	2.178	9

Appendix C

Rank Order of Factor Scale Scores on Freedom for Selected Groups

Group	Disci-plined	Condi-tional	Ego	Deprivation of Freedom
Yoga Training School				
Staff	1	32	62	59
Trainees	8	21	52	43
Nuns				
Monastery 1	2	53	61	56
Monastery 2	5	49.5	46.5	62
Monks				
Monastery 3	3	18	38	52
Monastery 4	4	32	41	51
Monastery 5	7	35.5	50	57
Monastery 6	9	45	43.5	58
Palisades	12	39.5	48	46
Monastery 7	14	32.5	56	37
Monastery 8	15	25	40	53
Monastery 9	27	49.5	46.5	42
Monastic Center				
Clergy	6	39.5	32	50
Married	16	34	30	47
Single	17	48	34	40
Staff Groups				
Women's Prison	10	10	8	12
Men's Prison, Administrative	13	2	2	6
Men's Prison, Custodial	39	14	20	10
Delinquent's School	19	16	42	39
Boarding School	24	41	39	19
Regimented Groups				
Drug Rehabilitation School	11	11.5	60	15
Women Military Cadets	18	46	53	24
Men Military Cadets	34	47	57	17.5
Fraternities				
Fraternity 2	20	13	23	32
Sorority 1	23	3	10	35
Fraternity 3	26	4	11	38
Sorority 2	28	9	21	44
Sorority 3	31	18	28	28
Fraternity 1	33	5	18	45

Group	Disci-plined	Condi-tional	Ego	Deprivation of Freedom
Communes				
Caphas Volunteers	21	6	14	61
Caphas Members	22	30	31	49
St. Samuel	25	7.5	33	17.5
Walden Two	37	11.5	13	41
Old Age Homes				
Dale	32	55	24	13
Tatt	35	35.5	25	20
Prisons and Students				
Women Prisoners	36	51	51	4
Boarding School	38	43	45	22
Delinquent School	46	57.5	26	5
Men Prisoners	49	62	55	1
Citizen Groups				
Parents of School Children	30	25	36	60
Police	40	27	19	23
Trailer Park	41	54	58	48
Suburban Community	54.5	18	7	54
Social Workers	61	60	54	29
Military Groups				
Medics	29	24	43.5	2
Women's Corps	42	32	17	8
Military Police	59	61	59	3
Student Groups				
Black Students	43	1	27	25
Scouting Fraternity	44	23	9	26
Women's Dorm 1	45	15	16	34
University Sample 1	47	20	3	36
Men's Dorm 1	48	37.5	22	21
Football Team	51	28	29	9
University Sample 2	53	52	49	14
Classroom	57	29	15	30
Women's Dorm 2	60	26	6	33
Men's Dorm 2	62	59	37	16
Cooperative Boarding Houses				
Anarch	50	22	1	31
Coop	52	44	4	55
Martin House	54.5	42	5	27
Housing Projects				
Candice	56	57	12	11
Carouthers	58	57.5	35	7

Appendix D

Opinions Concerning Chastity Among Palisades Monks, 1968

Opinion	Percent "Yes"
66. The celibate so consecrated by vow in religious life possesses a means for coming to know the meaning of love, a love that finds fulfillment in dispensing the love of Christ to His people.	92
70. The religious must be willing to take the risk involved in forming deeply personal and truly human friendships.	82
61. The vow to remain a celibate provides a specific structure for living a unique kind of love; it provides a frame for being present to the other, for encounter, for communication with another that can increase trust and reduce anxiety.	88
62. The great dignity of Christian chastity and its particular requirements are derived from a fundamental privilege: religious are wedded to the Word made flesh.	68
63. As Mary accepted the role of universal motherhood at the Incarnation, so the women religious, overshadowed by the Holy Spirit, consecrates her love to God for universal motherhood.	65
69. The traditional way of presenting chastity in religious life has allowed for the development of isolation and false mysticism among religious.	64
64. If a religious shuns involvement with persons I think the religious betrays the purpose of the vow of chastity.	58

Opinion	Percent "Yes"
67. The life of celibacy is an angelic life on earth.	23
68. Christian celibacy goes all the way along a road on which marriage stops half way	9
373. Do you think loneliness is inevitable with fidelity to the vow of chastity?	24
492. Do you think that the way the vow of chastity is treated in your spiritual formation is adequate?	48
Number	66

Source: Research Committee of CMSW 1969.

Appendix E

Attitudinal Differences for Religious Opinions, in Percent

Attitude or position	Yes or agree**	No or disagree**

Worldview:

164. The best way to improve world conditions is for every man to take care of his own corner of the vineyard.
39*   45

143. Every step in world history has been accomplished through the inspiration of reformers and creative men.
58*   35*

140. When you come right down to it, it's human nature never to do anything without an eye to one's own profit.
42   48*

H 144. With everything so uncertain in these days, it seems as though anything could happen.
43   51

Religious opinions:

125. The future is in God's hands, I will await what He sends and accept what comes as His will for me.
45*   44*

240. [Prayer is the] occasion to go down into myself and to be really present to myself.
51   42*

30. Religious have a greater call to holiness and apostolic responsibility than do Christian laymen.
42   47

540. Did you enter the religious life because a life apart from the world attracted you?
45   43

Attitude or position	Yes or agree**	No or disagree**

The Order and related structures:

(How do you feel about:)

596. The decision-making policy in your order. — 44* / 56*

398. Current unrest and focus on change has weakened the inner control of those who need a stricter discipline to remain constant; the impatient, the irresponsible, the immature, the psychologically too tense leave. — 50 / 47

The Local Monastery:

301. Change in the "climate" of communication, i.e., elimination of fear of disapproval and possible recrimination if grievances are made known, by redefining the subject-superior relation. — Needed: 51 / Not: 45

H 87. The only rules here are made for the good of the community. — 49 / 41

Personal opinions:

H 101. Sometimes I feel all alone in the world. — 47 / 49

540. Did you enter the religious life because a life apart from the world attracted you? — 45 / 43

H 102. I worry about the future facing today's children. — 43 / 51

---

*Indicates that 15 percent or more of those expressing a given position hold to that position "strongly" (e.g., "strongly agree" or "strongly disagree").

**Or equivalent

Numbers that are not prefixed by the letter "H" refer to the contemplative survey (Research Committee of CMSW 1969), N=66. Those prefixed by "H" refer to the page of the print-out of the Hillery 1970 Survey, N=49.

Appendix F

Attitudes toward Obedience

Questions	Percent "Yes" or equivalent	
	Total Sample of Trappists	Palisades
85. By the grace of office, superiors express the will of God for me.	51	45
86. In the life of the cloister there are still to be found age-old rituals governing the etiquette towards superiors, involving demands of respect from subjects, secretiveness appeals to higher wisdom. All this should be permitted to die out.	65	65
87. A truly obedient religious need seek no source other than his Rule and the will of his superiors to know what he should do.	11	11
88. Policy decisions and major community problems should be solved by superiors, and I should love and trust them enough not to criticize their decisions.	8	3
89. The superior should not try to give the impression that he acts under the immediate inspiration of the Holy Spirit, but should seek approval for commands by giving reasons for them.	76	82
90. The vow of obedience is a promise to listen to the community as it speaks through many voices.	38	38
How do you think regulations should be determined?		
314. By vote of all those in the house.	73	76
315. By vote of elected representatives on a house council.	21	24
317. By informal meetings with superior and house members.	62	67
These are some of the statements people have made about those in authority. To what degree do they correspond to your experience?		
321. They are too hesitant about correcting deviations.	56	59

Questions	Percent "Yes" or equivalent	
	Total Sample of Trappists	Palisades
322. They do not keep confidences.	28*	28*
323. They feel threatened when questioned.	52	44
324. They expect personal services.	24**	14**
325. They do not understand the individual's problems.	58	56
Consider the following statements with regard to obedience as it is practiced in your house:		
338. I feel that any initiative on my part is stifled.	7**	6**
340. I feel imprisoned in narrow legalism and red tape.	11	6
341. I feel that it has taught me to be responsible and cooperative.	50	62
343. I feel that it has helped me to be more humble and it has saved me from many mistakes.	40	41
344. I feel that I do not receive enough direction and guidance.	10	12
463. Do you think in your house there should be some kind of revision of the chapter of faults?	63	51
644. All authentic law is by its very nature flexible and can be changed by the community in which it is operative.	55	59
Number	235	66

*Chi-square significance of differences for the broader distribution (including "no" and "don't know"): .05 > p > .02.

In computing chi square for these differences, the Palisades population was subtracted from the total and differences were computed for Palisades vs. others. Minor categories ("no answer" and "does not apply") were excluded.

Source: Research Committee of CMSW 1969.

Appendix G

Discipline, Personal Responsibility, and Attitude toward Superiors

	Percent Responding "Good" or equivalent	
	---	---
Questions	Total Sample of Trappists	Palisades

At a time of evaluation it is important to make some assessment of our actual performance now in order to make useful suggestions for future planning. Looking candidly at life in your LOCAL COMMUNITY, how would you assess the following in the light of your present understanding of what community life is?

428. Communication with superiors.	55**	73**
439. The present system of delegation of authority by superior.	58*	76*
443. The encouragement of initiative of individuals in your local house by superiors and other religious.	45	49
616. More personal responsibility.	39	49
625. Community sharing in local house decisions formerly left to superiors.	54**	70**
Number	235	66

*Chi-square significance of differences for the broader distribution (including "so-so" and "quite poor"): .01 > p > .001.

**Chi-square significance of differences for the broader distribution (including "so-so" and "quite poor"): .001 > p.

Source: Research Committee of CMSW 1969.

Appendix H

Attitudes toward Prayer

	Percent	
Question	Palisades	Other Trappists

10--I usually think of my prayers as my spiritual
exercises.

(1) Yes	14	22
(2) No	76	65
(3) Undecided or uncertain	1	5
(4) The statement is irrelevant or meaningless in this form.	4	6
(5) The statement is so annoying to me that I cannot answer.	1	--

Is the way you usually think about prayer expressed
in the following items?

234-Set II A contemplative way of participating in
the salvation of the world by petitioning God for
the world's needs, thanking him for his kindness,
praising him for his creation, and making
retribution for the sins of man.

(1) This is my preferred way of thinking about prayer.	15	21
(2) Some of my thinking about prayer is expressed here.	79	71
(3) None of my thinking about prayer is expressed here.	1	2
(4) This is not my thinking about prayer and I would not like to think this way.	1	1
(5) This is not my way of thinking about prayer but I would like to think this way.	3	3

237-Set V Conversation with God

(1) This is my preferred way of thinking about prayer.	32	33
(2) Some of my thinking about prayer is expressed here.	56	53
(3) None of my thinking about prayer is expressed here.	3	4
(4) This is not my thinking about prayer and I would not like to think this way.	--	1
(5) This is not my way of thinking about prayer but I would like to think this way.	6	6

Question	Percent	
	Palisades	Other Trappists

238-Set VI Prayer is to the contemplative what the apostolate is to the active religious.

	Palisades	Other Trappists
(1) This is my preferred way of thinking about prayer.	18	25
(2) Some of my thinking about prayer is expressed here.	35	30
(3) None of my thinking about prayer is expressed here.	23	15
(4) This is not my thinking about prayer and I would not like to think this way.	17	24
(5) This is not my way of thinking about prayer but I would like to think this way.	3	4

239-Set VII A stillness which God fills.

	Palisades	Other Trappists
(1) This is my preferred way of thinking about prayer.	15	14
(2) Some of my thinking about prayer is expressed here.	49	49
(3) None of my thinking about prayer is expressed here.	11	15
(4) This is not my thinking about prayer and I would not like to think this way.	14	9
(5) This is not my way of thinking about prayer but I would like to think this way.	9	11

240-Set VIII The occasion to go down into myself.

	Palisades	Other Trappists
(1) This is my preferred way of thinking about prayer.	9	4
(2) Some of my thinking about prayer is expressed here.	42	40
(3) None of my thinking about prayer is expressed here.	20	20
(4) This is not my thinking about prayer and I would not like to think this way.	23	28
(5) This is not my way of thinking about prayer but I would like to think this way.	3	53

241-Set IX The meditative search for the meaning of life, through Scripture, especially, but other writing [as well] . . .

	Palisades	Other Trappists
(1) This is my preferred way of thinking about prayer.	32	18
(2) Some of my preferred thinking about prayer is expressed here.	53	60
(3) None of my thinking about prayer is expressed here.	5	8
(4) This is not my way of thinking about prayer and I will not like to think this way.	3	1

Question	Percent	
	Palisades	Other Trappists

Question	Palisades	Other Trappists
(5) This is not my way of thinking about prayer but I would like to think this way.	5	8
365--How do you feel about mental prayer?		
(1) I really enjoy it, looking forward to it every day.	23	24
(2) I value it deeply but have to work hard at it.	35	33
(3) It's a burden to me, though one I accept willingly as a necessary part of my spiritual life.	8	9
(4) My response is uneven. Sometimes it's fine; sometimes a burden.	30	33
386--Do you feel that your own prayer is contemplative in form?		
(1) Always	11	15
(2) Sometimes	62	59
(3) Occasionally	23	17
(4) Never	--	5
To what extent do you consider yourself well informed in . . . the following areas?		
588-Methods of mental prayer.		
(1) If you feel very well informed.	47	47
(2) Somewhat informed.	50	48
(3) Uninformed.	1	4

Percentages do not add to 100 since computations were made with categories of "No answer," "Irrelevant" statement, "Does not apply," etc., which are not shown in the table.

*Chi-square significance of differences: .01 > p.

Source: Research Committee of CMSW 1969.

Appendix I

Attitudes toward Silence

| | Percent | |
Question	Palisades	Other Trappists

358--Which of the following statements best describes your attitude toward periods of silence?

(1) In the life of a contemplative, silence should be total.	--	--
(2) Silence should be total except for set times of recreation.	5	1
(3) There should be specified periods and places for silence but outside of these talking should be permitted.	45	37
(4) The only silence that should remain in a contemplative house is silence of consideration, that is, silence should be observed when it is called for by charity or courtesy.	20	17
(5) Silence should be total except when there is a good reason for talking.	29	43

476--Which of the following statements best express what silence means to you:

(1) Silence is an aid to contemplation.	68	67
(2) Silence is an indispensable monastic discipline.	3	5
(3) Silence allows for distance from others.	--	1
(4) None of these statements express what silence means to me.	11	11
(5) All of these statements express what silence means to me.	17	15

How do you feel about conditions now existing in your order?

609--Manner of observing silence in your local house.

(1) If you are very satisfied.	27	27
(2) Somewhat satisfied.	39	40
(3) Mildly dissatisfied.	23	20
(4) Quite dissatisfied.	11	11

Question	Percent	
	Palisades	Other Trappists

What should be done about the following changes in your community?

611--Less silence.*

(1) We should have this.	5	2
(2) We should not have this.	1	5
(3) I think we have gone too far on this.	32	18
(4) I think we have not done enough on this.	3	17
(5) What we have done on this just about right.	59	56

Percentages do not add to 100 since computations were made with categories of "No answer," "Irrelevant" statement, "Does not apply," etc., which are not shown in the table. Computations of Chi square, however, are made without these categories. Chi square not shown where $p > .05$.

*Chi-square significance of differences: $.01 > p > .005$.

Source: Research Committee of CMSW 1969.

Appendix J

Attitudes Concerning Contemplative Life

	Percent	
	Palisades	Other Trappists

These are some statements people have made about different aspects of the contemplative life. To what degree do they correspond to your thinking?

303--Enclosure is a physical separation for the sake of a spiritual involvement with the world.

(1) High degree	27	33
(2) Somewhat	55	51
(3) Not at all	17	15

304--Once you become a cloistered religious it is better that no one sees you.

(1) High degree	3	1
(2) Somewhat	14	19
(3) Not at all	82	78

305--To seek to know outsiders well, even though you remain within the cloister is an infringement on the spirit of enclosure. **

(1) High degree	11	15
(2) Somewhat	24	43
(3) Not at all	64	40

Which of the following characteristics do you feel are essential to being a contemplative?

306--Withdrawal or hiddenness from the world. **

(1) Is essential	30	66
(2) Is not essential	39	18
(3) At present I am not really sure if this is essential or not.	29	13

308--Life of penance.

(1) Is essential	62	63
(2) Is not essential	18	18
(3) At present I am not really sure if this is essential or not.	17	17

370--How important is it to you as a contemplative religious to have periods of retreat in which you go apart completely from your service work for a lengthy period of time to spend a period in contemplation, e.g., a week or more? (Choose one only.)

(1) Important	39	41
(2) Because of the kind of person I am, not really important.	23	23
(3) Because of the nature of my work, not really important at all.	20	12
(4) None of these.	17	23

	Percent	
	Palisades	Other Trappists

375--Is contemplative life mainly a life of intensified prayer?

	Palisades	Other Trappists
(1) Yes	50	59
(2) No	39	30
(3) Don't know, not sure, perhaps yes or perhaps no	9	10

458--Is the essential nature of contemplative life to be of service?

	Palisades	Other Trappists
(1) Yes	30	29
(2) No	45	50
(3) Don't know for sure, perhaps yes or perhaps no	21	12

459--Should the central focus of our renewal be on the interior life?

	Palisades	Other Trappists
(1) Yes	58	68
(2) No	26	18
(3) Don't know for sure, perhaps yes or perhaps no	15	11

460--Do you think that major revisions should be made in the rules of contemplative orders?*

	Palisades	Other Trappists
(1) Yes	71	53
(2) No	15	27
(3) Don't know for sure, perhaps yes or perhaps no	12	18

What should be done about the following changes in your community?

630--More time for prayer.

	Palisades	Other Trappists
(1) We should have this.	12	15
(2) We should not have this.	1	3
(3) I think we have gone too far on this.	--	1
(4) I think we have not done enough on this.	20	21
(5) What we have done on this is just about right.	65	57

Percentages do not add to 100 since computations were made with categories of "No answer," "Irrelevant" statement, "Does not apply," etc., which are not shown in the table. Computations of Chi square, however, are made without these categories. Chi square not shown where $p > .05$.

*Chi-square significance of differences: $.05 > p > .02$.

**Chi-square significance of differences: $.005 > p > .001$.

***Chi-square significance of differences: $p > .001$

Source: Research Committee of CMSW 1969.

Glossary

Abbey: A monastery that is relatively independent and autonomous, ruled by its own abbot.

Abbot: The elected ruler, spiritual and temporal, of a monastery.

Agapé: Love that is spiritually based and is diffuse, unilateral, detached, inclusive, universalistic, and disciplined. See Chapter 3.

Agapé Love: See Agapé.

Anchorite: Hermit.

Angelus: A devotion made to the incarnation of Jesus and the Virgin Mary, accompanied by the ringing of a bell.

Brother: A monk who is not a priest.

Candidate: One who is interested in becoming a monk and who works and prays with the monks for a month in order to "try out" the life. He takes no vows. Formerly called "observer."

Canonical Hour: Certain times of the day designated for the singing of psalms, hymns, recitation of lessons, prayers, and so forth. There are seven canonical hours: Matins with Lauds, Prime, Terce, Sext, None, Vespers, and Compline.

Cantor: The leader of the monastic choir.

Cellarer: A monk appointed to oversee the material goods of the monastery.

Cenobite: A monk who lives in community with other monks.

Chapter of Faults: A meeting in which the monks accuse themselves (or "proclaim" others) of violations of the *Rule* and in which they are given various penances by the superior or abbot.

Choir Monk: A monk who sings in choir. Before Vatican II, he was intended also for the priesthood and was distinguished from the lay brother. This distinction is no longer maintained.

Cistercian: Pertaining to the Abbey of Citeaux, France, founded 1098 A.D. Also, a monk of that order.

Cloister: Strictly speaking, a covered walkway, open to the weather at least on one side, and quadrangular. It may be completely enclosed, and the term is also used to designate that part of the monastery reserved strictly for monks.

Commendum: Instead of being elected by the monks, abbots of monasteries "in commendum" were appointed by secular rulers. Such an abbot assumed control of all the monastery's resources. The practice no longer exists.

Compline: The last canonical hour.

Concelebrated Mass: A mass said jointly by two or more priests, with one monk serving as "president."

Contemplative: One who practices contemplative prayer.

Contemplative Prayer: An intuitive awareness of God in which the mind rests in the presence of God without attempting to reason about anything. The prayer is analogous to one sitting quietly in the presence of an old friend.

Dehy: An alfalfa dehydration machine at Palisades Abbey, eventually abandoned because it did not fit in with the monastic way of life.

Eucharist: The sacrament of the Lord's Last Supper; Holy Communion.

Enclosure: That part of the monastery that is separated from the "world." The enclosure is often indicated by a high wall or a locked door.

Eremitical: Referring to a hermit's way of life.

Exclaustrated: Referring to a monk who is temporarily out of the monastery.

Father Immediate: The abbot of a monastery that has founded other monasteries, called the daughter houses. This abbot is called the "Father Immediate" by these daughter houses.

Junior: A monk who has taken "simple" (annual) vows, that is, he is not yet a fully professed monk and has not taken solemn vows.

Lauds: See canonical hour.

Lay Brother: A monk who is not a priest or is not destined for the priesthood.

Lectio Divina: Literally translated, "spiritual" or "divine reading." It refers to the process of reading in which one is not attempting to reason something or to solve an intellectual problem but is simply allowing the material to dwell in one's mind.

Liturgical: Referring to public prayer and worship.

Matins: See canonical hour.

Monk: A member of a religious order, such as the Benedictines or the Cistercians, devoted primarily to contemplation and regular liturgical observances.

Night Office: The psalms, hymns, lessons, and so forth recited between midnight and dawn. Also called Vigils.

None: See canonical hour.

Novice: One who has been admitted to training for membership in a religious order. It follows postulancy.

Novice Master: One who is responsible for the training of Novices.

Novitiate: That part of the monastery assigned to the novices for residence and training.

Observer: See Candidate.

Office: The psalms, prayers, hymns, lessons, and so forth that a monk is bound to perform as a duty. The term may refer to all of the offices or to one of the canonical hours.

O.C.S.O.: Order of Cistercians of the Strict Observance.

Postulant: An applicant to a religious order who lives in the community for a trial period.

Prime: See canonical hour.

Prior: (1) Titular priors are the superiors of independent priories. (2) Cloistral priors are second in command to the abbot and are appointed by the abbot.

Priory: A religious house next below an abbey in rank.

Procurator: The business agent of the monastery, appointed by the abbot.

Refectory: The monastic dining room.

Religious: One who has taken religious vows.

Retreat: There are generally two kinds of retreats: (1) Directed retreats proceed according to a schedule of conferences, prayers, and so forth. (2) Undirected retreats allow the person on retreat to pray, read, or reflect under his or her own direction.

Second Vatican Council: A Council of the Bishops of the Roman Catholic Church called by Pope John XXIII. It began in October 1962 under John XXIII and ended in December 1965 under Paul VI.

Sext: See canonical hour.

Subprior: Third in command after the abbot; appointed by the abbot.

Superior: Ruler of the monastery. The abbot is elected by the monks of a monastery. Otherwise, the superior is appointed.

Terce: See canonical hour.

Thurible: A container for burning incense.

Usages: A collection of customs determining conduct in all aspects of monastic life.

Vatican II: See Second Vatican Council.

Vespers: See canonical hour.

Vigils: See Night Office.

References

Abbott, Walter M., S. J., and Very Rev. Msgr. Joseph Gallagher, eds. 1966. *The Documents of Vatican II*. New York: Guild Press.

Abbot General, O.C.S.O. 1956. Christmas letter.

Adler, Mortimer J. 1958. *The Idea of Freedom: An Examination of the Conceptions of Freedom*. Two volumes. Westport, Conn.: Greenwood Press.

Anonymous: A Father of the Abbey of Gethsemani, Kentucky, of the Order of Cistercians of the Strict Observance (Trappist). 1944. *Compendium of the History of the Cistercian Order*. Order of the Cistercians of the Strict Observance.

Anonymous. 1973. *The Cloud of Unknowing*. Edited by William Johnston. Garden City, N.Y.: Doubleday.

Azarya, Victor. 1984. *The Armenian Quarter of Jerusalem: Urban Life Behind Monastery Walls*. Berkeley: University of California Press.

Bales, Robert F. 1950. "A set of categories for the analysis of small group interaction." *American Sociological Review* 15:258–61.

Banfield, Edward C. 1958. *The Moral Basis of a Backward Society*. New York: Free Press.

Benedict, Saint. 1948. *Rule for Monasteries*. Translated by Leonard J. Doyle. Collegeville, Minn.: The Liturgical Press.

Benedictines of St. Meinrad's Abbey. 1937. *The Holy Rule of Our Most Holy Father St. Benedict*. St. Meinrad, Ind.: Abbey Press.

Bennett, J. W. 1975. "Communes and communitarianism." *Theory and Society* 2:63–94.

Blumer, Herbert. 1939. *Critiques of Research in the Social Sciences: I. An Appraisal of Thomas and Znaniecki's "The Polish Peasant in Europe and America."* New York: Social Science Research Council.

Boros, Ladislaus. 1973. *We Are Future*. Garden City, N.Y.: Doubleday.

Bridgewater, William, ed. 1960. *The Columbia-Viking Desk Encyclopedia*. Second edition. New York: Viking.

Browning, Elizabeth Barrett. 1932. "How do I love thee?" In Nella Braddy, ed., *The Standard Book of British and American Verse*. Garden City, N.Y.: Garden City Publishing Co.

Bulmer, Martin. 1986. *Neighbours: The Work of Philip Abrams*. Cambridge: Cambridge University Press.

Carden, Maren Lockwood. 1969. *Oneida: Utopian Community to Modern Corporation*. Baltimore: The Johns Hopkins University Press.

Chapter papers. 1971.

Choukas, Michael. 1935. *The Black Angels of Athos*. London: Constable.

Collins, R. 1975. *Conflict Sociology: Toward an Explanatory Science*. New York: Academic Press.

Creel, Austin B., and Vasudha Narayanan. 1990. *Monastic Life in the Christian and Hindu Traditions: A Comparative Study*. Lewiston, N.Y.: Edwin Mellen Press.

Curb, Rosemary, and Nancy Manahan, eds. 1985. *Lesbian Nuns: Breaking Silence*. New York: Warner Books.

Cuzzort, R. P., and E. W. King. 1989. *Twentieth-Century Social Thought*. Fourth edition. Chicago: Holt, Rinehart and Winston.

Dahl, Robert. 1961. *Who Governs? Democracy and Power in an American City*. New Haven: Yale University Press.

Dahrendorf, R. 1959. *Class and Class Conflict in Industrial Society*. Stanford: Stanford University Press.

Della Fave, L. Richard, and George A. Hillery, Jr. 1980. "Status inequality in a religious community: The case of a Trappist monastery." *Social Forces* 59 (September):62–84.

Denzin, Norman K. 1989. *The Research Act*. Third edition. Chicago: Aldine.

Dewey, Robert E., and James A. Gould, eds. 1970. *Freedom: Its History, Nature, and Varieties*. New York: Macmillan.

Domhoff, G. William. 1978. *Who Really Governs? New Haven and Community Power Re-examined*. Santa Monica, Calif.: Goodyear.

Doyle, Leonard J., trans. 1948. *St. Benedict's Rule for Monasteries*. Collegeville, Minn.: The Liturgical Press.

Dudley, Charles J., and George A. Hillery, Jr. 1979. "Freedom and monastery life." *Journal for the Scientific Study of Religion* 18(1):18–28.

Durkheim, Emile. 1915. *The Elementary Forms of Religious Life*. Translated by J. W. Swain. London: Allen and Unwin.

———. 1938. *The Rules of the Sociological Method*. Translated by Sarah A. Solovay and John H. Mueller. Edited by George E. G. Catlin. London: Collier-Macmillan Ltd., The Free Press of Glencoe.

Furlong, Monica. 1985. *Merton: A Biography*. San Francisco: Harper and Row.

Furnival, J. S. 1948. *Colonial Policy and Practice*. London: Cambridge University Press.

Gelineau, Joseph. 1963. *The Psalms: Singing Version*. Glasgow: William Collins Sons.

Giallombardo, Rose. 1966. *Society of Women: A Study of a Women's Prison*. New York: Wiley.

Giddens, A. 1973. *The Class Structure of the Advanced Societies*. New York: Harper and Row.

Gilbert, Dennis, and Joseph A. Kahl. 1987. *The American Class Structure: A New Synthesis*. Homewood, Ill.: Dorsey Press.

Gleick, James. 1987. *Chaos: Making a New Science*. New York: Viking.

Goffman, Erving. 1961. *Asylums*. Garden City, N.Y.: Doubleday.

Gold, Raymond L. 1958. "Roles in sociological field observations." *Social Forces* 36 (March):217–23.

Hart, Brother Patrick, ed. 1974. *Thomas Merton, Monk: A Monastic Tribute*. New York: Sheed and Ward.

Heilman, Samuel C. 1976. *Synagogue Life*. Chicago: University of Chicago Press.

Hill, Blake. 1967. "Women and Religion: A Study of Socialization in a Community of Catholic Sisters." Ph.D. dissertation, University of Kentucky.

Hill, Michael. 1973. *The Religious Order: A Study of Virtuoso Religion and Its Legitimation in the Nineteenth-Century Church of England*. London: Heinemann Educational Books.

Hillery, George A., Jr. 1955. "Definitions of community: Areas of agreement." *Rural Sociology* 20 (June):111–23.

———. 1968. *Communal Organizations: A Study of Local Societies*. Chicago: University of Chicago Press.

———. 1969. "The convent: Community, prison, or task force?" *Journal for the Scientific Study of Religion* 8:140–51.

———. 1971. "Freedom and social organization: A comparative analysis." *American Sociological Review* 36 (February):51–65.

———. 1972. "Social structure and resistance to change." *Sociologia Ruralis* 12:384–99.

———. 1973. "Families, communes, and communities." In Roland Warren, ed., *Perspectives on the American Community: A Book of Readings*. Chicago: Rand McNally.

———. 1976. "Conversations with the Monks." Unpublished manuscript.

———. 1978. "Freedom, love and community." *Society* 15 (May/June):24–31.

———. 1980. "A Christian perspective on sociology." In Charles P. De Santo, Calvin Redekop, and William L. Smith-Hinds, eds., *A Reader in Sociology: Christian Perspectives*. Scottdale, Penn.: Herald Press.

———. 1981a. "Freedom, love, and community: An outline of a theory," In Thomas Robbins and Dick Anthony, eds., *In Gods We Trust: New Patterns of Religious Pluralism in America*. New Brunswick, N.J.: Transaction Books.

———. 1981b. "Triangulation in religious research: A sociological approach to the study of monasteries." *Review of Religious Research* 23 (September):22–38.

———. 1982. *A Research Odyssey: Developing and Testing a Community Theory*. New Brunswick, N.J.: Transaction Books.

———. 1983. "Monastic occupations: A study in values." In Richard L. Simpson and Ida Harper Simpson, eds., *Research in the Sociology of Work: Volume 2*. Greenwich, Conn.: JAI Press.

———. 1984. "Gemeinschaft Verstehen: A theory of the middle range." *Social Forces* 63 (December):307–34.

———. 1985. "A theory of communal organizations." In Frank A. Fear and Harry K. Schwarzweller, eds., *Research in Rural Sociology and Development: Focus on Community*. Greenwich, Conn.: JAI Press.

———. 1991. "Several Loves." Unpublished manuscript.

Hillery, George A., Jr., and Paula C. Morrow. 1976. "The monastery as a commune." *International Review of Modern Sociology* 6 (Spring): 139–54.

Hillery, George A., Jr., Charles J. Dudley, and Paula C. Morrow. 1977. "Toward a sociology of freedom." *Social Forces* 55 (March):685–700.

Hillery, George A., Jr., Charles J. Dudley, and Thomas P. Thompson. 1979. "A theory of integration and freedom." *The Sociological Quarterly* 20 (Autumn): 551–63.

Hoffman, M. M. 1952. *Arms and the Monk! The Trappist Saga in Mid-America.* Dubuque, Iowa: Wm. C. Brown.

Horn, Walter, and Ernest Born. 1979. *The Plan of St. Gall.* Berkeley: University of California Press.

Hostetler, John A. 1974. *Hutterite Society.* Baltimore: The Johns Hopkins University Press.

Hummon, David. M. 1990. *Commonplaces: Community Ideology and Identity in American Culture.* Albany: State University of New York Press.

Johnston, William, ed. 1973. *The Cloud of Unknowing and the Book of Privy Counselling.* Garden City, N.Y.: Doubleday, Image Books.

Kanter, R. M. 1972. *Commitment and Community.* Cambridge, Mass.: Harvard University Press.

———, ed. 1973. *Communes.* New York: Harper and Row.

Kavanaugh, Kieran, and Otilio Rodriguez, trans. 1973. *The Collected Works of St. John of the Cross.* Washington, D.C.: Institute of Carmelite Studies.

Keating, Thomas. 1986. *Open Mind, Open Heart.* Warwick, N.Y.: Amity House.

Kelty, Matthew. 1971. "The monastic way of death." In *The Last Whole Earth Catalogue.* Menlo Park, Calif.: Portola Institute.

Kemper, T. 1976. "Marxist and functional theories in the study of stratification: Common elements that lead to a test." *Social Forces* 54 (March):559–78.

Kierkegaard, Soren. 1962. *The Works of Love.* Translation by Howard and Edna Hong. New York: Harper and Row.

Knowles, David. 1969. *Christian Monasticism.* New York: McGraw-Hill.

Kramer, Victor A. 1984. *Thomas Merton.* Boston: Twayne Publishers.

Kubler-Ross, Elisabeth. 1969. *On Death and Dying.* New York: Macmillan.

Lantz, Judith C. 1987. *Cumulative Index of Sociology Journals: 1971–1985.* Washington, D.C.: The American Sociological Association.

Lawrence, Brother. 1954. *The Practice of the Presence of God.* Fleming H. Revell.

Lawrence, Wayne E., and George A. Hillery, Jr. N.d. "Vertical integration in selected communities." Unpublished paper.

Lekai, Louis J. 1977. *The Cistercians: Ideals and Reality.* Kent, Ohio: The Kent State University Press.

Lenski, Gerhard. 1966. *Power and Privilege: A Theory of Social Stratification.* New York: McGraw-Hill.

Lewis, C. S. 1960. *The Four Loves.* New York: Harcourt Brace Jovanovich.

Lynd, Robert S., and Helen Merrell Lynd. 1956 [1929]. *Middletown: A Study in American Culture.* New York: Harcourt Brace Jovanovich.

———. 1965 [1937]. *Middletown in Transition: A Study in Cultural Conflicts.* New York: Harcourt Brace.

Manzaridis, G. 1975. "New statistical data concerning the monks of Mount Athos." *Social Compass* 22:97–106.

McCarthy, Colman. 1980. Untitled article in the *Washington Post*, March 23:G1, G5–7.

Merton, Thomas. 1948. *The Seven Storey Mountain*. New York: New American Library.

———. 1953. *The Sign of Jonas*. Garden City, N.Y.: Doubleday.

———. 1960. *The Wisdom of the Desert*. New York: New Directions.

———. 1962 [1949]. *The Waters of Siloe*. Garden City, N.Y.: Doubleday, Image Books.

———. 1966. *Conjectures of a Guilty Bystander*. Garden City, N.Y.: Doubleday.

———. 1969. *Contemplative Prayer*. Garden City, N.Y.: Doubleday, Image Books.

Mott, Michael. 1984. *The Seven Mountains of Thomas Merton*. Boston: Houghton Mifflin.

Neal, Sister Marie Augusta. 1970. *Final Report on the Survey for Contemplatives*. Dubuque, Iowa: New Melleray Abbey.

Nouwen, Henri J. 1976. *The Genessee Diary: Report from a Trappist Monastery*. Garden City, N.Y.: Doubleday.

O'Toole, Sister Mary George. 1964. "Sisters of Mercy of Main: A Religious Community as a Social System." Ph.D. dissertation, The Catholic University of America.

Parsons, T. 1953. "A revised analytical approach to the theory of social stratification." In R. Bendix and S. M. Lipset, eds., *Class, Status, and Power*. Glencoe, Ill.: Free Press.

———. 1960. *Structure and Process in Modern Societies*. Glencoe, Ill.: Free Press.

———. 1966. *Societies: Evolutionary and Comparative Perspectives*. Englewood Cliffs, N.J.: Prentice-Hall.

Parsons, T., and Neil J. Smelser. 1956. *Economy and Society*. New York: Free Press.

Pearsall, Marion. 1965. "Participant observation as role and method in behavioral research." *Nursing Research* 14(Winter):37–42.

Peck, M. Scott. 1976. *The Road Less Traveled: A New Psychology of Love, Traditional Values and Spiritual Growth*. New York: Simon and Schuster.

Peers, E. Allison, trans. and ed. 1960. The *Autobiography of St. Teresa of Avila*. Garden City, N.Y.: Doubleday, Image Books.

Pennington, W. Basil. 1982. *Centering Prayer: Reviewing an Ancient Christian Prayer Form*. Garden City, N.Y.: Doubleday.

Philippe, Thomas. 1990. *The Contemplative Life*. Trans. by Carmine Buonaiuto. Ed. by Edward D. O'Connor. New York: Crossroad.

Pippin, Roland. 1978. "Toward the Classification of Nomadic Gypsies: A Taxonomic and Theoretical Treatise." Unpublished Ph.D. dissertation, Virginia Polytechnic Institute and State University.

Price, Lorna. 1982. *The Plan of St. Gall: In Brief*. Berkeley: University of California Press.

Pruitt, Dean G., and Jeffry Z. Rubin. 1986. *Social Conflict: Escalation, Stalemate, and Settlement*. New York: Random House.

Ramold, Sister Mary Regis. 1964. "The Ursulines of Mount St. Joseph: A Religious Community as a Social System." Ph.D. dissertation, The Catholic University of America.

Reiss, A. J. 1961. *Occupations and Social Status*. New York: Free Press.

Renna, Thomas. 1980. *Benedict and His Monks*. Dubuque, Iowa: New Melleray Abbey.

Research Committee of CMSW. 1969. *A Report of the Survey for Contemplatives*. Boston: Department of Sociology, Emmanuel College. Sponsored by the Conference of Major Religious Superiors of Women's Institutes of the United States of America.

Roberts, Keith A. 1990. *Religion in Sociological Perspective*. Belmont, Calif.: Wadsworth.

Romanucci-Ross, Lola. 1973. *Conflict, Violence, and Morality in a Mexican Village*. Palo Alto, Calif.: National Press Books.

Rosenblatt, Roger. 1986. "Essay: Freedom of the damned." *Time* 128 (October 6):98.

Sampson, Samuel Franklin. 1968. "A Novitiate in a Period of Change: An Experimental Case Study in Social Relationships." Ph.D. dissertation, Cornell University.

Simmel, Georg. 1950. "The stranger." In Kurt H. Wolff, ed. and trans., *The Sociology of Georg Simmel*. New York: Free Press.

Sjoberg, Gideon. 1960. *The Preindustrial City: Past and Present*. Glencoe, Ill.: The Free Press.

Smith, Craig Allen. 1990. *Political Communication*. New York: Harcourt Brace Jovanovich.

Smith, M. G. 1965. *The Plural Society in the British West Indies*. Berkeley: University of California Press.

Sorokin, Pitirim A. 1937–41. *Social and Cultural Dynamics*. Four volumes. New York: American Book.

———. 1950. *Altruistic Love: A Study of American Good Neighbors and Christian Saints*. Boston: Beacon Press.

———. 1973. The Monastic System of Techniques: Monastic "Psychoanalysis," Counselling, and Therapy. Exerpted from P. A. Sorokin, *The Ways and Power of Love*, St. Meinrad, Ind.: Abbey Press.

Spiro, Melford E. 1956. *Kibbutz: Venture in Utopia*. Cambridge, Mass.: Harvard University Press.

———. 1958. *Children of the Kibbutz*. Cambridge, Mass.: Harvard University Press.

Steidle, The Reverend Basillius. 1952. *The Rule of St. Benedict*. Beuroner/Hohenzollern, Germany: Beuroner Kunstverlag.

Stein, Maurice R. 1964. *The Eclipse of Community: An Interpretation of American Community Studies*. New York: Harper and Row.

Strodtbeck, F. L, R. M. James, and C. Hawkins. 1957. "Social status in jury deliberation." *American Sociological Review* 22:713–19.

Sutherland, Anne. 1975. *Gypsies: The Hidden Americans*. New York: Free Press.

Teahan, John F. 1982. "Solitude: A central motif in Thomas Merton's life and writings." *The Journal of the American Academy of Religion* (December): 521–38.

Toennies, Ferdinand. 1957. *Community and Society (Gemeinschaft und Gesellschaft)*. New York: Harper and Row.

Van Zeller, Dom Hubert. 1959. *The Benedictine Idea*. Springfield, Ill.: Templegate.

Varenne, Herve. 1977. *Americans Together: Structural Diversity in a Midwestern Town*. New York: Teachers College Press.

Vidich, Arthur J., and Joseph Bensman. 1960. *Small Town in Mass Society*. Garden City, N.Y.: Doubleday.

Warren, Roland. 1978. *The Community in America*. Third edition. Chicago: Rand McNally.

Weber, Max. 1930. *The Protestant Ethic and the Spirit of Capitalism*. Translated by Talcott Parsons. London: Allen and Unwin.

Williams, Melvin J. 1943. "Catholic Sociological Theory: A Review and Prospectus." *American Catholic Sociological Review* 4:137–43.

Willis, Cecil L. 1977. "Definitions of community II: An examination of definitions of community since 1950." *The Southern Sociologist* 9 (Fall):14–19.

Wrong, D. 1964. "Social inequality without social stratification." *Canadian Review of Sociology and Anthropology* 1:5–16.

Zablocki, Benjamin D. 1971. *The Joyful Community*. Baltimore: Penguin Books.

Index

ABOUT THE AUTHOR

GEORGE A. HILLERY, JR., is Professor of Sociology at Virginia Polytechnic and State University. He has spent forty years researching communities, and has published several studies on the topic, including *A
Research Odyssey: Developing and Testing a Community Theory* and *Communal Organizations: A Study of Local Societies*.